What Caesar Did for My Salad

The Secret Meanings of our Favourite Dishes

ALBERT JACK

PENGUIN BOOKS

PENGUIN BOOKS

Published by the Penguin Group
Penguin Books Ltd, 80 Strand, London WC2R 0RL, England
Penguin Group (USA) Inc., 375 Hudson Street, New York, New York 10014, USA
Penguin Group (Canada), 90 Eglinton Avenue East, Suite 700, Toronto, Ontario, Canada M4P 2Y3
(a division of Pearson Penguin Canada Inc.)
Penguin Ireland, 25 St Stephen's Green, Dublin 2, Ireland
(a division of Penguin Books Ltd)
Penguin Group (Australia), 250 Camberwell Road, Camberwell, Victoria 3124, Australia
(a division of Pearson Australia Group Pty Ltd)
Penguin Books India Pvt Ltd, 11 Community Centre, Panchsheel Park, New Delhi – 110 017, India
Penguin Group (NZ), 67 Apollo Drive, Rosedale, Auckland 0632, New Zealand
(a division of Pearson New Zealand Ltd)
Penguin Books (South Africa) (Pty) Ltd, Block D, Rosebank Office Park, 181 Jan Smuts Avenue,
Parktown North, Gauteng 2193, South Africa

Penguin Books Ltd, Registered Offices: 80 Strand, London WC2R 0RL, England

www.penguin.com

First published by Particular Books 2010
Published by Penguin Books 2012

1

Copyright © Albert Jack, 2010

All rights reserved

The moral right of the author has been asserted

Designed and typeset by Dinah Drazin

Printed in Great Britain by Clays Ltd, St Ives plc

978-0-141-04344-9

www.greenpenguin.co.uk

ALWAYS LEARNING   **PEARSON**

Contents

This book is dedicated to all cooks everywhere.
What would we do without you?

Acknowledgements

Thanks in the first place should go to chef Liam Tomlin for all the advice and encouragement during the early days. Not to mention access to the best food-history library I have ever seen. Thank you, Chef! Also to the lovely Jan Tomlin, who enthused and encouraged and kept giving me other new ideas to go and look up. Dimo Papachristodoulou, my favourite Mexican, helped too, as did Candice Kalil with her angry pasta, and thank you, Celeste Perry, for allowing me to use your restaurant in Cape Town as an office. For further ideas and research kindly provided from those across the world, thanks to Louise De Jager in Australia and Jessica Rohrer in South Africa

Peter Gordon returned to the team this year with the now famous Morecambe and Wise incident. One Saturday morning, two years ago, as I stayed with him for a few days en route from America to South Africa, we were so engrossed in discussing this book that it was after midday before we realized we were both still in our pyjamas. Although at the kitchen table, mind you, and not in bed like Morecambe and Wise.

And finally I would like to thank my long-term team at Penguin, especially Georgina Laycock, who has put as much effort into *What Caesar Did for My Salad* as anyone; I count myself lucky to have her on my side. Kate Parker, the clever copy-editor. You worked very hard on this one – thanks so much for your brilliant efforts. And then in no particular order: senior production controller Rita Matos, editorial assistant Caroline Elliker, editorial manager Rebecca Lee, cover designer Richard Green, text designer Dinah Drazin and, last but by no means least, my new publicist Lyndsey Ng. Thank you all.

Introduction

Food is just as entitled to a proper history as castles, wars, kings, queens, art, literature or the bubonic plague. But the book world is now so saturated with celebrity chefs trying to show the working woman or man how to rub garlic on a ciabatta or break lime leaves over a piece of raw fish that we've lost sight of many of our best-loved dishes, not to mention the stories behind them showing how they became such classics in the first place. And while I don't ride around London on a scooter with my mates or swear at incompetent sous-chefs for a living – I don't in fact know one end of a pork loin from its elbow – I do love history and I especially love food. The history behind our favourite dishes is fascinating and full of surprises – from the Buddha's obsession with **porridge** to the dying playwright Molière dosing himself with **Parmesan** rather than medicine (it didn't work, in case you're wondering). It's also sadly overlooked and so I wanted to find out more.

In the Monty Python film *The Life of Brian* the would-be rebels ask: 'What have the Romans ever done for us?' Well, one unexpected answer I discovered in my research is that, among many other things, they invented **fast food**. To save you cooking, you could dash out from your high-rise apartment (they invented these too) to your nearest street vendor to grab a takeaway. And what about that beloved staple of the modern takeaway, the Indian curry? This dish, in all its many guises, turns out to be the very tasty result of centuries of wars, invasions and trading missions. Did you know, for instance, that **biryani** came from the Persians and **vindaloo** from the Portuguese, while **mulligatawny** was concocted by the stiff-upper-lipped Brits of the Raj who insisted on still having a hot soup course in the midst of the sweltering heat? Moving back to Europe, it's amazing to see how much food has changed yet how it has stayed the same: how the peasants of the Middle Ages scraped by on sludgy **pease pudding** (healthier fare, even so, than the meat-rich dishes of their wealthy overlords), while today's modern-day peasant, the penniless student, survives on the tastier but not dissimilar **baked beans** on toast.

This dish, as I discovered, might well hail from France – an offshoot of **cassoulet**, their classic bean stew – and that country, with a bit of help from Italy, has had a huge influence on European cooking. But rather than just explaining how cooking techniques have evolved over the centuries, I wanted to tell the stories about the people behind the food we eat every day. Who was **Margherita**, for instance, and why was the world's most famous pizza named after her? And what about **Suzette**: why do pancakes flambéed in Grand Marnier bear her name? We've all enjoyed **peach Melba** at some point, or spread some butter on a piece of **Melba toast**, so wouldn't it be a great idea to tell the story of the demanding diva, Dame Nellie Melba, for whom these dishes were created? And, of course, no history of food would be complete without the tale of how that inveterate gambler the Earl of **Sandwich** came up with the snack that bears his name and now forms the mainstay of every lunchbox and **buffet**.

Once I'd started my research, all sorts of intriguing questions kept popping up. Why do we call our favourite kinds of coffee **espresso** or **cappuccino**, for instance? Did medieval Turkish soldiers really invent the **kebab** by threading bits of meat on to their swords and balancing them on top of their campfires? What exactly does **horseradish sauce** have to do with our equine friends, if anything, and who put that **toad in the hole**? Turn over a few more pages and you'll find the answers to all these questions and many more.

You can look up a dish or type of food in the index or just turn to a relevant 'meal'. As you'll see, I have structured this book around the eating day, starting with a chapter on breakfast and ending up with cheese as the final course for dinner. These days we eat all kinds of foods at all kinds of day and so the chapters aren't completely rigorous in their organization: appetizers are fairly interchangeable with starters, for instance, while the aforementioned horseradish – accompanying roast beef here – could equally well belong in the section on sauces.

The meals we eat and when we eat them has shifted over the years to reflect our increasing mobility and changing lifestyle. But they can still be a reflection of who we are. For example, everybody knows what breakfast is and, in that sense, we are all the same. If you call it 'brunch', then either you should get up earlier or you're reverting to an older practice (see below). Do you have 'elevenses'? Then you are either retired or in hospital.

Do you call your midday meal 'lunch'? If so, you are probably middle class, reasonably well off and would spend all afternoon over it if you didn't have to go back to work. If you call it a 'business lunch', then you've clearly no intention of going back at all.

If you call it 'luncheon', then, Lady Whatever-Your-Castle-Is, you should definitely read this book as you'll discover how some of the world's most expensive and sought-after dishes are not quite as smart as they appear but have a decidedly bloodthirsty and often revolutionary history ... And if you call lunch 'dinner', then you are either working class or at school, or you live in the north.

Interestingly, this is actually the meal with the longest pedigree. At the beginning of the sixteenth century, the main meal of the day took place at around 11.00 a.m., for rich and poor alike, and was called 'dinner', thanks to the Old French word *disner*, deriving in turn from *desjeuner* and meaning 'to break the fast' (as well as providing the modern French word for 'breakfast').

The day ended with 'supper' or, as it came to be known in the north, 'tea', which was a light snack eaten as the sun went down and just before everybody went to bed. The introduction of artificial light meant that meals no longer had to be take place in daylight hours: generally the richer you were the more candles you could afford and the later you ate dinner (i.e. the main meal of the day). Hence the middle- and upper-class obsession with dinner and why it and supper have become pretty much synonymous.

Incidentally, if you call a meal with friends a 'dinner party', then you probably also call lunch 'lunch'. But you should definitely be wary of guests who throw their keys into a bowl when they arrive. The last time that happened I ended up with my own set.

As you make your way through this book, you will see how food has affected the course of history (the Boston Tea Party, for example, or the Irish Potato Famine) and how it has, in turn, been affected by history. You'll see, for instance, how Prohibition brought out the resourcefulness of American chefs, in the form of various dishes from **Caesar salad** to **fruit cocktail**; how the traditional rivalry between the Welsh and the English gave us **Welsh rabbit**; and how the rising price of **pepper** was the real reason behind Columbus's voyage to America. You'll see how the world of the arts has inspired a large number of dishes, such as **omelette Arnold Bennett**, for instance, **Jenny Lind soup**, named after the Swedish opera singer, or the meringue dessert celebrating the Russian ballerina Anna **Pavlova**. And interspersed among the entries on food you'll find everyday phrases relating to the things we eat, and the stories behind them, from *just desserts* to *humble pie*.

En route, you may be interested to discover how many national dishes actually turn out to come from somewhere entirely different: those all-American favourites the **hamburger** and the **hot dog** are, in fact (ahem), German; France's beloved **croissant** actually hails from Austria; **Scotch eggs** are not from Scotland; and all the words we British use to describe our **best cuts of beef** turn out to be French. You'll also see what lengths people go to during times of war to rechristen a dish so that it *isn't* associated with a particular country – hence 'hot dog' instead of the German-sounding **frankfurter** or **Salisbury steak** instead of 'hamburger'.

So, dear readers, a cookbook this is not. But while the chefs among you will learn little here about how to assemble a particular dish, you might enjoy such stories of culinary invention as the one surrounding **chicken Marengo**, for instance. Following victory at the Battle of Marengo, Napoleon ordered his cook, Dunand, to prepare a celebration meal. But having lost half the kitchen in the confusion of the battle, the chef had to knock something together for his emperor with whatever came to hand. Not an easy task in the circumstances, which is why such unusual ingredients as chicken, eggs, crayfish and toast sit together on the same plate. Meanwhile, less confident cooks should take heart from finding out how a cooking disaster inspired Alfred the Great's eventual victory against overwhelming odds, and from discovering just how many of the world's best-loved dishes arose as the result of mistakes or missing ingredients.

I've enjoyed researching and writing this book enormously and I hope you find it a satisfying read. I'd love to hear your thoughts and your own food-history stories, so why not contact me at caesar@albertjack.com. Inevitably, there wasn't room to include every dish I wanted to cover in this book, but you never know – there might be a second sitting …

Albert Jack
May 2010
Cape Town

1
Breakfast

Coffee: The Drink that Speeded Up the World

Raising a Glass to Toast

What is the Connection between Marmalade
and a Sick Queen?

The Full English Breakfast

'The Name's Benedict, Eggs Benedict'

The Noble Story of French Toast

Who was the First Person to Pronounce on Porridge?

Kippers: When is a Herring Not a Herring?

Devilled Kidneys and Canned Ham

The Surreal History of Breakfast Cereal

Arnold Bennett the Famous Omelette

How Did the Croissant Get Its Shape?

My wife and I tried two or three times in the last forty years to have breakfast together, but it was so disagreeable we had to stop.

WINSTON CHURCHILL

To eat well in England, you should have breakfast three times a day.

W. SOMERSET MAUGHAM

Coffee: The Drink that Speeded Up the World

It's thought that the word **coffee** may derive from the Arabic *kahwa*, a type of wine, which in turn derives from a word meaning 'to have no appetite' – appropriate when you think how the day's first cup of coffee often takes the place of breakfast. This galvanizing drink is believed to have originated nearly twelve hundred years ago in Ethiopia, in the region of Kaffa – which has also been suggested as an alternative derivation of the word. According to legend, a shepherd guarding his flock noticed how jumpy his sheep became after eating the red berries that had fallen off a nearby bush. When he sampled some himself, he was amazed to feel a similar surge in energy. Word got about and soon the monks at a nearby monastery were gathering the fruit for themselves and, after many attempts, ended up with a murky brown beverage that they came to rely on to keep them awake for their nightly prayers. But it wasn't until much later, in the thirteenth century, that coffee became a truly palatable drink: it was the Arabs who discovered that roasting coffee beans, grinding them and steeping the grounds in boiling water produced the best flavour, and the world has been hooked ever since.

ESPRESSO: COFFEE IN THE AGE OF STEAM

Throughout the nineteenth century, the era of industrialization when steam power was all the rage, people tried brewing coffee using hot water vapour. Indeed, a steam-brewing contraption at the 1896 World's Fair is said to have made 3,000 cups per hour. Unfortunately, steam-brewed coffee tastes awful since coffee needs to be made at just below boiling for it to be at its best. The first coffee machine to use steam to force hot water through very finely ground beans – a much more acceptable method – was invented by Frenchman Louis Bernard Rabaut back in 1822 but it took almost another eighty years to really catch on, and it was the Italians rather than the French who popularized it. Espresso means 'fast' so it's a little ironic that it took such a long time. It wasn't until 1901, when the definitive machine was designed by Italian inventor Luigi Bezzera, that **espresso** became a café staple, speeding up life for everybody.

CAPPUCCINO: PUTTING A TONSURE ON YOUR CUPPA?

Contrary to popular opinion, this type of coffee, with its distinctive layer of frothy milk, is not named after the coffee bean used, but another group of coffee-obsessed clerics – the Capuchins. Originally part of the Franciscan order of monks in Italy, they broke away in 1520 out of a desire to get back to basics and return to the life of solitude and prayer formerly practised by their founder, St Francis. But the religious authorities took a dim view of this and the heretic monks were forced into hiding. They were given refuge by the Camaldolese monks, however, and to show their appreciation began to wear the hooded *cappucio* cloaks favoured by that order. The hood also helped them to stay out of trouble, serving as useful camouflage by allowing them to blend in with their hosts. Eventually the new order became respectable in the eyes of the Church, so much so that a sister order of nuns was also formed and they all settled together in Naples in 1538.

It was there, legend has it, that the Capuchins developed the method of making their morning coffee by steaming goat's milk and pouring the froth over a mug of cold coffee drawn from a barrel. They had discovered that the foam acted as insulation and heated up the liquid beneath as they sipped it on those cold monastic mornings. **Cappuccino** means 'little Capuchin', either after their coffee-brown robes or because the white foamy top of a cappuccino with its ring of brown resembles the monks' traditional tonsure – shaven on top of the head with a ring of hair around the edge.

There is a counter-story that it was a Capuchin monk, Marco d'Aviano (1631–99), who came up with the first cappuccino – directly after the Battle of Vienna in 1683 (obviously a key event for breakfast inventors: see also the story of the CROISSANT). As spiritual adviser to the Holy Roman Emperor Leopold I, he would certainly have needed a reviving cuppa after all those hours spent on his knees, praying for victory. But as the first time such a claim was made was during the celebration of the battle's tricentenary in 1983 by the Austrian press, this should perhaps be taken with a pinch of salt (if not a teaspoon of sugar).

As with all monastic orders, the Capuchins' numbers have dwindled drastically over the centuries but, to this day, the group, who also gave their name to a monkey and a squirrel, still have around six active houses in Britain, twelve in Ireland and approximately two hundred missionary stations across the world. Perhaps they should have stuck to coffee making as Starbucks have over 25,000 of their own outlets around the globe from which an estimated 7.5 million cappuccinos are sold every single day. Now, that should cheer the Capuchins up, don't you think?

Raising a Glass to Toast

In the beginning there was bread – which was revolutionized by the ancient Egyptians around six thousand years ago
when they realized that if they let the dough sit around in the
warm sunshine, it would become naturally leavened by the
yeast spores in the air and once baked it would retain its risen
shape. Shortly afterwards there was **toast** – when, after a few
days in the dry desert air, the bread became hard and unpleasant to eat. Toasting it was a means of making stale bread edible again. The Romans spread the idea of toast throughout
Europe, including Britain. The word 'toast', in fact, comes
from the Latin *tostus*, meaning 'scorched' or 'burned'. Toast
is essentially burned bread, so the name makes sense. 'Tost'
was a great favourite in the Middle Ages when 'sops' of bread
were used to soak up wine or sweet liquids and then toasted
against the heat of an open fire (see also FRENCH TOAST,
MELBA TOAST and WELSH RABBIT).

But what is the connection between a slice of cooked bread
and raising your wine glass and toasting someone? We need
to look back once again to the Romans, who had a strange
practice of adding a small chunk of burned bread (toast) to
each glass. Some historians have suggested that this was to
add flavour to the wine or to give each guest a small 'treat'–
like a crouton in soup. A more likely reason is that it was to
remove impurities and improve the flavour of poor wines.
Burned toast was like a crude form of the 'activated charcoal' used in modern-day water filters to do the same job of
absorbing impurities and enhancing flavour.

The habit of quaffing wines from a glass with a piece of
toast in it persisted and by the sixteenth century 'drinking
a toast' became the same as saying 'drinking a glass of wine
with a chunk of toast at the bottom'. The term 'toast' then

stretched to the act of drinking itself, regardless of whether there was any toast in your glass, and then to the entire ceremony and even the person being honoured by it. Drinking a toast became all the rage in the seventeenth and eighteenth centuries: the precursor of today's drinking games. Everyone in the room would be separately toasted and it was impolite not to drink to each of them in turn. When the party ran out of physical attendees to toast, they would then raise a glass to absent friends and then all manner of absurdly unattainable ambitions, simply as an excuse to keep drinking.

What is the Connection between Marmalade and a Sick Queen?

There is an old story that the word **marmalade** derives from *Marie malade* ('ill Mary', in French), referring to how Mary, Queen of Scots (1542–87), used it to settle her stomach during a bout of seasickness when sailing from France to Scotland. This is certainly the derivation that respected etymologist Michael Caine (you know who I mean: 'You're only supposed to blow the bloody doors off' – that Michael Caine) once revealed on the Michael Parkinson show. Yet the word was already in use well before Mary's time – first appearing in the English language in 1480, according to the *Oxford English Dictionary*. A simple linguistic confusion may be responsible for its association with a seafaring queen: the word *mar* means 'sea' in Spanish, close to *mer* in French, while *malade* does indeed mean 'sick' in that language, hence the connection between seasickness and Queen Mary. But, long before she was vomiting up her state banquet into the English Channel, *marmelada* was the Portuguese name for a sweet quince paste (quince is *marmelo* in that language) that was imported as a luxury to Britain from the late Middle Ages onwards. So expensive that it was only used by royalty and the well heeled, *marmelada* was nonetheless in great demand. Tudor cooks invented a more affordable version by boiling up the cheaper imports of lemons and bitter Seville oranges into thick, solid conserves they called 'marmalades', which were cut into slices and eaten as sweets. The closest thing we have to it today is Turkish delight.

When marmalade changed from a sweet into a jam is hard to pinpoint, but evidence suggests its having happened in money-conscious Scotland. In the eighteenth century, Scottish recipes included a much higher proportion of water (possibly spearheaded by a Mrs Janet Keiller, the founder of Keiller's marmalade, in the 1790s) and changed marmalade from an expensive Portuguese dessert into a common British condiment. It was also a clever way of making sure that expensive ingredients were stretched as far as possible – something of a noble art north of the border – by spreading it on a piece of TOAST. That way the sensation of eating a chunk of Tudor marmalade was preserved at a fraction of the price and became a breakfast staple that British empire-builders, many from Scotland, spread around the world.

During the Middle Ages, pork was one of the few types of meat that was widely available and affordable throughout rural England. Indeed, for many, it was the only meat they ever had to eat. **Bacon** wasn't just the most delicious way to eat it: the smoked and salting process it went through meant that, unlike pork, it didn't need to be eaten immediately and a side of bacon could keep a hungry family fed (just a small piece of bacon could make PEASE PUDDING taste much better) for a whole winter.

From this it's easy to see how ***bringing home the bacon***, as the expression goes, would have been quite an event and acquiring a pig for the family pot a much sought-after prize. Catching a greased pig, one possible origin of the phrase, was popular at country fairs up and down the land: men would chase the animal around a ring and the winner, who finally caught and held on to the pig, was then given it to take home.

A rather more likely explanation for the phrase originates from a traditional event known as the Dunmow Flitch Trials. Established by a noblewoman called Juga in 1104, at Great Dunmow in Essex, this was a challenge to all married couples in England to live for a year and a day in complete harmony, without so much as a cross word between them. The prize offered was a flitch of bacon (a whole side) but, and this doesn't surprise me, in over five hundred years there were only eight winners. The tradition was re-established in 1855 and nowadays the trials are held every four years, often with celebrities taking part, probably in aid of some fashionable charity or another. Claimants of the flitch are required to stand in front of a jury of twelve (six maidens and six bachelors of Great Dunmow) and prove their worthiness during a daylong family event. The winners 'take home the bacon'. Or they do in theory: these days, it would seem, conjugal harmony is just as rare as it ever was.

The Full English Breakfast

The British breakfast, I swear on my honor as a scholar,
is without a peer on this globe's crust. I mean, of
course, the kind of breakfast that was *de rigueur* when
I was a student of Oxon in the balmy days before the
world wars had done their worst ... It was a parade of
the ultimate subtleties in meats and fish and fruits. It
weighted a man naturally towards poetry and philosophy. It broadened him out, not only in girth, but in the
circumference of friendliness.

ROBERT P. TRISTRAM COFFIN (October 1948)

For a meal that has become world famous, strangely little is
known about the evolution of the English breakfast. Until the
mid seventeenth century, most people would have had two
substantial daily meals: lunch (known as 'dinner' – see page xiii)
in the late morning and supper in the early evening. Breakfast
was not recognized as a meal and was only recommended to
children, invalids and the elderly, who were advised to eat
small meals at regular intervals. But as lunch moved to later
in the day, people became hungrier first thing in the morning,
especially when their evening meal was relatively small. In
countries where the evening meal was larger, breakfast did
not become quite so important; indeed, in southern Europe
it is still not a proper meal, but merely COFFEE and perhaps
a piece of bread or pastry (see CROISSANT). In England and
northern Europe, by contrast, the pattern has been quite
different for hundreds of years. By the 1700s, breakfast in
Britain was taken at around 9.00 or 10.00 a.m. and consisted
of ale, bread and beef. But, with an act of culinary genius,
it was the Victorians who turned what was still essentially a
snack into a full-scale meal and so the medieval 'dinner' was

transformed into the **full English breakfast**, served BUFFET-style throughout the grand houses of the nation.

Why this meal then caught on so strongly around the world has a lot to do with the simultaneous rise of the middle classes and the British Empire. One division between the poor and the wealthy has historically been that the latter group was able to afford to eat as much meat as it liked. And the new Victorian middle classes felt the need to prove, or at least feel, they were on a similar social level to the grandiose upper classes. The Industrial Revolution lent a hand, leading to greater social mobility in which once humble families were now headed by captains of industry far wealthier than their noble counterparts. It was these upstart folk, with their growing country estates, who initiated the buffet breakfast, with its vast array of dishes, for their regular guests to enjoy when they rose in the morning, thus establishing the 'traditional' English breakfast.

As the British Empire stretched across the world, so this habit spread with it – taken by the empire's administrators to India, South Africa and Australia and retained in memory of an idealized mother country whose customs and traditions they were anxious to impose upon the inhabitants of those less enlightened (as they saw it) corners of the globe. They didn't want to integrate: they wanted to claim the world for Britain. Hence starting the day with an enormous meaty breakfast (especially in a hot climate to which such a meal was incredibly unsuited) became almost an act of faith.

So what should it actually consist of? Mrs Beeton gives the following advice in her celebrated *Book of Household Management* (1861):

> The following list of hot dishes may perhaps assist our readers in knowing what to provide for the comfortable meal called breakfast. Broiled fish, such as mackerel, whiting, herrings, dried haddocks, &c.; mutton chops

and rump-steaks, broiled sheep's kidneys, kidneys à la
maître d'hôtel, sausages, plain rashers of bacon, bacon
and poached eggs, ham and poached eggs, omelettes,
plain boiled eggs, oeufs-au-plat, poached eggs on toast,
muffins, toast, marmalade, butter, &c. &c.

No wonder old atlases showed the territories of the British
Empire coloured a dark dyspeptic pink! Scanning Mrs Beeton's monumental list, we can spot some ingredients still on
the menu today and forming the core of the modern full English: BACON and eggs, sausages and TOAST. Later additions
on the healthier side of things are: tomatoes, mushrooms and
BAKED BEANS. And then it's up to the cook to check the
leftovers from the night before and decide whether to add
BUBBLE AND SQUEAK, fried potatoes or BLACK PUDDING.
The decline of the British Empire may well have had more to
do with the fact that today we are far more likely to start our
day with a bowl of CORN FLAKES (see BREAKFAST CEREAL
for more on the American breakfast counter-revolution) than
a plate of bacon and eggs with all the trimmings, unless you
are in a roadside café, where you would be chased out for asking for cereal, let alone anything as effete as a muffin.

There is a sense of slight embarrassment about the perfection of a good full English that is entirely characteristic of
the English, but the meal should be properly celebrated. One
of the most enjoyable things is that no two breakfasts are the
same and as most British workers and tradesmen start the day
with one, it has quite literally fuelled our economy for generations. In all the hotels around the world that I have stayed in,
the queue for the full English is always longer than the one for
the yoghurt and fruit in the morning, I promise you.

There are different regional variations, and Scotland,
Wales and Northern Ireland, not to mention southern Ireland, all have their own versions.

FULL SCOTTISH BREAKFAST

A **full Scottish breakfast**, along with the usual eggs, bacon and sausage, has black pudding (ingredients: blood, pork rind and barley), HAGGIS and potato scones. It may also include white pudding (basically black pudding without the blood) and oatcakes. Another favourite ingredient is square sausage – a kind of sausage burger – also known as Lorne sausage.

FULL WELSH BREAKFAST

The unusual ingredient in the **traditional Welsh breakfast** – otherwise identical to the full English – is laverbread, a purée of boiled reddish seaweed which is then mixed with oatmeal, formed into patties and fried in bacon fat. It's been eaten in Wales since the Middle Ages.

ULSTER FRY

Northern Ireland's **Ulster fry** makes a full English look positively healthy. It has seven key ingredients: bacon, eggs, sausages, farl soda bread (a triangular-shaped flat bread, split in half and fried), potato bread, black pudding and tomatoes, all fried together, preferably in one large pan.

THE IRISH BREAKFAST

I should disclose at this point that there is, of course, a **full Irish breakfast**, one that my friends in Dublin claim was the very first and that the English stole from them. But we know that during the eighteenth and nineteenth centuries, the English were, by and large, landowners while the Irish, in general, worked on that land and were always complaining of being hungry. And we know it was the great potato famine of 1845 that drove millions of the Irish to North America (see 'How the Potato Killed a Million People', page 154), so it's somewhat unlikely they were enjoying many full Irish breakfasts prior to then. Therefore, with respect to fine Irish chefs around the world who insist the English stole their breakfast, I'm afraid I can't endorse that claim.

'The Name's Benedict, Eggs Benedict'

The world's favourite brunch dish, **eggs Benedict** comprises an English muffin cut in two, each half topped with ham, a poached egg and a dollop of HOLLANDAISE SAUCE. A number of Benedicts claim to have invented it. In 1942, the *New Yorker* published an interview with one Lemuel Benedict, a retired New York stockbroker, who told the story of his breakfast one day at the Waldorf Hotel back in 1894. Unimpressed by the menu and with a thumping hangover, he asked for 'buttered TOAST, poached eggs, crispy bacon and a hooker of hollandaise'. According to Benedict, the maître d', Oscar Tschirky (see also THOUSAND ISLAND DRESSING and WALDORF SALAD), was so taken with the dish that he immediately included it on the hotel menu, replacing the TOAST with a muffin and the BACON with ham.

But this is disputed by a letter sent to *The New York Times* in September 1967 by Edward P. Montgomery, who suggested the dish was in fact the idea of Commodore E. C. Benedict, a yachtsman and retired banker, who died at the age of eighty-six in 1920. Montgomery insisted he had the original recipe, which he included in his letter, saying it had been given to his uncle, a close friend of Benedict. Publication of this letter prompted another one, from Mabel C. Butler of Massachusetts, in which she claimed that the 'true story' behind the original recipe was 'well known to the relations of Mrs Le Grand Benedict', of whom she was one. According to Mabel Butler, when the Benedicts lived in New York City, at the turn of the century, their habit was to dine regularly at Delmonico's

Restaurant. One morning Mrs Benedict complained that the menu had become too familiar and suggested more variety. As she was a regular customer, the head chef asked the good lady what she had in mind, to which she replied: 'I would like poached eggs on toasted English muffins with a thin slice of ham, hollandaise sauce and a truffle on top.'

Each tale was firmly believed by its narrator but it is equally likely that all three were referring to a dish that had been around for a lot longer, probably going by a different name. What is certain is that printed recipes for eggs Benedict were beginning to appear from the turn of the twentieth century. In *Eggs, and How to Use Them*, published in 1898 and subtitled (clearly with Mrs Benedict in mind) 'A Guide for the Preparation of Eggs in Over Five Hundred Different Styles', the reader is encouraged to 'split and toast some small muffins; put on each a nice round slice of broiled ham, and on the ham the poached egg; pour over some creamy Hollandaise sauce'. Meanwhile, in 1900, the *Connecticut Magazine* printed a similar recipe, suggesting readers should 'Broil a thin slice of cold-boiled ham ... toast a slice of bread, butter it and moisten with a little water; lay the ham on it and on that a poached egg'.

However, it turns out that this all-American dish could well have been European in origin. Elizabeth David, in *French Provincial Cooking* (1960), refers to a traditional French dish called *oeufs à la bénédictine* and consisting of puréed fish and potatoes on fried bread with a poached egg on top. So maybe eggs Benedict was originally a sort of full French breakfast enjoyed by Benedictine monks on days when they were forbidden to eat meat? (They'd have been tucking into a FULL ENGLISH otherwise, given half a chance.)

These days there are many variations on the theme, including EGGS FLORENTINE (the ham substituted by spinach), **seafood Benedict** (the ham replaced with crab, lobster or prawns) and **waffle Benedict** (with a waffle instead of the muffin and lashings of maple syrup in addition to the hollandaise). **Eggs Benedict Arnold**, in which the muffin is replaced by an American biscuit (a bit like an English scone) and the hollandaise sauce with gravy is very curiously named for such a staunchly American dish. Benedict Arnold was a general during the American Revolutionary War of 1775–83 who famously switched sides and fought for the British. One of the most hated figures in US history, his name has since become a byword in America for treason.

The Noble Story of French Toast

What we call **French toast** is known as *pain perdu* ('lost bread') in France itself. Like TOAST, it is regarded as a way of using stale (or 'lost') bread, slices of which are softened by being dipped in a mixture of egg, milk and sugar before being fried in butter. In Britain, it was actually referred to as **German toast** until the First World War when anti-German sentiment caused the name to be changed. In a similar vein, the British royal family changed its surname from Saxe-Coburg-Gotha to Windsor (see BATTENBERG CAKE and SALISBURY STEAK) and the German shepherd dog became known as an Alsatian at around the same time. In a further, somewhat ironic twist, French toast briefly became known as **freedom toast** in America following French disapproval of the invasion of Iraq in 2003 (see also FRENCH FRIES).

The actual German name for the dish is *arme Ritter* or 'poor knights', echoing its much older English name, **Poor Knights of Windsor**. The original Poor Knights were veterans of the Battle of Crécy in 1346, one of the most important battles of the Hundred Years' War (1337–1453). Although the English won the battle, thanks to the introduction of the fearsome longbow, many knights were still captured and held for ransom by the retreating French. Forced to sell their grand estates to raise the money, twenty-six noble knights eventually returned to England alive and free but penniless. King Edward III (1312–77) then provided the veterans with a pension and accommodation at Windsor Castle and they became known as the Alms Knights, or the Poor Knights of Windsor, establishing a centuries-long tradition.

At one point, during the 1830s, the Poor Knights objected to their name – perhaps because by then they were much more affluent, they no longer appreciated sharing a name with stale, sugary egg-soaked bread – and King William IV (1765–1837) officially changed their title to the Military Knights of Windsor. Their duties are to pray for the sovereign on a daily basis and escort the Knights and Ladies of the Garter into St George's Chapel, Windsor, during processions and services held by the Order of the Garter (also established by Edward III). It's perhaps the association between the Poor Knights and the French that has led to the modern English name for the dish.

Who was the First Person to Pronounce on Porridge?

If I asked you to visualize the earliest scene from the history of **porridge**, I imagine you'd picture a Scottish peasant stirring a big pot on a chilly morning and not the Buddha (566–486 BC) fasting in sun-soaked India. But the making and eating of porridge is in fact central to his story. In his search for enlightenment, the Buddha did without food for so long that he fainted and a peasant girl brought him back from the brink of death with a little milk and a bowl of rice porridge. Thanks to the young girl's ministrations, he was soon strong enough to take his seat under the Bodhi Tree, where he finally achieved enlightenment.

In his teachings, first collected orally and then written down by his followers, the Buddha went on to explain the five benefits of porridge. As it turns out, these five benefits are somewhat less than transcendental and already long acknowledged by porridge eaters (Buddhist or otherwise) the world over: namely that it improves digestion, quenches thirst, suppresses hunger and reduces constipation and flatulence. And anything that does that can only be a good thing. (For more on the Buddha and food, see the box on page 239.)

Kippers: When is a Herring Not a Herring?

Am I the only one who has ever wondered why, when we eat smoked herring for breakfast, we change its name to **kipper**? Etymologists argue about where the word comes from: whether it's *kipe*, a creel used to catch fish, *kippian*, the Old English verb for 'to spawn', or *kip*, the small beak a male salmon develops during the spawning season (hence another kind of 'kipper' – live and unsmoked). And there are various stories about who first turned herring – or indeed any fish caught in large numbers and in need of preserving – into kippers (see also PICKLED HERRING and RED HERRING). Northumbria claims it was one John Woodger of Seahouses, who in around 1843 left some split salted herring in a shed where a fire had burned all night. It was thought that all the fish had been 'ruined' by the smoke. However, one was tasted, declared 'delicious', and so the kipper was born.

But this turns out to be a rural (rather than an urban) legend. As Mark Kurlansky explains in *Salt: A World History* (2002): 'Smoked foods almost always carry with them legends about their having been created by accident – usually the peasant hung the food too close to the fire, and then, imagine his surprise the next morning when etc. etc....' The one thing that etymologists can agree on is that the word 'kipper' is far older than even the oldest story of how smoked herring first came about. The process of 'kippering', salting and smoking fish or meat, goes back a very long way, probably to prehistoric times, or ever since people started using salt to preserve food. The kipper could well be the oldest British dish of all.

Devilled Kidneys and Canned Ham

To 'devil', according to the *Oxford English Dictionary*, is a culinary term for 'cooking something with fiery hot spices. The term was presumably adopted because of the association between the devil and excessive heat in Hell.' The practice of devilling food is an old one: James Boswell (1740–95), the famous diarist and Dr Johnson's official biographer, frequently noted a passion for 'devilled bones' for his supper. Presumably that was a dish of spicy spare ribs rather than anything more sinister.

Devilled kidneys became an extremely popular ingredient in the FULL ENGLISH BREAKFAST from the nineteenth century onwards. Anything devilled, or heavily spiced, might be served at breakfast, including devilled eggs, ham, chicken or mushrooms. An article published in *The Jewish Manual* in 1846 and ascribed to 'A Lady' (identity unknown) explains how 'Devilling, or broiling with cayenne pepper, is also a good expedient to coax the palate when you have relics of poultry or game.'

In 1868, an American food distributor based in Boston, the William Underwood Company – a major supplier to Union troops during the American Civil War (1861–5) – began experimenting by mixing ground ham with hot spices, including mustard and cayenne pepper. They christened this process 'deviling' (to use the American spelling – preparing ham in this way was an innovation, even if the word itself was much older) and their product, **Underwood Deviled Ham**, soon found its way all over America, thanks largely to the canning process (see CHICKEN KIEV) and the growing rail networks. Their famous red devil logo was trademarked in 1870, the oldest food trademark in America, and the canned ham remains popular in that country to this day.

The Surreal History of Breakfast Cereal

The brightly coloured cereal packets on your breakfast table, full of chocolate and sugar and covered in cartoon elves and grinning tigers, are in fact the unlikely last remnants of a bizarre, long-running battle that raged in nineteenth-century America between an equally unlikely set of combatants: vegetarians, water-cure fanatics and the Seventh-day Adventist Church.

It was all powered by a growing obsession with regulating bodily functions. At the time, most Americans ate a FULL ENGLISH BREAKFAST – a substantial meal, heavy on pork and other meats and very low in fibre. As a consequence, many were very constipated and suffered painful gastric disorders.

But, being the nineteenth century, nothing happened by halves. The first spokesman in the health-food revolution was the Reverend Sylvester Graham (1794–1851). A vegetarian with no medical training, he was determined that wholemeal flour was the answer, and his very profitable **Graham bread** and **Graham crackers** followed as a result. Vegetarianism and temperance became wildly popular for a while: meat-eating was declared to be unhealthy – not to mention productive of equally negative carnal desires – and coffee and tea were condemned as poisons. It wasn't long before Graham's supporters were declaring that their search for 'healthy' substitutes based on grains and cereals was for the common good, some no doubt recognizing how this might earn them very healthy sums of money in the process.

In 1858, Dr James Caleb Jackson (1811–95) took over an unsuccessful water-cure resort in New York, renaming it 'Our Home Hygenic Institute'. Patients were subjected to a punishing regime of baths and unpleasant treatments and fed a restricted diet based on various grains, like farm animals. In 1863, Jackson created the first **breakfast cereal**, which he called **Granula**, but it was hardly fast food; it had to be soaked overnight in milk before it was even possible to chew the stone-hard crumbs. Even so, Granula caught on, earning Jackson ten times the amount of cash he had invested in developing it.

In Battle Creek, Michigan, the Seventh-day Adventists ran a health institute, the Battle Creek Sanitarium, where the latest in dietary reform was practised, but it didn't really catch on until John Harvey Kellogg was put in charge. Dr Kellogg (1852–1943) had been hand-picked for the job and his medical and spiritual training had been supervised at every stage by the Adventists. Following his experience of living in a boarding house during training, where cooking was impossible and restricted to the vegetarian diet required by his religion, the hungry young man recognized the need for a ready-cooked breakfast cereal that required no preparation. In 1880, he came up with a mixture of wheat, oat and maize meal baked in little biscuits, which he cheekily called **Granola**, and it became a huge success, in the land of overnight successes.

A few years later, in 1893, a Denver lawyer called Henry D. Perky (1843–1906; no relation to Pinky) invented a completely different product to cure his indigestion that he called **Shredded Wheat**. The wheat was steamed until thoroughly softened, then rolled between grooved rollers to form strands that were then pressed together and cut into biscuits, referred to by Perky as 'my little whole wheat mattresses'. Unfortunately, the process didn't work as the moist wheat biscuits soon perished. Kellogg then went to see the disillusioned inventor and offered Perky $100,000 for the patents he had taken out for manufacturing his cereal, but then he lost his nerve and retracted the offer. He would later regret this, however, particularly since in his conversation he had shared his secret of how Kellogg products were dried by slow heating so that they remained in perfect condition for a long period of time. Armed with this knowledge, Perky tinkered with his machinery, began to dry his Shredded Wheat and sat back to watch the dollars roll in, becoming immensely rich in the process.

Kellogg was naturally envious and, after a long period of experimentation, came up with a process in which wheat was cooked, flattened into flakes and then dried. **Granose Flakes**, as he called them, would soon prove to be a significant commercial discovery, but not for the good doctor. With no real head for business, he was mostly interested in his sanatorium and for a while his patients were the only people who could buy his products.

The man primarily responsible for speeding breakfast cereal out into the grocery stores of the nation was Charles William Post (1854–1914). He entered the cereal business after a string of entrepreneurial failures that led to a physical collapse. As a patient at Kellogg's sanatorium in 1891, he didn't find a cure, but he did come to realize that health foods and, in particular, coffee substitutes were potential goldmines. The idea alone must have been enough to cheer him up a bit. After leaving the sanatorium, he started his own health institute in Battle Creek and within four years he had developed Postum, a wheat- and molasses-based hot drink. Using everything he knew about sales, Post then mounted an advertising campaign and his product became a success.

There was, he said, no limit to the number of physical and moral ills (even divorce or juvenile delinquency) that were caused by coffee, but it could all be banished with Postum, the beverage that promised to 'make red blood'. Two years later, he launched what would prove to be an even bigger hit. **Grape Nuts** had been a failure as a grain beverage, as it was originally marketed, but rebranded as a breakfast cereal it quickly became a bestseller. (It was sweetened with maltose, which Post called grape sugar and which he thought had a nut-like flavour – hence the name.) By 1902, Post was making over a million dollars a year – a lot of money now but a huge sum in those days.

J. H. Kellogg's younger brother and general office assistant at the sanatorium, Willie Keith (1860–1951), followed with an improvement on the Granose idea – flakes made from corn. Eventually, the two Kellogg brothers fell out and in 1906 W. K. (whose signature still appears on every cereal packet as the company's trademark today) founded the great Kellogg breakfast food empire with his toasted **Corn Flakes**. Originally called the Battle Creek Toasted Corn Flake Company, it was renamed the Kellogg Company in 1922, while the product on which it was founded became what must be the most celebrated breakfast cereal in the world. At the time of its conception, hundreds of other would-be cereal pioneers had leapt into the field as well, many journeying to Battle Creek itself to start their businesses. Soon thirty different cereal flake companies, most of them fly-by-night operations, had crowded into the small town. And Americans had scores of cereals to choose from, each promising to cure their every ailment.

But despite their origins in the health-food movement, breakfast cereals have no special nutritional value, beyond the food value of the grain they are made from – hence the fact that so many today are artificially 'fortified' with extra vitamins. It is the milk they are eaten with that provides most of the nutrients they otherwise lack.

Arnold Bennett the Famous Omelette

Today Arnold Bennett (1867–1931) is probably better known for the omelette named after him than for any of his thirty novels and other writings. Originally Bennett had intended to follow his father and practise law at the family business in their home town of Hanley, in an area of Staffordshire known as the Potteries, but in 1888 he took the brave decision to move to London.

When his first novel, *A Man from the North*, was published to critical acclaim in 1898, he felt vindicated and became a full-time writer. Bennett's books poured out, many of them set in a thinly veiled version of the Potteries called the Five Towns, earning him tremendous popularity with the public, although his attitude to his work displeased many of his literary contemporaries (in particular Virginia Woolf), who accused him of forsaking art in the interest of quantity and income, criticizing him for his conventional writing style and choice of material. Bennett himself made no apologies: he simply regarded himself as a working writer, once even commenting, 'Am I to sit still and see other fellows earning two guineas for stories that I can do better myself? Not me. If anyone imagines my sole aim is art for art's sake then they are cruelly deceived.'

And as the money rolled in, his work rate never diminished and he even managed to produce five new books in the last three years of his life. It was while completing one of them, *Imperial Palace* (1930), that Bennett checked into the Savoy Hotel, where he ended up staying until he finished the entire story. During this period, the hotel's chefs turned his favourite breakfast of eggs and smoked haddock into the famous **omelette Arnold Bennett**, still to be found on the hotel menu eighty years later.

How Did the Croissant Get Its Shape?

The **croissant**, cornerstone of the 'continental' breakfast the world over, first came about during the late 1830s, when August Zang, an Austrian artillery officer, founded a Viennese Bakery at 92, rue de Richelieu in Paris. Zang's shop sold all kinds of Viennese delicacies, including the **kipferl**, a crescent-shaped pastry common in Austria since at least the thirteenth century. His kipferl was so popular that bakers all over Paris rushed to make their own French version and the croissant (meaning 'crescent') was born.

There are all kinds of culinary legends explaining the unusual shape of the kipferl and hence croissant, mostly connected to the fact that the symbol of Turkey, and thus Islam, is a crescent moon. One story says it was invented in Germany to celebrate the Muslim defeat at the Battle of Tours in 732; others suggest that it dates from the Crusades. But my favourite is that it celebrates the failure of the Turkish siege of Vienna in 1683 (see also CAPPUCCINO), when bakers, up in the middle of the night to prepare their bread for baking, heard the Turks digging a tunnel under the city walls and quickly raised the alarm. The Turks, taken by surprise, were soundly beaten. The crescent-shaped pastry the bakers then made to mark the Turkish defeat allowed the Viennese to relive their victory every time they tore one in half or dipped it into a cup of coffee. But whichever story is the true one, and however the croissant acquired its distinctive shape, it remains a fact that the definitive French pastry is not French in origin but Austrian.

2
Lunchbox

Could a Cornish Pasty Really Save Your Life?

Do Scotch Eggs Come from Scotland?

Did a Satanist Really Invent the Sandwich?

Don't be Fooled by a Ploughman's Lunch

Who Invented the Picnic?

Ship's Biscuit: When Did a Snack Take
the Place of Lunch?

Whatever You Do, Don't Mention
the Quiche (Lorraine)

A Brief History of the Pie

Ask not what you can do for your country. Ask what's for lunch.

ORSON WELLES

Could a Cornish Pasty Really Save Your Life?

The earliest written description of a meat and vegetable pasty dates from the reign of Henry III (1207–72) and Chaucer refers twice to venison pasties in the fourteenth-century *Canterbury Tales*. Originally a luxurious dish enjoyed by the nobility, who discarded its tough outer pastry to eat the tender filling (see 'A Brief History of the Pie', page 39), the pasty was a humbler version, made with whatever vegetables and meat were available, and extremely popular among working people from the sixteenth century onwards.

But of course the pasty is principally associated with Cornwall, attaining this identity over the last two hundred years. Indeed, it was already regarded as traditional Cornish fare in the beginning of the nineteenth century and described as such in Worgan's *Agricultural Survey* of the county in 1808. The Cornish were famous fishermen and notorious smugglers but the industry that really supported their economy was tin mining. This was harsh and dangerous work and **Cornish pasties** suited the conditions of the mines perfectly. The thick pastry acted as part thermos, part lunchbox, keeping the contents of the pasty secure and warm. The pasties were easy to carry and, full of meat, vegetables and carbohydrate, they were a meal in themselves, providing the miners with enough energy to pass a gruelling day down the pit. Often one end of a pasty would contain fruit or jam, by way of a dessert. Housewives used to make one for each member of the household and mark their initials on one end of the pasty, thus avoiding many a lunchtime fist fight at the pit head.

And when it comes to how Cornish pasties could save your life ... there was a superstition among miners that it was unlucky to eat the thick crimped crust and it should be thrown to the 'knockers' (the spirits of the tin mines). As so often with superstitions, there was a practical reason lurking behind this one: miners used the crust as a handle to hold the pasty while they ate it and so avoided transferring arsenic, a deadly poison present in the mines, from their hands and into their food.

When foreign competition put Cornish mining out of business in the late nineteenth century, workers were forced to emigrate to America, Australia and South Africa. In the first six months of 1875, no fewer than ten thousand Cornish miners boarded the boat towards a new life and they took their Cornish pasty with them all over the globe.

Do Scotch Eggs Come from Scotland?

The **Scotch egg** is a strange-looking food – a hard-boiled egg wrapped in sausage meat, dipped in breadcrumbs and then deep-fried – and it has an unusual history. Food historian Alan Davidson argues that it is descended from the Indian dish *nargisi kofta*, eggs covered in minced lamb and cooked in curried tomatoes. Brought home by returning soldiers of the British Empire, it later evolved into **curried Scotch eggs**, with spices being added to the mincemeat and no sauce. Various other individuals and institutions, all non-Scottish, have laid claim to the Scotch egg, including the famous London department store Fortnum & Mason, which called its 1738 version of the dish 'bird's nests' and used plover's rather than hen's eggs.

The first printed recipe for what we'd recognize as Scotch eggs (but which didn't call them Scottish) appeared in *A New*

System of Domestic Cookery by English gentlewoman Mrs Maria Rundell (1745–1828), which was a huge hit when first published in 1806. A forerunner of the much more celebrated Mrs Beeton, Mrs Rundell was nonetheless a bestselling author in her day – her cookbook reprinted sixty-five times and sold over half a million copies.

But the first time they were actually called Scotch eggs in print was by one Meg Dodds, landlady of the Cleikum Inn at St Ronan's, near Peebles in Scotland. It was she who apparently first used the term in her *Cook and Housewife's Manual* (1826), where she recommended they be eaten hot with gravy. So far, so Scottish ... However, although there is indeed a Cleikum Inn – albeit at Lochgelly, Fife, many miles from Peebles – it turns out that Meg Dodds herself never actually existed. She is in fact a character in Sir Walter Scott's very popular novel *St Ronan's Well*, published two years earlier. Many have speculated that it was Scott – a prolific writer who found fame during the early 1800s with his books *Rob Roy* (1817) and *Ivanhoe* (1819) – who had written *Cook and Housewife's Manual* himself, using Meg Dodd as a nom de plume, and it is he who is therefore responsible for the rise in popularity of the humble Scotch egg. Hence it is this particular Scot who can lay claim to Scotch eggs – or Scott's eggs, as they should perhaps be called – ensuring that a little piece of Scottish heritage would appear at every British petrol station and budget wedding reception some two hundred years later. And this has nothing to do with the crumbs on the coating being so obviously ginger.

Did a Satanist Really Invent the Sandwich?

Sandwich is, believe it or not, not really even a proper word. It is a proper name, however. The village of Sandwich, first recorded in AD 642, is a picturesque and historic place in Kent: its name evolved from the Old English words *sand* and *wic*, meaning 'Sand Village' or 'Town on the Sand'. Now two miles from the sea, it was once a thriving seaport – the first captive elephant was landed there in 1255, before being delivered as a gift to Henry III – and the home of King Charles II's naval fleet under the command of Sir Edward Montague. When in 1660 his grateful king made Montague an earl, the latter pondered which of the great ports he would honour with his new title. Bristol was one option and Portsmouth another, but the naval commander settled for Sandwich and so his hereditary title became the Earl of Sandwich.

To date there have been eleven earls but the most famous of them, the one who provided the key ingredient for every packed lunch in the Western world, was number four. John Montague (1718–92) was, like his great-grandfather, First Lord of the Admiralty but unlike him he was both corrupt and incompetent. The navy was in a state of complete disarray by the time it was called into action during the American Revolutionary War (1775–83): the eventual defeat of the British forces was regarded by many as his fault. And hardly surprising as the earl was far more interested in his life outside work, particularly gambling. Indeed, it was this that gave rise to the great culinary legend forever associated with him. According to the famous story, he was once playing cards long into the wee small hours in 1762 with friends. Drunk and on a winning streak, Sandwich decided he needed some food and ordered waiters to bring him some meat but 'between two slices of bread'. This was to prevent his fingers from becoming greasy and marking the cards, helping his opponents to figure out his gaming pattern. The strategy worked and the snack soon caught on at the great gaming tables and gambling clubs of England, the 'sandwich' quickly becoming part of the English way of life.

It didn't help his reputation that Sandwich was also a member of the notorious Hellfire Club, a gentlemen's society set up to ridicule organized religion. No one knew what went on at their meetings – members didn't discuss them – but rumours were rife of orgies and satanic rituals. It was reputedly at one of these meetings that he became the victim of one of history's great one-liner putdowns. Sandwich is said to have abused Samuel Foote: 'Sir, I don't know if you will die on the gallows or of the pox.' To which Foote shot back: 'That, my lord, depends on whether I embrace your principles or your mistress.' The story was speedily spread around London by his many enemies.

By his death in 1792, Sandwich had become the most unpopular man in England. Even friends suggested his epitaph should read: 'Seldom has any man held so many offices and yet accomplished so little.' Yet the sandwich is not his only legacy to history. As First Lord of the Admiralty, Sandwich was one of the sponsors of the voyage Captain James Cook made to the New World in 1778. On 14 January, Cook became the first European to visit the Hawaiian Islands, which he originally called the Sandwich Islands in honour of his benefactor. Although the islands changed their name a century later, the South Sandwich Islands and the Sandwich Straits still bear the name of the old gambler, and inventor of the sandwich, to this day. Not to mention the expression it has given rise to, in the sense that we can now find ourselves **sandwiched** between two objects or two business appointments or, as I would much prefer, between two cocktail waitresses in a Las Vegas casino. I'm just relieved that the first earl selected Sandwich for his title. I'm not sure I'd fancy a cheese and CHUTNEY bristol, or a ham and tomato portsmouth. Would you?

WHAT ABOUT THE OPEN SANDWICH?

The **open sandwich**, particularly favoured in Nordic countries (see SMORGASBORD) and consisting of a single slice of bread with food items arranged on top, is a much older concept than the double-slice variety. It goes back to the Middle Ages, when a large chunk of bread called a 'trencher' was used as a plate to hold other food. At the end of the meal, the bread could be eaten or, if the diner had had enough, left on the floor for the dogs to devour.

AND WHY IS IT A CLUB SANDWICH?

A **club sandwich**, also known as a **clubhouse sandwich**, has its origins in America. Usually made with three slices of bread, this double-decker sandwich traditionally consists of bacon, chicken, lettuce and tomato, always on toasted bread. The sandwich was apparently made famous by the exclusive Saratoga Springs gaming club in New York during the late 1800s, when it became a firm favourite on the menu. Ever since the Americans had added MAYONNAISE and all sorts of sauces to the common sandwich, greasy fingers were evidently once again a problem for card players, which the toasted version helped to solve.

Don't be Fooled by a Ploughman's Lunch

We all know a **ploughman's lunch** is made up of fresh bread, hard cheese, onion and pickles and is a fixture of just about every British pub menu, including those where there is no ploughed field in sight. It is often mistaken for a genuinely old dish, harking back to simpler, rosier-tinted times when the ploughman pulled up his horses in a shady furrow and unpacked his humble lunch. Sadly, it has nothing to do with the traditional rural way of life. 'Ploughman's lunch', referring to a specific type of dish, is a modern term, coined during the late 1960s and early 1970s by the English Country Cheese Council as part of a marketing campaign to encourage people to eat more cheese and launched after an article was published about it, written by the chairman of the council, Sir Richard Trehane.

The Cheese Handbook, written by B. H. Axler and published in 1969, quotes Trehane (who provides a preface to the book): 'English cheese and beer have for centuries formed a perfect combination enjoyed as the Ploughman's Lunch.' The phrase itself may indeed be old. It first appeared in print in John G. Lockhart's *The Life of Sir Walter Scott*, published between 1837 and 1839, which describes how 'the surprised poet swung forth to join them, with an extemporized SANDWICH, that looked like a ploughman's luncheon, in his hand' (see also SCOTCH EGG). The *Oxford English Dictionary* notes this as the first recorded use of the expression, although whether it was a cheese and pickle sandwich is, of course, unknown.

The Cheese Council may also have been inspired by the **ploughboy's lunch**, recorded to have been served in pubs in some parts of rural England during the period of rationing immediately after the Second World War and consisting of a hunk of bread, a slab of local cheese, some pickled onions and a pint of beer. The marketing campaign was clearly a major success as the 'ploughman's' soon caught on and was being enjoyed in pubs throughout the land, as reflected by Paul Theroux who, in his 1973 novel *Saint Jack*, describes how 'We had a ploughman's lunch in the village – beautiful old pub – and went back to London.' By 1975, the mighty *Times* newspaper was informing its readers: 'The pubs specialize in lunchtime catering and you can get a decent "ploughman's" for between 20p and 30p.' Those were the days.

Who Invented the Picnic?

At the end of the eighteenth century, a new fashion crossed the English Channel. The French were having a new type of informal party, known as a *pique-nique*, in which the guests would bring along a share of the food and wine so that the burden of providing would not be left to only one family. Consequently, these social get-togethers were often held in outdoor public places, and to this day **picnic** is used to describe an outdoor meal, usually with friends.

It has been suggested that the word 'pique' might derive from one of the senses of the French verb *piquer*, 'to pick', while 'nique' is something 'irrelevant' or 'of no importance'. This is just speculation, however, as according to the *Oxford English Dictionary* the origin of the word isn't known. It was first used in English during the mid eighteenth century, associated initially with poker playing and later to describe a meal of cold foods eaten outside during a hunt – a tradition dating back to the mid 1300s and usually involving game pies and roasted or baked meats.

When the great royal parks of Paris were opened to the public for the first time, following the Revolution in 1793, *pique-nique* culture took off with a vengeance and London-ers who were used to looking to Paris for the latest fashions in clothes and culture promptly set up their own version, the 'Picnic Society', whose members would each arrive with their share of the overall feast. The nationwide enjoyment of picnicking was firmly established in England by the mid 1800s and many of the great writers of that era and later, including Charles Dickens and Arnold Bennett (see also OMELETTE ARNOLD BENNETT), helped to popularize the custom in their fiction.

Ship's Biscuit: When Did a Snack Take the Place of Lunch?

Now, luckily for you, this is not something you'd recognize as a lunchtime dish. But in the past when sea voyages could last months or even years and with a decided lack of stor-age space for fresh food aboard ship, this unappetizing dried bread formed the major part of a sailor's daily ration. When Richard the Lionheart set off on the Third Crusade in 1190, he loaded his ships with an early form of **ship's biscuit**, which he called 'biskit of muslin'. By the time of the Spanish Armada (1588), a sailor's daily ration was one pound of bis-cuit and one gallon of beer. Sailors gave it all kinds of nick-names, from 'hard tack' ('tack' was their word for food) to 'sheet iron' and 'tooth dullers'. Ship's biscuit was made edi-ble only by being dipped in a liquid or some kind of gravy.

At Chatham in Kent, the Royal Navy actually built its own bakery at the Royal Docks, devoted entirely to supplying every crew member with his staple diet. The *Encyclopaedia Britannica* of 1773 notes: 'Sea biscuit is a type of bread much dried by passing the oven twice to make it keep well for sea service. For long voyages they bake it four times and do so six months before embarkation and it will hold good for a whole year.' Incidentally, it's also the ancestor of today's WATER BISCUIT.

Made from the cheapest flour (the captain's and officers' rations were from finer), ship's biscuit was notorious for supplying an unintended source of protein: weevils and maggots. It certainly explains why sailors traditionally ran riot and drunk themselves blind as soon as they got off their ships. They were probably trying to block out the memory of months of gnawing on maggoty ship's biscuit.

Whatever You Do, Don't Mention the Quiche (Lorraine)

The Second World War ended over sixty years ago, but the Germans remained very unpopular in France for many years. After D-Day (6 June 1944), the French punished any kind of fraternization with the occupying enemy extremely sternly and there was a wave of executions without trial, public humiliations, assaults and detentions of suspected collaborators – all of which makes the real history of their most popular lunchtime dish a tad embarrassing for them, which is exactly why I am telling it.

Located in the north-east of the country and now firmly French, Lorraine has always been the subject of territorial disputes, and over the last couple of hundred years has been occupied by both the Prussians and the Germans on many an occasion. Lorraine's very name is Germanic, coming from Lothringen, a German kingdom of the Middle Ages, but this doesn't often come up in polite conversation with its pro-French inhabitants. During the Second World War, the fight to drive the German army out of France was so intense that

General de Gaulle chose the Cross of Lorraine as the symbol of the French Resistance. Consequently, Lorraine is now host to the largest American military cemetery in Europe. And yet the region has long been strongly influenced by the culture and cuisine of its German neighbours, as is shown by its most famous export, **quiche Lorraine**. Its pastry case was originally baked in the same cast-iron tin as German custard tarts – indeed the filling, made with eggs and milk or cream, is a type of savoury custard. The word 'quiche' actually derives from the German word *Kuchen* for 'cake' or 'tart', later mangled into *Kische* and then *quiche* by the French. Thus the most famous French dish in the world is actually a garbled version of the German phrase the 'cake of Lothringen'.

Although the recipe for quiche was first developed as a simple meal to cater for people on religious fasting days when abstinence from meat was essential, the key ingredient of Lorraine's quiche is bacon. A favourite staple of Allied soldiers fighting on the Lorraine battlefields, who brought the recipe back home with them in the late 1940s, it has been available in just about every supermarket in Britain and America ever since.

A Brief History of the Pie

Pies are an essential part of the cuisine of central and northern Europe and occur elsewhere (such as North America) only as introduced dishes, probably spread by the Romans, who in turn pinched the idea from the ancient Greeks. Food historian Alan Davidson, in *The Penguin Companion to Food* (2002), suggests that the derivation of the word may be from 'magpie', shortened to 'pie'. These birds are known to collect a variety of things and it was an essential feature of the earliest pies that they contained a variety of ingredients. It's only been more recently that pies have contained one chief ingredient, such as **apple pie**.

The first pies as we'd recognize them were eaten by the nobility and were called 'coffins' (which formerly just meant a container). Very large and filled with assorted meats in a sauce, they were baked like a modern casserole but using the crust itself as the pot. The tough (almost inedible) pastry, called 'huff paste', was discarded after the filling had been eaten (rather like bread trenchers – see OPEN SANDWICH) or given to the servants. As time went by, pies became smaller and the pastry tastier (often enriched with butter) and they were no longer just the preserve of the aristocracy. (For the pie as a precursor of the tin can, see POTTED SHRIMPS.)

Humble pie is not a real dish, of course, but a type of apology in which the person apologizing usually has to accept some sort of humiliation in the process. The expression dates back to the Middle Ages and the banquets held after a long day hunting. During the feast the lord of the manor and his noble guests would expect to be served the finest cuts of venison, while the deer's entrails, or offal, known as 'umble' or 'numble' (from the French *nomble*), would be baked in a pie and served to lower-class folk, or perhaps to those who were out of favour with the lord. Hence a higher-class diner seated at the wrong end of the table (accidentally or as a deliberate snub) would be forced to eat **umble pie** and endure the consequent humiliation.

DON'T TELL ANY PORK PIES

The **pork pie** is essentially an edible fossil: although its pastry is edible, its stiff texture and sheer sides evoke the huff paste 'coffins' of yore. Made from a hot-water paste of flour, lard and boiling salt water, the pastry case is filled with roughly chopped pork and baked in a supportive mould that is removed towards the end of cooking to let the pie brown evenly. Once the pie is baked and while it is still hot, rich stock made from trimmings is poured in through the small hole in the lid. As the stock cools, it turns into a protective jelly. The pork pie has proved so enduringly popular that it has inspired the cockney rhyming slang for 'lies', as in: 'That policeman thought I was telling him porkies, but I wasn't.'

There are many imitators but the traditional home of the very best pork pies is Melton Mowbray in Leicestershire. The common-or-garden pork pie uses cured meat, frequently enhanced with artificial colouring, to ensure that the meat filling is pink; the meat in a **Melton Mowbray pie**, by contrast, is grey because it's made from fresh rather than cured pork. But there could be another reason why its makers don't feel the need to artificially heighten the colour of the pork in a Melton Mowbray pie, one relating to a popular legend associated with the town.

Melton Mowbray used to be a focal point for fox hunting – perhaps helped by its pork pies being the perfect portable snack for the hungry huntsman. It is reputed that in 1837 the 3rd Marquis of Waterford, Henry de La Poer Beresford (1811–59), a well-known rascal with a passion for heavy drinking and high jinks, had enjoyed a successful hunt with a group of his noble friends and rode into Melton Mowbray to celebrate. As the evening progressed and the group moved from pub to pub, somebody discovered a few tins of red paint which the marquis then daubed liberally across the door of every tavern they visited. As the night wore on, more doors were painted, along with the water pump, the post office and several other public amenities. On his way out of town, the marquis even painted the tollgate and, according to some accounts, the toll keeper himself.

Naturally the incident was widely reported after it appeared in the *London Examiner* and the expression **painting the town red** is still used to describe a roisterous night out. Traces of red can still be seen in Melton Mowbray if you stroll down the high street. But unlike the town and the average pork pie, the Melton Mowbray is untainted by any red colouring and remains the tastiest pie in the kingdom.

3
Sunday Lunch

What are the Origins of the Sunday Roast?

Where Do the Noble Names for Beef Come From?

What Does a Yorkshire Pudding Have
to Do with Yorkshire?

Does Horseradish Sauce Have Anything
to Do with Radishes, or Horses?

At length Jones made a full stop, and turning about, cries, 'Who knows, Partridge, but the loveliest creature in the universe may have her eyes now fixed on that very moon which I behold at this instant?' 'Very likely, sir,' answered Partridge; 'and if my eyes were fixed on a good sirloin of roast beef, the devil might take the moon and her horns into the bargain.'

HENRY FIELDING, *Tom Jones*

What are the Origins of the Sunday Roast?

On 7 March 321, the Emperor Constantine (*c.*272–337), a convert to Christianity, passed the first law marking out Sunday as a day of rest: 'On the venerable Day of the Sun let the magistrates and people residing in cities rest, and let all workshops be closed.' As Christianity became an integral part of Western life – indeed, it was under Constantine's rule that it became the dominant religion in the Roman Empire – more rules were passed, banning all kinds of activities on Sunday, except, of course, eating. Sunday was a special day, the one day off in the week for working people, and the main meal should be special too. Everyone was expected to attend church on a Sunday morning and the slap-up meal they enjoyed on their return home – often the one meal of the week where they ate meat – was a reward for behaving so virtuously. During the Middle Ages, the lord of the manor would provide a roast ox for his serfs, thus initiating the tradition of the **Sunday roast**.

It wasn't until the twentieth century that it was common for every home to have its own oven. Prior to that, the poorer families of the parish often stopped off at bakeries on their way to church and placed joints of meat in the large bread ovens that were still cooling down from Saturday night's baking. They could then pick up the meat, roasted to perfection, on their way home.

Roasting meat was something the British were traditionally supposed to excel at, as acknowledged by the Swedish scientist and explorer Pehr Kalm (1716–79) on a visit to England:

'the English men understand almost better than any other people the art of properly roasting a joint.' He did go on to point out that the only other dish they were any good at making was PLUM PUDDING – but the compliment was in there, somewhere.

For many, **mustard** is the key condiment to have with their SUNDAY ROAST. But where does the expression *as keen as mustard* come from? It is commonly believed to have originated with the famous mustard manufacturing company Keen & Sons, founded in 1742 and eventually acquired by Colman's in 1903. But the expression (and the love of mustard) is much older than that. The Romans were the first to import mustard plants to Britain, where they have been grown ever since. The seeds of the plant could be cracked or ground and added to food to give it a spicy kick, but unlike peppercorns, which had to be expensively imported from the East, the plants could be grown anywhere and were thus accessible to everyone. Mustard became associated with vigour and enthusiasm because it added zest and flavour to a meal. Hence if someone was 'as keen as mustard', they were lively and sparky; Keen & Sons were simply picking up on a saying that was already well known to suggest that their mustard was the best – and sharpest – there is.

Where Do the Noble Names
for Beef Come From?

No wonder the French gave the British the not overly fond nickname *les rosbifs*. The long-standing enthusiasm for the SUNDAY ROAST was real, as reflected in the words of Richard Leveridge's 1735 song 'The Roast Beef of Old England':

> When mighty Roast Beef was the Englishman's food,
> It ennobled our brains and enriched our blood …

If *rosbifs* is not meant politely, it's hardly surprising as the song – which used to be sung by theatre audiences before and after a new play and is still performed at Royal Navy mess dinners – goes on to be quite rude about the French:

> But since we have learnt from all-vapouring France
> To eat their ragouts as well as to dance …
> [We're] A sneaking poor race, half-begotten and tame,
> Who sully the honours that once shone in fame.

Which is somewhat ironic, considering how the names of the very **best cuts of beef**, as we shall see, all derive from that nation of dancing ragout eaters.

SIRLOIN

Taken from the rear back portion of the animal, **sirloin** is one of the most prized cuts of beef. According to folklore, Henry VIII (1491–1547), renowned for his love of food and drink, once so enjoyed a loin of beef that he bestowed a knighthood upon it. And so, much to the great amusement of his court, the favoured cut became known thereafter as Sir Loin. I would love that story to be true, but, sadly, it is far more likely that the term is Old French in origin, from *surlonge*, meaning 'above the loin'. The sirloin is, after all, the 'upper' cut of the loin of beef.

BARON OF BEEF

The **baron of beef**, a large joint consisting of two sirloins left uncut at the backbone, would have been roasted at the great banquets of days gone by. The first written reference to a baron of beef is from around 1745, ruling out any connection to King Henry by around two hundred years, although the king Georges, who reigned for most of the eighteenth century, were known to enjoy a banquet or two. Indeed, legend has it that the expression arose as an extension of the Sir Loin joke. In reality, the French were behind this one too: the word 'baron' here comes from the French term *bas-rond* (lower or hind round part).

CHATEAUBRIAND

A **chateaubriand**, a thick cut of tenderloin steak that is usually broiled or grilled, is also French in origin, named in honour of the celebrated writer François-René de Chateaubriand (1768–1848). Oppressed by his gloomy, slave-trading father, Chateaubriand didn't get off to a happy start in life, the only relief being provided by long country walks with his sister Lucile, with whom he had an unnaturally close relationship. At seventeen, he left to join the army and in two years was promoted to captain, but a year later, in 1788, he suddenly lost interest in his military career after meeting several leading French authors. When the French Revolution broke out, Chateaubriand was so appalled at the violence he saw in Paris that he left for America, where he settled in the Deep South in 1791.

He had all kinds of adventures there, later claiming to have lived with Native American Indian tribes, an experience that inspired his third published work, *René* (1802), a painful, strangely familiar-sounding, tale of an unhappy Frenchman living with the Natchez tribe of Louisiana after fleeing an intense, possibly incestuous, relationship with his sister Amélie. *René* was an immediate success, cited as a major influence on the group of poets, painters and writers of what would later become known as the Romantic Movement. These included the likes of Percy Bysshe Shelley and Lord Byron, who became as famous for their fussy ruffled shirts as they did for their work. If these artists regarded Chateaubriand as the father of Romanticism, then that must make him the grandfather of New Romanticism and the rash of frilly-shirted, floppy-haired pop bands that burst forth in the early 1980s.

Chateaubriand returned home from America following an amnesty issued by Napoleon to all those who had fled France during the Revolution, and secured his fame with his next book, *The Genius of Christianity*, published in 1802. This took the form of an apology for the Christian faith and the part it had played, or not played as the case may be, in the Revolution. Napoleon, who was keen to appease the Catholic Church, heartily approved and soon appointed the writer as secretary of the legation to the Holy See (the Vatican) and Chateaubriand embarked on a long career as a writer and politician, rising to the role of state minister in 1815.

However, his refusal to swear an allegiance to King Louis-Philippe in 1830 ended his political career and Chateaubriand spent the rest of his life writing controversially about the new monarch, disparaged as the 'bourgeois king', and other sensitive issues of the day. While his influence as a writer continued to grow – a young Victor Hugo once wrote, 'to be Chateaubriand or nothing' – his fans were not just literary ones. It is reputedly while he was serving as French ambassador to London in 1822 that his chef, Montmireil, famously christened a dish – beef tenderloin served in a sauce of white wine, shallots and tarragon – after his adored master. Although more often served with BÉARNAISE SAUCE today, chateaubriand steak continues to be enjoyed as it has been, by Romantics old and new, for some two hundred years.

When you are ***given the cold shoulder***, it is obvious you are not welcome any more. Like 'humble pie' (see the box on page 40), this phrase can be traced back to the great banquets of medieval England. During the feasts, which could last for days, lavish dishes were washed down with lashings of wine and ale, while travelling musicians, dancers and jesters entertained the guests. But all good things have to come to an end and it was customary for the host to conclude the festivities by asking his cooks to serve slices from shoulders of cold beef, mutton or pork. It was useful shorthand for the host to send the message in this way rather than to visit all his many guests in person to inform them the party was over. This tradition then passed to lower-class meals, where the host would serve guests who had outstayed their welcome from a **cold shoulder** of mutton. These days to be 'given the cold shoulder' is perceived as unkind treatment, although in medieval times it was regarded as a civilized and polite gesture.

What Does a Yorkshire Pudding Have to Do with Yorkshire?

Made from a batter of eggs, flour and milk (a thicker version of the recipe for pancakes) and cooked in a shallow tin containing extremely hot beef dripping, batter puddings have been a staple part of the British diet for centuries. They evolved in the thrifty north of England, where a pan of batter was placed under the joint of meat cooking on a roasting spit, making use of the fat that dripped into the pan. A recipe for 'Dripping Pudding' was first published in 1737 in the wonderfully titled book *The Whole Duty of a Woman*, which gave the following instructions:

> Make a good batter as if for pancakes; put it in a hot toss-pan over the fire with a bit of butter to fry the bottom a little, then put the pan and batter under a shoulder of mutton, instead of a dripping pan, keeping frequently shaking it by the handle and it will be light and savoury, and fit to take up when your mutton is enough; then turn it in a dish, and serve it hot.

Ten years later, Hannah Glasse published *The Art of Cookery Made Plain and Easy* and included the dish, giving it the title **Yorkshire pudding** for the first time and noting: 'It is an exceeding good pudding, the gravy of the meat eats well with it.' The book was an instant bestseller in both Britain and America, ensuring her recipe quickly spread, and the dish has remained a favourite accompaniment for the SUNDAY ROAST – now eaten with roast beef rather than mutton – ever since.

But why *Yorkshire* pudding? Hannah Glasse was born in London and her father was a Northumberland landowner with no known connections to the county. Jennifer Stead, discussing the history of the pudding in *Traditional Food East and West of the Pennines* (1991), agrees that batter puddings were made throughout the British Isles, but that those from Yorkshire were renowned for their lightness and crispiness. She suggests that their mastery of the technique may be tied in to the regional personality:

> This accords with their fabled brusque temperaments: the fact that they require spanking hot fat, explosions as the batter hits it, fierce heat, and crisp results, may explain why it has often been said that only Yorkshire folk – those possessing the Yorkshire temperament – can make a true Yorkshire pudding.

AND WHAT ABOUT TOAD IN THE HOLE?

Batter puddings could have other ingredients added to them, often incorporating leftovers for a cheap and nutritious meal. *The Diary of Thomas Turner* (1754–65) includes a reference to sausages cooked in a baking tin with batter poured all around them, but without calling it **toad in the hole**. Instead, the earliest reference to this poor man's Sunday lunch dish is found in the 1787 edition of the *Oxford English Dictionary*, which defines 'a dish called toad in the hole' as 'meat boiled in a crust'. It has been suggested that the dish acquired its somewhat unappetizing name from the way the meat sticking out of the crispy batter resembles a toad poking its head out of a marshy hole. In 1861 Mrs Beeton revealed rather contentiously that toad in the hole was a 'homely and savoury dish of steak and kidney, although any leftover meat could be used'. It was during the First World War that sausages became the central part of the dish, possibly in an attempt to cook them without exploding (see BANGERS AND MASH), and have remained our favourite version ever since.

Does Horseradish Sauce Have Anything to Do with Radishes, or Horses?

Many people wouldn't eat their roast beef without a good dollop of this fiery condiment made from grated horseradish root, mixed with cream and vinegar. The first reference to the plant was made by Roman scholar Pliny the Elder (AD 23–79) in his *Natural History*, published in AD 77–9, where he recommended it for its medicinal qualities; indeed, the roots and leaves of the plant were still used for this purpose during the Middle Ages. While it belongs to the same family of Asian plants, also including MUSTARD, broccoli and cabbage, horseradish is not actually a radish, although the name may have arisen because people regarded it as a hotter, coarser version of the smaller plant. Equally, the name may relate to the old European method of processing the vegetable by crushing it under a horse's hoof. More likely is the suggestion that it arose as a mistranslation of the German term *Meerrettich* as 'mare radish'. The correct translation would be 'sea radish', reflecting how the plant grows wild in coastal areas. So the only horses there would be the proverbial white ones crashing on the beach nearby.

4
Teatime

The Secret of a Nice Cup of Tea

Should It Really be Alfred the Cake?

In Remembrance of Cakes Past: The Petite Madeleine

The Story of the Bun: Sally Lunn, Chelsea
and Hot Cross

Love, War and the Bakewell Tart

The Foreign Origins of the Lamington,
Australia's Favourite Cake

The Bitter Rivalry of the Eccles Cake Makers

Why One Maid of Honour is Never Enough

Garibaldi: A Very Revolutionary Biscuit

How a Biscuit Helped Maintain the Anzac Spirit

The Battenberg: A Royal Cake Left
Behind by History

There are few hours in life more agreeable than the hour dedicated to the ceremony known as afternoon tea.

HENRY JAMES, *The Portrait of a Lady*

The Secret of a Nice Cup of Tea

The relationship between **tea** and the British is so intense and enduring that it is almost impossible to imagine one without the other. In *Asterix in Britain* (1966), the Britons asking for Gaulish help in fighting the Romans, fifteen hundred or so years before the formal introduction of tea leaves to Britain, habitually drink cups of hot water with a spot of milk. When Getafix the Druid adds a special herb (tea) to the hot water, it has the same rallying, galvanizing effect on the Britons as his magic potion has on the Gauls. A cup of tea may have become a British tradition, but in fact tea is the most commonly consumed hot beverage in the world. The original tea leaf was cultivated from the *Camellia sinensis* bush, in Yunnan Province, China, where humans first came up with the idea that eating the leaves or boiling them in water might be enjoyable.

One early legend, dating back to the Tang Dynasty nearly five thousand years ago, claims that it was Bodhidharma, the founder of Chan Buddhism, who discovered tea. According to the story, he fell asleep while meditating one morning and stayed asleep for nine whole years. When he finally woke up, he immediately cut off his eyelids to punish himself for such idleness. He then cast them away, where they took root in the soil and grew into tea bushes.

In case that puts you off tea for ever, there is another, less disturbing, legend which tells of Shennong, Emperor of China, who was drinking boiled water when leaves from a nearby tree flew into his bowl, changing its colour to an amber brown. Sipping the brew, the emperor was pleasantly surprised and so the cup of tea was born.

Tea became fashionable in Britain with the arrival of Catherine of Braganza (1638–1705), the Portuguese princess who married Charles II in 1662. When she moved into the king's court she introduced her favourite drink, which soon became popular with the nobility and the wealthy classes of England. About that time, the first advertisements for tea appeared in London newspapers and tea began arriving in Britain by the shipload. Tea drinking became even more popular when Queen Anne (1665–1714) chose tea over ale as her regular breakfast drink. By 1750, it had become the principal drink of all the social classes in Britain, even though it was very expensive, a pound of the cheapest tea costing about one-third of a skilled worker's weekly wage.

There are two ways in which the British managed to make the cup of tea their own. The first was through their unusual preference for adding milk. In the seventeenth and eighteenth centuries, the china cups tea was served in were so delicate, they often cracked when boiling tea was poured straight into them. Milk was therefore added to cool the liquid and stop the cups from cracking. At first a necessity, this soon became a preference and is the reason why, even today, many people add milk to their cups before pouring in the tea. The second was through the invention of **afternoon tea** (see also the box on page 67). Legend has it that in the 1840s Anna, 7th Duchess of Bedford – one of Queen Victoria's ladies-in-waiting – came up with the idea of a late afternoon meal to overcome the 'sinking feeling' she felt during the long gap between lunch and dinner. At a time when men were traditionally out of the house, either drinking at their club, hunting or – if middle class or below – actually doing some work, this became a very feminine ritual, celebrated with special china tea services and daintily presented cakes and SANDWICHES, and providing an amazing forum for uninterrupted gossip. By 1880, tea was a huge event. People would dress up for the occasion and afternoon tea dances, often accompanied by a live orchestra, became extremely popular.

Tea was so important that it had even kicked off a war between the Americans and British. Disgruntled American settlers threw tons of the stuff into the sea at Boston following the decision by the British government to impose a very high tax on it. The settlers objected to having to pay tax to the rulers of a far-off land rather than to their own elected representatives. Indeed, they were furious enough to start a war over it, and what became known as the Boston Tea Party led to the Revolutionary War (1775–83), eventual independence and America's emergence as the leading economic power in the world. I should probably point out here that that is the real reason for the Boston Tea Party and not, as I told a group of Japanese tourists the last time I was in Boston, because a Mr Starbucks and a Mr Nescafé got together and tossed all that tea into the harbour.

WHO WAS EARL GREY?

There are four classifications of tea: green and white, both unfermented; oolong, which is semi-fermented; and black, which is fully fermented. From these basic varieties thousands of different blends are produced worldwide. The most popular form of black tea has not only a very unusual taste but a rather strange name, **Earl Grey**.

Charles Grey, the 2nd Earl Grey (1764–1845), was prime minister between 1830 and 1834, a significant time in British politics. Despite strong opposition to his policies by the previous prime minister, the Duke of Wellington (see BEEF WELLINGTON), the first announcement Earl Grey made on replacing the Iron Duke was a pledge to carry out wide-ranging parliamentary reform that included allowing one out of every six men (from a population of 14 million) to actually vote. Previously it had been nearer to only one in twenty.

During his short time as prime minister, Grey also earned the distinction of abolishing slavery throughout the British Empire, but it was his removal of the East India Company's complete monopoly on trade with China in 1834 that led to his immortalization. This opened up the tea trade routes and ushered in the era of the tea clipper, ships packed with just that one product, such was its boom in popularity. In China the tea export business was suddenly hugely profitable and a grateful Chinese ambassador presented the prime minister with an entirely new blend of tea which included distinctive oil extracted from the rind of the bergamot orange. As a further compliment to the earl, a cup of Earl Grey also has a greyer tone than ordinary tea. Try looking at it alongside a cup of builder's tea and you'll see what I mean.

Should It Really be Alfred the Cake?

If you're not much good in the kitchen, never fear. For it was a cooking disaster that proved to be the turning point in Alfred's path towards becoming the only English king in history to be called 'Great'.

When he took the throne in 871, it looked like his reign would be short and unsuccessful as the invading Danes were already running the kingdoms of Mercia, East Anglia and Northumbria. And all that stood against complete Viking control of England was the sickly 21-year-old King of Wessex in the west of the country. Over the next few years, Alfred tried a mixture of attacks and bribery, but nothing worked for long and any truces with the Vikings were promptly broken. After a surprise night-time attack on his camp at Chippenham, Alfred was pushed back into a small area of the

Somerset marshes known as the Isle of Athelney. During the
winter of 877, the whole area was flooded and could only be
navigated by natives. It was here that Alfred found sanctuary
while he regrouped, reorganized and re-supplied his army in
readiness for a counter-attack on the Danes.

Things had been pretty desperate up to that point. On
first fleeing to the marshes, the king had been forced to travel
in disguise, staying in humble lodgings among the peasant
people as he hid from the Viking invaders and it was then
the famous incident occurred that is forever associated with
him. Early in the king's flight, as the story goes, he was given
shelter by a peasant woman and instructed to watch over her
cakes (probably an early kind of scone), which were cooking
over the fire. But so preoccupied was Alfred with his trou-
bles that he forgot to watch them and the cakes all burned.
Not knowing who he really was, the peasant woman scolded
her guest for not paying proper attention to what he was
doing, which jolted the young man from his daydreaming,
inspiring him to prepare and plan his attack on the Vikings
far more carefully than before. As winter gave way to the
spring, he was ready to advance upon the Danish warlord,
Guthrum, using the Roman tactic of fighting from behind
a wall of shields, and on 6 May 878 managed to shatter his
previously invincible enemy. Guthrum and his surviving
army fled to their stronghold at Chippenham, where Alfred
laid siege to the Vikings, who eventually surrendered after
fourteen days.

Alfred went on to become a wise and effective ruler, who
encouraged education, revised his kingdom's legal system and
improved its military structure. A learned and pious man, he
was later made a saint by the Catholic Church and is commemorated in statues and stained-glass windows throughout
the land. But a more unlikely memorial to the great monarch,
and to that celebrated turning point early in his reign, can be

found in nature. In both Europe and North America there is an inedible fungus, *Daldinia concentrica*, which grows on dead and decaying wood and which has historically been used as tinder to start fires. Black and lumpy, it goes by the common name of **King Alfred's cakes** because of its uncanny resemblance to a pile of burned scones.

In Remembrance of Cakes Past: The Petite Madeleine

> She sent out for one of those short, plump little cakes called 'petites madeleines', which look as though they had been moulded in the fluted scallop of a pilgrim's shell. And soon, mechanically, weary after a dull day with the prospect of a depressing morrow, I raised to my lips a spoonful of the tea in which I had soaked a morsel of the cake. No sooner had the warm liquid, and the crumbs with it, touched my palate than a shudder ran through my whole body, and I stopped, intent upon the extraordinary changes that were taking place ... at once the vicissitudes of life had become indifferent to me, its disasters innocuous, its brevity illusory ...

Small sponge cakes baked in distinctive shell-shaped moulds, **madeleines** are now among the most recognizable cakes in the world thanks to Marcel Proust (1871–1922) and his *In Search of Lost Time*. Eating a madeleine (in the passage from the book quoted above) sends the narrator off on a (very) long journey into involuntary memory. But who was the original Madeleine that they were named after? Some sources suggest that she was a French pastry chef working for the deposed king of Poland, Stanisław Leszczyński. Forced by an assassination attempt to seek exile in France, he and his family moved to the Château de Commercy in the commune of Commercy in north-eastern France. When in 1755 Madeleine Paulmier became his pastry chef, she supposedly invented the cake to cheer up the exiled king.

But the cakes are much more likely to be named after a very different Madeleine, for Madeleine is also the French name for Mary Magdalen, the former prostitute and follower of Jesus. Several orders of nuns have taken her name and that, twinned with the cake's distinctive scallop-shell shape (the traditional symbol of a Catholic pilgrim, as Proust himself points out above), would suggest that the cakes were originally baked with a more religious purpose in mind, perhaps to remind those who ate them that while, like Mary/Madeleine herself, we are all sinners, we are also pilgrims on a hopeful journey to find God.

The Story of the Bun: Sally Lunn, Chelsea and Hot Cross

In America, **bun** is a generic name for a bread roll of some kind, either sweet or savoury, whereas British buns are much sweeter and richer. The word has been used since at least the fifteenth century and is derived from the French *bugne* or 'swelling', referring to its bulging shape. There are many kinds of bun. Here are three of the most interesting.

THE SALLY LUNN

During the seventeenth century, the Protestant Huguenots were persecuted by the Catholic Church (see HOLLANDAISE

SAUCE and MORNAY SAUCE) and many caught the boat to England. The Huguenots were respected as skilled lace-makers, weavers and merchants, mainly specializing in silk. And they soon became an important part of English society at a time when the English were emerging from the cheerless grip of Oliver Cromwell's Puritan regime (1649–60). The Huguenots wielded vast influence in terms of business, finance and physical support for the new monarchy, restored under Charles II (although many Huguenots were to later fight for the Protestant William of Orange against the English king during the Glorious Revolution of 1688, which must have made Charles, who had invited them in the first place, turn in his grave).

The influence of the Huguenots also extended to British cuisine. One of the new settlers was a pretty young girl called Solange Luyon, who relocated to Bath in Somerset and soon found work at a bakery in Lilliput Alley (a narrow street now known more prosaically as North Parade Passage). Almost immediately she began baking a light, round teacake that became the talk of the town as locals would queue up at breakfast time for one of 'Sollie's' cakes. Bath and nearby Bristol both being a hub for travellers, word soon got about and the anglicized **Sally Lunn bun** became hugely popular throughout Georgian England. Today the original recipe is passed along with the deeds to the bakery, now known as Sally Lunn's and thought to be the oldest house in Bath. Visitors can still buy a Sally Lunn bun at the tea shop/museum, safe in the knowledge that some things will never change.

THE CHELSEA BUN

One of the most popular buns of all, the **Chelsea bun** was created and sold exclusively at the Chelsea Bun House in Pimlico, London, from the beginning of the 1700s. A glazed square bun made from a spiral of dough flavoured with lemon peel, cinnamon and other spices, it was popular with royals and commoners alike. Mad King George III (1738–1820) was a regular customer, often popping in for a Chelsea bun on his way from the palace to the nearby Pleasure Gardens, and the bakery became unofficially known as the Royal Bun House. Despite the original business closing in 1840 when the building was knocked down, the legend of the Chelsea Bun House lived on and its replacement, the Real Old Chelsea Bun House (which, of course, it wasn't), proved to be equally popular.

The bakery and its famous buns were subsequently commemorated in literature. In 1840 (the year of its closure), Charles Dickens drew attention to the bakery in *Barnaby Rudge*, his account of the Gordon Riots (1780), describing in one passage how the Royal East London Volunteers marched in 'glittering order to the Chelsea Bun House and then regaled in the adjacent taverns until dark'. In 1855, Anne Manning, prolific author of some fifty-one works, called one of her novels *The Old Chelsea Bun House: A Tale of the Last Century*, while in one of his short stories from *A Tangled Tale* (1880), Lewis Carroll has one of his characters exclaim: 'Give her a Chelsea bun, miss! That's what most young ladies like best!' The man, a street hawker with a 'rich and musical' voice, goes on to display his wares:

> the speaker dexterously whipped back the snowy cloth that covered his basket, and disclosed a tempting array of the familiar square buns, joined together in rows, richly egged and browned and glistening in the sun.

Needless to say, the young lady in question is sorely tempted, but gets whisked away by her fierce aunt before she can succumb.

THE HOT CROSS BUN

For many people the **hot cross bun** epitomizes Easter, particularly Good Friday and the crucifixion of Jesus Christ, in commemoration of which the bun is said to have been created. According to Elizabeth David in *English Bread and Yeast Cookery* (1977), sweet, spiced buns have been popular since Tudor times but were permitted only on special occasions. In 1592, during the reign of Queen Elizabeth I, the following decree was issued by the London Clerk of the Markets:

> That no bakers, etc, at any time, or times hereafter, may make, utter or sell by retail within or without their houses, unto any of the Queen's subjects any spice cakes, buns, biscuits, or any other spice bread (being bread out of size and not by law allowed) except it be at burials, or on the Friday before Easter, or at Christmas, upon pain of forfeiture of all such spiced bread to the poor.

It is not known exactly why such a decree should have been made but that seems to be when our tradition for spiced buns on Good Friday began, although the first recorded use of the term 'hot cross bun' wasn't until 1733. The custom was clearly well established later in the century, however, such that by 1791 James Boswell was referring to it in his *Life of Samuel Johnson*, recalling how in 1773 that 'being Good Friday I breakfasted with him [Johnson] and Hot Cross Buns'.

The tradition of eating special food at Easter actually goes back much further, to the time of the Anglo-Saxons, who worshipped a goddess of the dawn, Eostre, from whom the words 'east' and 'Easter' derive. It's believed that the Saxons offered small cakes to the goddess on her feast day at the spring equinox, a custom going back to the ancient Greeks and Romans, who both had traditional spring festivals involving bread offerings to their gods.

These days hot cross buns are sold all the year round, thanks to the unstoppable rise of the supermarket. However, there is one place in Britain where spiced buns are still associated with special days of celebration, albeit in rather a strange way. In Abingdon in Oxfordshire, to mark important events such as coronations and royal jubilees, local dignitaries all assemble on the roof of the county hall and pelt buns at the populace assembled in the market square below. (Needless to say, everyone immediately scrambles for them and a literal bun fight ensues – see the box below.) The county hall, now a museum, holds a collection of buns, dried and varnished, that have been thrown through the ages. Not sure I'd care to be on the receiving end of one of those.

The term ***bun fight*** is an expression, used tongue in cheek, for any grand occasion at which people dress up and food is served. Focusing on the 'fight' element, the term is also used in a rather different sense, to mean a heated exchange, generally one that has no real importance except to the participants – ***a storm in a teacup***, you might otherwise say (using another teatime analogy). The term is believed to go back to the nineteenth century and the elaborate AFTERNOON TEAS that used to be served in well-to-do Victorian households. These meals traditionally consisted of a whole range of buns, scones and teacakes – all conveniently missile-shaped. Hence, if the diners were children, it's easy to see how things might degenerate if Nanny lost control.

Love, War and the Bakewell Tart

Two desserts have come out of one quiet Derbyshire town: the **Bakewell tart** (made with shortcrust pastry) and the **Bakewell pudding** (made with puff pastry). The former has become world famous; the latter, although not so well known, has a surprisingly romantic history for such a solid (though tasty) dish.

Haddon Hall is a stately Tudor pile a short horse ride along the river from Bakewell and the traditional home of the Vernon family. Back in the sixteenth century, in the days before daughters were allowed to choose their own husbands, Sir George Vernon was determined that his two daughters, Margaret and Dorothy, should marry well. For Margaret, the elder of the two, he selected the son of Lord Stanley, owner of vast estates in Lancashire and therefore a highly desirable match. But his younger daughter, Dorothy, had ideas of her own and wouldn't fall so easily into line. She had succumbed to the charms of John Manners, the son of a much lesser aristocrat and despised by her father as 'that nobody, the second son of a mushroom earl'. Indeed, so displeased was Sir George and so determined to keep the lovers apart that he incarcerated Dorothy in the Hall, forbidding her access to the outside world.

But love will always find a way and Lady Dorothy eventually made good her escape. One evening in 1563, while festivities were being held to celebrate Margaret's forthcoming marriage, Dorothy took advantage of the general carousing and merrymaking and slipped unnoticed out of the house to her suitor hiding in the garden. John Manners had a pair of horses with him, ready to sweep them away to Aylestone, in Leicestershire, where they were secretly married. The couple lay low until Sir George's wrath had eventually abated and Dorothy was able to win him round. The story goes that, when she eloped, she took with her the recipe for her favourite dish, Bakewell pudding, so as not to lose touch with her beloved home town. Indeed, the legend of their elopement is commemorated in a memorial at All Saints Church in Bakewell. There is also a historical novel, *Dorothy Vernon of Haddon Hall* (1902), based on her story and a bestseller in its day, and a 1924 film of the same name.

Dorothy may have cherished the recipe for Bakewell pudding but it wasn't published until much later, in Meg Dodds' 1826 *Cook and Housewife's Manual* (see SCOTCH EGG). The story told around the Peak District, however, is that earlier in the nineteenth century a certain Mrs Greaves, landlady of the White Horse, a busy coaching inn at the centre of Bakewell, left a recipe out for her new assistant cook to make jam tarts. The inexperienced cook spread the jam at the bottom of the pastry case, placing the almond and egg mixture on top instead of stirring it into the pastry as instructed, so that what was meant to be a tart turned out to be a pudding. These new puddings immediately became favourites with many visitors to the inn, who then carried the recipe back to all corners of England, ensuring its rapid rise to fame.

Jane Austen stayed in Bakewell in 1811 while writing her masterpiece *Pride and Prejudice*; it is reputed that she even stayed at the White Horse Inn, where she may well have eaten their signature pudding. In the book, her spirited heroine Elizabeth Bennett visits Lambton, a fictional town clearly based on Bakewell, with her aunt and uncle and then undergoes a softening of heart towards her rejected suitor, Mr Darcy. The book doesn't say, of course, but her good mood may well have been enhanced by good pudding, her stay in the town leaving her as determined as Dorothy Vernon to fight for the husband she wanted.

The history of the Bakewell tart is rather more prosaic. Its origins can be traced back as far as the fifteenth century when 'flathons', or flans, became popular. And the frangipane filling, a paste-like mixture of eggs and almonds, has been used across Europe in cakes and tarts since earlier times still. Even so, the Bakewell tart owes its unusual name not to the process of overcooking the crust ('bake well') but to the place where it was first made. (The pun hasn't gone unobserved, however: a visitor to the town is supposed to have suggested it was a 'well-baked tart from Bakewell'.) In 1845, the poet-turned-cookery-writer Eliza Acton published her recipe for the dish, noting that it 'is famous not only in Derbyshire but in several of our northern counties where it is usually served on holiday occasions'. In 1861, Mrs Beeton published her own version of the recipe and a century later Mr Kipling introduced the rest of the Western world to the glories of the icing-topped **cherry Bakewell**.

But while the Bakewell tart is the best-known dessert to come out of the town, the Bakewell pudding remains its bitter rival. To this day, a long-running, very civilized war has been waged between tart lovers and devotees of the original pudding. Their headquarters are the Bakewell Tart and Coffee Shop and the Old Original Bakewell Pudding Shop respectively. Both establishments guard their original recipes in fireproof vaults and compete, hopefully in a good-natured middle England way, for loyal customers and supremacy. Why not go there and try them for yourself?

The Foreign Origins of the Lamington, Australia's Favourite Cake

A **Lamington** is a small sponge cake covered in chocolate icing and rolled in desiccated coconut that is hugely popular throughout Australasia. No arguing about the origins of this one (see PAVLOVA) as it is definitely Australian, although New Zealand's strawberry version is widely claimed to be better. (Don't they ever stop arguing, that lot?)

The cake owes its name to one Charles Wallace Alexander Napier Cochrane-Baillie (1860–1940), more conveniently known as the 2nd Baron Lamington. Thanks largely to the old boys' network, he became assistant private secretary to the British prime minister, Lord Salisbury, in 1885. In 1890, the government sent him to Vietnam and Siam (now Thailand) in an attempt to discourage the French from extending their colonies and in 1896 he replaced Sir Henry Norman as Governor of Queensland in Australia. The name of the cake is deceptive, however, as it wasn't the baron or his wife who came up with it but their chef, Armand Galland.

Like many of the best dishes, the invention of the Lamington arose from a desperate attempt to remedy a kitchen disaster against the clock (see also CAESAR SALAD, CRÊPES SUZETTE and TARTE TATIN). Called upon to quickly create a cake for unexpected guests at Government House, Armand Galland slightly burned his vanilla sponge and, with no time to spare, rolled slices of it in chocolate sauce and coconut in an attempt to cover up his error. The unusual cakes went down a treat. Lady Lamington, who is known to have taken a keen interest in all things culinary from her letters to renowned food writer Hannah MacLurcan, was so pleased with the result that she asked for them to be served to guests on all official occasions. The first known recipe for Lamington cake appeared in the *Queenslander Magazine* in 1902, while seven years later Amy Schauer, an authority on rich cakes and desserts, included the recipe in *The Schauer Australian Cookery Book*.

It's not just New Zealand that has muscled in on the Lamington; some Scottish historians have also since tried to climb on to the bandwagon, suggesting that a sheep shearer's wife from the village of Lamington once made the cake for other travelling sheep shearers, but there is no evidence to support this. In 2006, the National Trust of Queensland declared the Lamington a state icon, while 21 July has been designated National Lamington Day.

It seems strange that the Lamington, Australasia's most popular teatime cake, should have become definitively Australian thanks to a highly unpopular British Governor of Queensland and his French chef. Ironically, Lamington himself hated the cakes that have become his enduring legacy, describing them as 'those bloody poofy woolly biscuits'. That sounds about right for an Australian national dish.

The Bitter Rivalry of the Eccles Cake Makers

Many traditional and popular English cakes and buns were originally named after the town in which they were first made, such as Oxfordshire's **Banbury cakes** and Lancashire's **Chorley cakes**. Many remained popular only locally while some, like the **Eccles cake**, were enjoyed so much by visitors from further afield that the recipe for them was subsequently spread up and down the country. The first reference to the Eccles cake in print is in Mrs Raffald's very popular cookery book of 1769, and by 1818 they were being exported abroad, throughout the empire, suggesting a rapid increase in business for the town of Eccles around the early nineteenth century – all thanks to a small sweet pastry filled with mincemeat or (in the modern version) currants.

But to sample the best Eccles cakes, you have to visit the small town near Manchester. By the end of the eighteenth century, local baker James Birch was renowned as the premium maker of the Eccles cake. The cakes proved so popular that a former employee, James Bradburn, opened a rival bakery in 1813. Birch soon began to place adverts claiming to be the original Eccles cake maker 'removed from across the way'. Bradburn then responded by advertising 'the only old original Eccles Cake shop, never removed!' By his wording he was implying his was the original and Birch had left to set up a new shop on the other side of the road. Their comic rivalry was, in the end, to both of their advantage: customers bought from both shops to sample the rival wares in the long-running debate as to whose were the original, and best.

Why One Maid of Honour is Never Enough

Another cake with a local historic connection is the **maid of honour** – a small tart with a curd cheese filling – famous in London and especially around the adjoining districts of Richmond and Kew. Local legend claims Henry VIII himself named the cake in honour of Anne Boleyn, maid of honour to Catherine of Aragon and, in time, Henry's second wife. Apparently, she and several other ladies-in-waiting were eating them from a silver tray when she and Henry first met at Richmond Palace. The cakes soon became a firm favourite throughout the royal household, especially with the king who, according to local legend, ordered the recipe to be locked away in the palace and the chef who created them locked away too, to preserve the secret recipe.

That obviously meant that everyone who was anyone wanted to try these cakes and the bakers of Richmond and Kew spent years experimenting until they had managed to work out the royal recipe. People would travel from far and wide to try their cakes. And as the practice of afternoon tea became more and more common, a maid of honour was the perfect accompaniment, the first advert for one appearing in a 1769 copy of the *Public Advertiser*. In 1850, Robert Newens opened his eponymous shop, moving in 1860 to larger premises in Kew, where the Maids of Honour bakery and tearooms is still run by his descendants who continue to feed visitors to Henry VIII's nearby palace of Hampton Court with the king's favourite cake.

To become a maid of honour was a highly sought-after role at the royal court. The maids were unmarried women of noble blood who waited on the Queen of England, who usually had eight to run around for her. The position at court provided an opportunity for a young woman to find a noble husband, or for an ambitious girl like Anne Boleyn to get much better acquainted with the king. But Anne should have realized from the start that Henry was far too greedy to be satisfied with just one maid and their marriage lasted for only three years, until 1536, when Henry had her executed on trumped-up charges so he could marry another maid of honour – Jane Seymour.

Garibaldi: A Very Revolutionary Biscuit

At the beginning of the nineteenth century, Italy was a collection of warring states. The person responsible for drawing them into one country was Giuseppe Garibaldi (1807–82), who is credited with being the first international revolutionary, a nineteenth-century Che Guevara and a pretty unusual inspiration for a biscuit.

As a young man, Garibaldi joined the Carbonari (the 'Charcoal Burners'), a secret revolutionary organization dedicated to Italian nationalism (for more on it, see CARBONARA), but in 1834 he fled to South America when his part in a failed revolution led to his being condemned to death in his absence by a Genoese court. He went on to fight in the Uruguayan Civil War, earning himself a reputation for bravery by leading uphill bayonet charges against forces far greater in number.

Garibaldi's heart never strayed from his home country, however, and the revolutions of 1848 finally tempted him home to Italy. When the French, under the command of the future Napoleon III, sent forces to Rome, Garibaldi's republican army found itself fighting the imperialists on far too many fronts. He was forced to withdraw his 4,000 men and head north to Venice, and from there into exile in America. During this time his romantic profile as a freedom fighter was increasing daily, especially in Britain where Italian exiles frequently wrote about his exploits.

On 24 March 1854, the famous Italian revolutionary sailed into Tyneside, where, cutting quite a dash in his red silk shirt, poncho and sombrero, he was greeted with huge enthusiasm. By mixing with the working classes rather than hobnobbing with local dignitaries, he further enhanced his reputation in the eyes of the public. Staying in England for only a month, Garibaldi toured the country, and thousands of Londoners were at Nine Elms station to greet his train when he arrived in the capital. He was hailed in the newspapers as the 'Italian lion' and 'the noblest Roman of them all'. Thousands lined the streets, chanting 'We'll get a rope and hang the Pope, so up with Garibaldi' as the Italian hero passed by. This adulation was not shared by the British establishment, who were mightily relieved when the man they considered to be nothing more than a rabble-rousing terrorist returned, once again, to his homeland, with Queen Victoria declaring, 'Garibaldi, thank God, has gone.'

Garibaldi was so popular that some hotels even made a profit from selling his bathwater and hundreds of Italian café and tavern owners renamed their establishments after him. But the most lasting testament to the boy-band level of hysteria that gripped Britain in April 1854 was provided by cake makers Peek Frean, who later cooked a biscuit in his honour. Claiming it was based on the raisin bread he provided for his marching troops, they still produce the famous **Garibaldi biscuits**, or **squashed fly biscuits**, today.

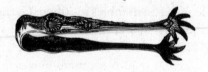

How a Biscuit Helped Maintain the Anzac Spirit

Originally known simply as **rolled oat biscuits** (rather like OATCAKES), these are made from a simple recipe of oats, GOLDEN SYRUP and coconut. At the beginning of the First World War, women in Australia and New Zealand began baking huge numbers and shipping them off to the soldiers of the Australian and New Zealand Army Corps. They chose this variety of biscuit because it would keep well during the long journey. The military, meanwhile, stamped the crates 'ANZAC' to ensure they reached the correct regiments on arrival, and the name stuck. Soldiers eagerly awaited their **Anzac biscuits**, because they made a nice change to their usual rations and reminded them of home.

In 1921 the recipe appeared in a New Zealand cookbook for the first time as **Anzac crispies**. At around the same time, commercial production of the biscuit began to raise funds for the Returned and Services League of Australia (RSL) and the Royal New Zealand Returned and Services' Association (RSA) and there is now a traditional association between the biscuit and Anzac Day, the day of remembrance held on 25 April each year. That is the date of the beginning of the doomed Gallipoli campaign in 1915, during which over 10,000 men died but in the process demonstrating a courage, stoicism and good humour later characterized as the 'Anzac spirit'. The Anzac trademark is protected by Australian law, meaning that, technically speaking, if you make these at home you are not allowed to call them Anzac biscuits without the permission of the Australian government. But I promise not to tell anyone if you do.

To *take the cake* is an American expression, although also commonly used in the UK, meaning to be outrageous enough to deserve merit. A stunt pilot or racing driver, for example, might 'take the cake' for his audacity. It has been recorded that this phrase originated in the late nineteenth century among black slaves working on the southern plantations in America. It seems they devised a game whereby couples would parade arm in arm around a barn and were judged by the others on the style and grace of their walk. The winning couple would be given a cake as a prize and the most flamboyant and entertaining of them could expect to hear cries of 'they take the cake'. This pastime was known as the *cakewalk*, which is also a well-known expression for something that is easy to achieve.

However, it is quite possible that the root of this expression goes back much earlier, to the Bible in fact. As missionaries converted large parts of Africa to Christianity, teaching from the Bible became widespread. For most inhabitants of the region it was likely to have been the only book they had ever read; thus its influence was profound. There is one story, for instance, telling how a biblical knight would be rewarded with a cake made of toasted cereal, sweetened with honey, if he was judged the most successful knight either in battle or in the workplace. There is strong evidence to suggest that African Americans adopted this reward after learning about the tale. However, anybody competing in the cakewalk who was considered rather too flamboyant and cheeky would be brought back down to earth by being awarded a biscuit instead. They had ***taken the biscuit*** (gone too far).

The Battenberg: A Royal Cake
Left Behind by History

It's easy to forget that our current royal family was originally from Germany and that the first king among them to take power, George I (1660–1727), couldn't even speak English. By the beginning of the twentieth century, thanks in large part to Queen Victoria, her German husband and her many children, all the royal families of nineteenth-century Europe and Russia were extremely closely interrelated – dangerously so as the recurrence of haemophilia and madness proves. The **Battenberg cake**, a sweet, oblong-shaped sponge of variegated pink and yellow covered in marzipan, was invented to

celebrate the marriage of Victoria's granddaughter Princess
Victoria of Hesse and by Rhine to her cousin Louis of Battenberg, a German prince, in 1884. The four pink and yellow squares of the cake, as they appeared when the cake was
cut in cross-section, represented each of the four Battenberg
princes. But the closeness of the ties between the German
and British royal families was to become extremely problem-
atic when the First World War broke out.

Battenberg had moved to England on his marriage and
joined the navy. His naval career had flourished since his
marriage; he had earned no less than twenty military awards
and had risen to the rank of admiral of the fleet by the time
Germany and England had erupted into war in 1914. With
anti-German sentiment rising among the people, and open
resentment growing towards him in the elite gentlemen's
clubs of London, Winston Churchill, then the First Lord
of the Admiralty, strongly advised Battenberg to resign his
position. Although Battenberg was reluctant at first, he soon
agreed, writing to Churchill in October 1914: 'I beg of you
to release me. I am on the verge of breaking down & I cannot
use my brain for anything.' But he remained bitter about the
situation, writing to Churchill's naval secretary, Rear Admiral Horace Hood, on 13 November: 'It was an awful wrench,
but I had no choice from the moment it was made clear to me
that the Government did not feel themselves strong enough
to support me by some public announcement.'

As the war progressed, persistent rumours of the British
royal family's pro-German sentiments flourished and their
popularity declined. Even so, it still took the king until 17
July 1917 to officially drop the family's German surname,
Saxe-Coburg-Gotha, and adopt a very English-sounding one
instead – Windsor, after his favourite castle. He also aban-
doned his subsidiary German dynastic titles, a clear indication to the public of his loyalty to the British. At the same

time, in an attempt to improve his reputation, Battenberg anglicized his own name by changing it to Mountbatten, after considering 'Battenhill' for a short while. The king's other relatives did likewise and all over Europe the name 'Battenberg' disappeared from aristocratic families loyal to the British king, leaving only the distinctive cake to remind us of a time gone by.

5
Fast Food

A hot dog at the ballgame beats roast beef at the Ritz.

HUMPHREY BOGART

A Quick History of Fast Food

Fast food goes hand in hand with urban living – people lacking the space or time to prepare food for themselves – and as the Romans are credited with the invention of the town, so it is most likely they who first came up with the idea. In Roman cities much of the poorer population were packed into *insulae* ('islands' in Latin), multi-storey apartment blocks built out of cheap materials – proving that high-rise accommodation is not such a new concept either. With little opportunity to cook for themselves without burning down the neighbourhood, many had to depend on food vendors for their meals. This wasn't what we would recognize today as fast food – in the mornings, bread soaked in wine was eaten as a quick snack and cooked vegetables and stews were in demand later in the day – but the idea behind it is the same.

By the Middle Ages, all large towns and urban areas supported numerous vendors, providing a huge range of dishes. As in the cities of antiquity, these establishments catered for those without cooking facilities: workers, the poor, travellers and pilgrims. At a time when the daily diet of most people living in the British countryside consisted of simple fare such as PEASE PUDDING, the food on offer would have seemed highly sophisticated: the pilgrims in Chaucer's *Canterbury Tales* (1387–1400), for instance, are constantly talking about snacks, and munch their way through everything, from pasties and roasted onions to sweetmeats such as blancmange.

This kind of food fascinated people living in rural areas, who had a much more limited and unimaginative diet. Even

quite lowly folk in the cities had access to a huge variety
of speedy meals: then as now, it was all part of the instant
gratification of urban life. 'London Lickpenny', a popular
fifteenth-century poem, picks out many of the cries of the
food sellers on the streets, who offer the narrator a whole
range of cooked food, from 'hot sheep's feet and oysters' to
'ribs of beef and many a hot pie'. These precursors of the
burger bars, fried-chicken outlets and KEBAB shops that lit-
ter (quite literally) today's inner cities had only their owners'
voices and distinctive jingles to make them stand out from
the crowd. As a consequence, London became notorious for
the constant racket from vendors trying to drown each other
out. As Joseph Addison wrote in the *Spectator* in 1711: 'there
is nothing which more astonishes a foreigner, and affrights a
country squire, than the Cries of London.' Street hawkers
were also a popular subject for artists and by the middle of
the 1700s engravings of the 'Cries of London' had become
all the rage. Likewise their attention-grabbing cries were
written down and collected, such as this one, taken from an
eighteenth-century primer:

> 'Hot Mutton Dumplings – Nice Dumplings, all Hot.
> Hot Mutton Dumplings,' this man cries.
> 'What more could one desire,
> To save the trouble of making pies,
> Or puddings, and save your fire?'

The modern version of the hawker's cry is, of course, the
advertising jingle, but the intention is just the same – to get
us to part with our money for an alluring snack or ready-
cooked meal, which these days can be popped in the micro-
wave and heated in the blink of an eye.

FAST FOOD TAKES OVER AMERICA

Skipping (we are talking about *fast* food here) over the Atlantic to a different continent altogether, we arrive at what must be the home of fast food today – America. A hundred years ago, on 7 July 1912, a fast-food restaurant called the Automat opened in New York. The Automat was a revolutionary cafeteria with ready-prepared foods on sale behind hinged windows which the customer then purchased by inserting coins in a machine. This really was instant gratification and it wasn't the first of its kind – its owners Joseph Horn and Frank Hardart had set up their first in Philadelphia in 1902 – but New York's Automat created a sensation. The demand was so great that huge queues snaked back down Broadway and in fact it could take rather longer to get your food than in a conventional restaurant, but its fans didn't care: food had finally moved into the twentieth century. Numerous Automat restaurants were built all around the country to deal with the demand. The company also popularized the notion of **takeaway food**, with their slogan 'Less Work for Mother', although the idea wasn't a novel one: German immigrants had been preparing and selling their cooked sausages (see HOT DOG) for half a century by then. Soon another concept altogether became popular and the Automat was relegated to a mere footnote in the history of fast food. And that concept was the HAMBURGER restaurant.

Two brothers from New Hampshire, Dick and Mac McDonald, opened a BARBECUE drive-in in 1940 in San Bernardino, California, and after discovering that most of their profits came from hamburgers, the brothers reopened their restaurant in 1948 as a stand offering a simple menu of hamburgers, FRENCH FRIES, milkshakes and Coca-Cola, all served in disposable cartons. The McDonalds wouldn't have seen it like this as, in their eyes, their approach was ultramodern, but by drastically simplifying their menu, they were going back to the model of the medieval food vendors who had concentrated on one key product they excelled at. As a result, the brothers were able to produce hamburgers and fries constantly, without waiting for customer orders, and could serve them immediately; and their hamburgers were only 15 cents, about half the price they would have cost at a typical diner.

The transformation of the McDonalds' hamburgers into a global phenomenon wasn't down to the brothers, however, but to ferocious businessman Ray Kroc, who had originally specialized in milkshakes. Kroc bought the brothers out in 1954 (later refusing to pay the royalties that had been verbally agreed at the time) and then introduced two things that were to make McDonald's a world leader: production lines inspired by Henry Ford's car factories that meant the food was perpetually being replenished; and a ruthlessly maintained policy of standardization that ensured that every branch would serve exactly the same food in exactly the same way. It was so successful that all other fast-food chains promptly followed suit and American fast food proceeded to take over the world.

A **bistro** is a FAST-FOOD café, or at least it was until ultra-fast-food outlets began to dominate our high streets in the 1970s. After the defeat of Napoleon at the Battle of Waterloo in 1815, troops from all over Europe began to occupy Paris, particularly the Russians. Naturally the French cafés were soon bustling with new visitors, trade was roaring and one of the most frequent shouts to be heard at the time was '*Bweestra! Bweestra!*', which means 'Quickly! Quickly!' in Russian. Hence the word soon became associated with cheap bars, small clubs and cafés.

The Hamburger: From German Snack to American Icon

The **hamburger** is commonly acknowledged as America's signature dish and it's estimated that Americans eat over 14 billion of them every year. So you can see how being the home of the hamburger could mean big business, and this is indeed the claim of the small town of Seymour in Wisconsin. Seymour's Hamburger Hall of Fame celebrates the history of burgers, while the town's annual one-day Burgerfest includes parades and competitive events themed on burger-related condiments, including the famous Ketchup Slide. In 1989, the world's largest hamburger was produced during the festival, weighing in at a queasy 5,500 pounds. Back in 1885, as the town informs its visitors, fifteen-year-old Charles Nagreen was selling minced-meat patties from his stall at the very first Seymour Fair. Hamburger Charlie, as he became known, soon worked out that why his meatballs weren't selling was that customers weren't able to easily walk around eating them. So Charlie flattened his meatballs, serving them between two slices of bread and naming them hamburgers after the hamburger steaks that were already popular in the northern states.

Charlie Nagreen continued to sell hamburgers at county fairs for the rest of his life and became a local celebrity, claiming right up to his death to be the inventor of this form of FAST FOOD. But there is a rival claim, also dating from 1885. According to this story, sausage-making brothers Frank and Charles Menches were accidentally sent beef instead of pork by their supplier. Short of time and with limited resources, they decided to cook up the beef instead and serve it in sandwiches at the Erie County Fair, naming their new concoction the hamburger sandwich after their home town of Hamburg in the state of New York.

And there are all kinds of other counter-claims: no less an institution than the US Library of Congress has credited Louis' Lunch, a restaurant in New Haven, Connecticut, with making America's first burger in 1895. But eminent hamburger historians (and yes, they *do* exist) have begged to differ, citing instead Old Dave's Hamburger Stand at the 1904 World Fair in St Louis, run by Fletcher Davies, a restaurant owner from Athens in Texas. So convincing was their argument, in fact, that the Texas State Legislature then confirmed Athens as the 'Original Home of the Hamburger' in November 2006. They take this all very seriously over in America.

While they argue it out among themselves, let us take a look instead at the northern Europeans, who have been eating minced, salted and preserved steak ever since Genghis Khan hacked his way around the continent during the early 1300s (see STEAK TARTARE). Nineteenth-century German immigrants used ships of the Hamburg America Line, which began crossing in 1847. The immigrants took their favourite recipes with them and their easily prepared fast food of minced meat and bread was soon in demand along all the busy ports of the East Coast. Incoming passengers on the Hamburg Line, referred to as Hamburgers, called their favourite snack of ground meat served in a round bun a *Brötchen* ('roll' in German), although these were soon being called hamburgers by New Yorkers after the travellers who were eating them. We know this because by the mid nineteenth century (well before any of the 'official' claims) food vendors along New York Harbour were advertising 'steak cooked in the Hamburg style' to attract newly arrived German passengers and crew. As early as 1802 the *Oxford English Dictionary* had been defining **Hamburg steak** as a type of salted beef.

On reflection, it is fair to suggest that, with the rapid spread of the Hamburg steak throughout America, one man alone is unlikely to have come up with the notion of slipping meat into a bun. After all, back in England and rather earlier, in 1762, John Montague had had the same idea himself (see SANDWICH) and the British aristocracy has never been known for its inventiveness. It's true that, as America expanded and the rail and road networks granted travellers easier access over greater distances, so the food-on-the-move industry exploded into life (see FAST FOOD). Yet the famous meat-filled bun that fuelled that expansion can most likely be traced not to a single American but to a host of northern European migrants leaving the port of Hamburg for the Brave New World.

Salisbury Steak: The Food Fad that Rescued the Hamburger from the Enemy

Basically a HAMBURGER without a bun, the **Salisbury steak** was the invention of one eccentric man, the Dr Atkins of the nineteenth century: Dr J. H. Salisbury (1823–1905). A trained doctor and chemist, Salisbury joined up as an army medic when the American Civil War broke out in 1861. After some time he noticed that the main medical problem for soldiers in the field was not bullets but diarrhoea – due, in his view, to a poor diet (although I'd have put my money on anxiety in the face of the enemy as the most likely cause). Salisbury believed that a healthy diet was directly responsible for a healthy body. These days, of course, all of us are aware of how important our diet is for health, but back in 1861 this was radical thinking. Salisbury's conclusions were treated with suspicion to begin with until it soon became evident that the regular intake of minced steak, onions and coffee he recommended led to a huge improvement in the health of the rank and file (or perhaps they'd just got over their battle fright by then).

Salisbury also believed (somewhat less sensibly) that vegetables and starchy foods could produce substances in the digestive system which poison and paralyse the tissues, leading to heart disease, tumours, tuberculosis and mental illness. He maintained that our teeth were principally 'meat teeth' and our digestive systems designed to digest lean meat, hence fruit and vegetables, fats and starches should make up only a third of our diet. Starch was digested slowly, so it would ferment in the stomach and produce vinegar, acid, alcohol and yeast, all of which were harmful to our systems. The cult of Salisbury flourished and by 1888 he was prescribing his special recipe, now called Salisbury steak, to be eaten three times a day, together with lots of hot water to rinse out the digestive system, as a 'meat cure' for rheumatism, gout, colitis and anaemia.

But if it weren't for the outbreak of the First World War, it is unlikely that the Salisbury steak would be well known today. During the war, most English-speaking nations began renaming anything that sounded remotely German, to the extent that the British royal family changed its surname (see BATTENBERG CAKE) and America's favourite dish, the hamburger steak, instead became known as Salisbury steak among the Allied forces, the term subsequently spreading throughout the English-speaking world.

Not to mince your words is to speak plainly, frankly and with brutal honesty. The phrase is always used in the negative sense, as in 'not to' – we never hear anybody complaining of someone 'mincing their words', after all (we're clearly all amenable to a spot of flattery or economizing with the truth). The first recorded use of the expression can be traced to Joseph Hall's *Cases of Conscience* (1649), making it one of our older sayings. Some things we are told are unpleasant and difficult to take in and perhaps need to be made more 'digestible' – hence the analogy with butchers mincing cheaper cuts of meat, often full of bones and gristle, to make them easier to swallow. It has always been felt that a person 'not mincing his/her words' is making no effort to soften their impact.

From Swords to Skewers: The Rise of the Kebab

Legend has it that the **kebab** was born over the open fires of medieval Turkish soldiers, who impaled meat on their swords and then grilled it. References to skewers of grilled meat go back far further, however: ancient Greeks from Homer to Aristophanes wrote about an earlier variant of the kebab, the *obeliskos* (meaning 'little spit', it's also the origin of the word 'obelisk', a narrow thin monument such as Cleopatra's Needle on the Embankment in London). Yet the dish was old even then. After all, when you think about it, the cooking of meat over a fire must date back to approximately the day after prehistoric man first discovered how to light one.

However, while most of our culinary techniques, such as

roasting, toasting and baking, are centuries old, grilling meat kebab-style was largely unknown in Western Europe until around thirty years ago. That is because the nature of the dish reflects the differences in cuisine and lifestyle between West and East. In Europe, where the weather is cooler, it would have been easier to store whole joints of meat for roasting. In the Near East, by contrast, where before refrigeration the hotter temperatures would have meant meat went off much faster (the Jewish prohibition of pork and shellfish began as an entirely sensible rule for a tribe of desert-dwelling nomads), smaller cuts would have been more practical. In addition, fuel has long been in short supply in the hotter, drier Near East, with fewer trees to chop down for firewood, but used to be superabundant in Europe. Traditional European cookery therefore comprises methods that use much more fuel, such as baking and roasting, while Near Eastern cuisine has concentrated on much quicker methods, such as grilling and frying.

The word 'kebab' has an interesting history, deriving from *kababba*, an ancient Arabic word, meaning fried – not grilled – meat. A fourteenth-century Arabic dictionary describes a *kabab* as a dish of fried chunks of meat with some liquid. The Arabic word for grilled meat, by contrast, was *shiwa*. The Turks then took both words and combined them into the **shish kebab**, in which the liquid element of the *kabab* has been transmuted into a marinade that renders the meat more succulent and stops it from drying out when it is cooked over an open fire.

Now the term has become central to Arabic culture and cuisine. In Persian poetry, *jeegar kabab kardan*, meaning to break somebody's heart, translates literally as 'to grill liver', while in Iran the word for 'kitchen' used to be *kabab khaneh*, literally 'grill house' or 'kebab house'.

WHERE DOES THE DONER KEBAB COME FROM?

Kebabs come in many different forms but the shish and doner kebabs are the best-known varieties. The drunker a kebab-shop's customer is the more likely he is to order a **doner kebab**. Translated as 'rotating roast', its origins lie in the expansion of the Ottoman Empire into Europe and their picking up the European habit, when roasting larger joints of meat over a fire, to slice cooked strips off the outside of the joint, allowing the raw meat underneath to take its turn. Descendants of the Ottomans running modern kebab restaurants in high streets all over Europe slow-roast their meat in just this way.

The idea behind roasting the meat vertically, in what is known fondly by fans everywhere as 'an elephant's leg', is a modern method of self-basting, dating from the nineteenth century. It is intended to coat and infuse the roasting meat with dripping fat for a longer period than horizontally roasted meat. The greyish meat of an average doner kebab is undoubtedly of poor quality but the suggestion that its name refers to the notorious Donner Party of 1846 (led by George Donner), where starving American pioneers snowbound in the Sierra Nevada resorted to cannibalism, is just a scurrilous rumour. Likewise nobody has recorded how or why the word 'kabab' evolved into 'kebab' throughout the high streets and laybys of modern Europe, but presumably it's because, after eight lagers and at two in the morning, it's marginally easier to say.

How Eating Fish and Chips Became a Religious Experience for the British

Until the middle of the sixteenth century, eating meat on a Friday was an offence punishable by hanging. But with the British genius for turning the unpleasant into a treat, this led directly to our national habit of eating **fish and chips** on that day.

The law originated with the Christian tradition that believers must abstain from eating meat on a Friday. Jesus Christ was executed on Good Friday and for hundreds of years Christians have honoured his sacrifice and atoned for their sins by denying themselves meat on that day of the week. (Incidentally, this is also where the expression *Friday-faced*, for someone who looks depressed, comes from.) Luckily for hungry Christians everywhere, the Church, like many supposed vegetarians, doesn't regard fish as meat, so that is why you now see huge queues outside fish and chip shops all over the country every Friday, although I doubt many realize that, by not eating meat, they are honouring or atoning for anything.

There has long been a link between fish and Christianity. Not only were some of the Apostles fishermen but, back in the days when conversion to Christianity was punishable by death, the secret sign for the religion was a simple drawing of a fish: the Greek word for 'fish' was also an acrostic that spelt out 'Jesus Christ, God's Son and Saviour'. There is a more pragmatic story that the Church invented the rule purely to boost fish sales, but sadly there is no evidence to back it up.

Fish fried in batter was originally a Jewish dish, one that became increasingly popular in the East End of London where many Jews settled during the early nineteenth century. Charles Dickens refers to a fried fish warehouse in *Oliver*

Twist (1839) and Henry Mayhew, in his epic four-volume survey of London (1851–62), estimated there to be already around three hundred fried-fish sellers in the city.

Fried chipped potatoes (see also FRENCH FRIES) go back further, probably dating from the late eighteenth century, and chip sellers were traditionally Irish (see 'How the Potato Killed a Million People', page 154, for more on Ireland's dependence on this vegetable). Previously the most popular form of potato-based FAST FOOD had been the baked potato, but in the nineteenth century the taste for chips spread, particularly in Scotland and the north of England: they became a complete craze in the mill towns of Lancashire. Interestingly enough, it was Dickens once more who was the first to call this snack 'chips' in print: the *Oxford English Dictionary* cites his description in *A Tale of Two Cities* (1859) of 'husky chips of potatoes, fried with some reluctant drops of oil'.

A wave of chip shops spread down from the north and a wave of fried-fish shops spread up from the south until eventually the two overlapped. In 1860, a Jewish immigrant called Joseph Malin opened a shop, on Cleveland Street in the East End of London, selling fried fish 'in the Jewish fashion' alongside fried chipped potatoes for the first time. Demand was so great for this new, cheap 'fast food' that Malin soon opened fish-and-chip shops all over London. In 1863, Mr Lee's chippy opened for business in Oldham Market in Lancashire and soon he also had a chain of shops, expanding across the north of the country.

But it was the arrival of the steam-powered fishing trawlers in 1877 that really revolutionized the industry, allowing owners of fish-and-chip shops to buy cheaper fish in much greater quantities. By the end of the century, fish-and-chip shops were as much a part of British culture as steam trains and working-class poverty. By 1925, there were 35,000 shops, accounting for two-thirds of all the fish caught around the

British Isles. Essayist and general expert on British poverty
George Orwell rated fish and chips first among the home
comforts in his book *The Road to Wigan Pier* (1937), going as
far as to say that the dish had 'averted revolution' (and perhaps inventing the concept of 'comfort food' in the process).

The government were clearly paying attention for, during the Second World War, fish and chips were judged so
important to the national morale that they were one of the
few foods to avoid rationing (helped by the fact that Britain
didn't need to import either fish or potatoes). Although our
enthusiasm for Indian, Italian and Chinese takeaways (see
chapters 12–14) have led to a reduction in the number of old-
fashioned British chippies, there are still nearly nine thousand left in Great Britain. And that is over seven times the
number of McDonald's restaurants (see HAMBURGER). Fish
and chips now accounts for 20 per cent of all takeaway meals
bought on a Friday, and it's estimated that in excess of 250
million fish-and-chip suppers are eaten throughout the UK
every year, which makes them something of a national institution. Now, that is something worth celebrating.

Jellied Eels: Traditional London Fast Food Guaranteed to Make You Squirm?

The only English king to die from something he ate was Henry
I (*c.*1068–1135), who reputedly fell victim to food poisoning
after indulging in a 'surfeit of lampreys' (eels). Anyone who
has ever tried London's traditional fast food of **jellied eels**
may well understand why.

Eels, now an endangered species, were once so common in
the Thames that nets were set as far upriver as London itself,
and consequently they became a staple dish for the poor, particularly in the East End. Eels would be chopped up, boiled
in stock and allowed to cool, forming a jelly (they are natu-

rally gelatinous – though I'm not sure that makes them any more appealing). **Eel pie** was also a popular dish, in which the eels were cooked beneath a pastry lid. There is even an Eel Pie Island in the Thames at Twickenham (also the site of the Eel Pie Island Hotel, once a celebrated venue for jazz and rock bands), so called in commemoration of the dish and the eel fishing that formerly took place there. These days, however, cooked eels, either jellied or in a pie, are a rare sight on restaurant menus. There used to be over a hundred eel-pie-and-mash houses in London and many more street vendors (see also FAST FOOD): the few that remain now do a roaring trade in beef pies, mashed potato and liquor (a kind of parsley sauce). While few people are brave enough to go back for a second helping of jellied eels, this delicacy nonetheless remains a favourite of the true Londoner (see also PICKLED COCKLES and WHITEBAIT).

The Sausages Whose Bark is Worse than Their Bite

The **hot dog** feels like a very modern snack and under that name it does indeed date back only to the twentieth century. But under its alternative name of **frankfurter** it has a much longer pedigree.

Immigrants from Germany brought their favourite sausage to America with them: one that they had been eating since the Middle Ages. Indeed, Frankfurt celebrated the frankfurter's five hundredth birthday in 1987. By 1564, when Maximilian II was crowned Holy Roman Emperor, the snack was sufficiently established for it to be given out to the people of Frankfurt in celebration. The association between 'sausage' and 'dog' is more recent, however, dating back to the early nineteenth century when a talented Frankfurt butcher, Johann Georg Lahner (1772–1845), created a new recipe that gave his sausages such a distinctive smooth brown appearance that he called them 'dachshunds' or 'little dogs'. (That also works in reverse, of course: as dachshunds look so very much like frankfurters, perhaps that's how they acquired their nickname of 'sausage dogs'.)

But it was only after it moved to America that the frankfurter really came into its own. As the Germans settled all over that country, they introduced their favourite dishes to their new neighbours and the frankfurter became extremely popular. There are claims from all over the States as to who was the first to put it into a roll, including at least two versions of an unlikely story that the original frankfurter vendors lent their customers white gloves to eat the hot sausages with, to stop them burning themselves, but as customers kept walking away with them, they decided to offer them bread instead. While it may be open to debate who actually came up with the idea of putting sausages into rolls, there is little doubt about how the frankfurter hit the big time and who was behind it. When Christian von der Ahe (1851–1913), another canny German, bought the St Louis Brown Stockings baseball team in 1882, one of his first ideas was to set the ticket price at just 25 cents, ensuring full crowds who would consequently spend much more money on his beer and frankfurters, a move leading to the birth of the long association between the sport of baseball and hot dogs, one that endures to this day.

The term 'hot dog' is popularly believed to have been coined during a baseball game, in fact, between the New York Yankees and the Giants in 1901. It was a chilly day and concessionaire Harry Stevens decided to buy up all the dachshund sausages he could find, his vendors offering them for sale with the following cry: 'They're red hot! Get your dachshund sausages while they're red hot!' Observing the vendors, newspaper cartoonist T. A. Dorgan sketched a dachshund dog inside an elongated roll and, apparently unable to spell 'dachshund', used the caption 'hot dog' instead, a term that quickly caught on.

Dorgan wasn't the first person to play around with the notion of an actual dog in a bun, as attested by this satirical poem that appeared in a Yale student rag six years before:

> 'Tis dog's delight to bark and bite,'
> Thus does the adage run,
> But I delight to bite the dog
> When placed inside a bun.

This reflected the suspicion at the time that the best cuts of meat weren't always finding their way into the cheap sausages, which, for all one knew, might actually contain dog meat. Whatever they contained, hot dogs clearly didn't taste too bad as consumption of them never let up. Manufacturers of frankfurters initially tried to avoid the term but, with anti-German sentiment running high during the Second World War (see also FRENCH TOAST and SALISBURY STEAK), 'frankfurter' was dropped in favour of 'hot dog'* and, under this name, quickly rose to become the American icon it is today.

---

*During the First World War, dachshunds (the actual dogs, that is) had been renamed 'liberty pups'.

French Fries: What Did the
Belgians Ever Do for Us?

CHIPS, or **French fries** as they call them in the States, represent the perfect balance between the Old and the New World. America supplied the potato, imported in the sixteenth century by Spanish explorers. The earliest specimens, like the tomato (see GAZPACHO), were initially used medicinally, in small quantities, as an ingredient in pills, salves and therapeutic potions. But then Europe supplied the perfect cooking method. Belgian historians have found evidence that inhabitants of the Meuse Valley near Liège were cutting potatoes into strips and frying them as long ago as 1680. The French love their *pommes frites* but even they admit the recipe is Belgian in origin. And then America re-imported the recipe and their (and subsequently our) favourite side dish of all time was born.

But so why aren't they called Belgian fries? One story goes that the French fry was given its name by American GIs stationed in Belgium at the end of the Second World War. Thinly cut crispy chips garnished with mayonnaise are a Belgian speciality they would have been able to buy from any street corner. Apparently this delicacy was then incorrectly named 'French' because the bemused GIs thought that, as the Belgians were speaking French, they must be in France.

However, the real story goes back rather further, originating with one of America's great heroes, Thomas Jefferson (1743–1826), a founding father of the United States and author of the Constitution. Long before the days of being branded as cheese-eating surrender monkeys, the French had a very close relationship with the Americans. They had helped in the American Revolutionary War against the British and Jefferson then spent five happy years, between 1784 and 1789, as ambassador to France. During that time Jefferson grew to love its culture and cuisine and encouraged his servants to study French ways. As a result, the ambassador returned to America with a wide range of ideas that he was eager to introduce to the New World.

When he became president in 1801, he hired a French chef, Honoré Julien, to work at the White House and his resulting banquets were reported in great detail to a fascinated public. At one of them Jefferson introduced a food he called 'potatoes fried in the French manner', which was subsequently shortened to 'French fries'.

The term has been used in the US ever since, that is until a few years ago, when the decision was made in 2003 to invade Iraq. When France objected, this led to a big dip in enthusiasm among some Americans for all things French, including various foodstuffs. Inspired by the renaming of German-sounding items that took place in Britain and America during the two world wars (see BATTENBERG CAKE, HOT DOG and SALISBURY STEAK), restaurant owners rebranded various French-sounding foods (see also FRENCH TOAST), and plain old chips were suddenly transformed into **freedom fries**.

The word **barbecue** was first used in England during the mid 1600s to describe a wooden framework for sleeping on, the term evolving over the years to mean a framework for laying out and drying fish as a means of preserving them. Just as the origin of MARMALADE has been ascribed to the French for a seasick queen, so it is tempting to assume 'barbecue' must be from the French *barbe à queue* ('beard to tail'), referring to an animal being cooked whole. But sadly this is not the case. It actually derives from the Spanish *barbacoa*, adopted

from the term used by the Arawak Indians of the Caribbean to refer to a wooden grill for cooking meat. Upon
this framework a large animal would be roasted over
an open fire, leading directly to that strange obsession
among Englishmen for eating undercooked chops and
burned chicken on a cold summer's afternoon.

An interesting modernization of the word exists in
aerospace technology. As a spacecraft rotates to allow
heat from the sun to be spread evenly over its surface, it
executes what is termed the 'barbecue manoeuvre' or is
deemed to be in 'barbecue mode'. Although, considering the queasiness that must induce in the astronauts, I
think I'd have called it the DONER KEBAB manoeuvre or
mode.

6
Aperitifs and Appetizers

Eating's Cheating: The Sickly History of the Aperitif

How Mother's Ruin Became the Sahib's Saviour:
The Story of the Gin and Tonic

Shaken Not Stirred: The Martini

The Bloody Mary: Drinking to a
Brutal English Queen?

Waiter, There's a Mosquito in My Canapé …

… And an Outhouse in My Hors d'Oeuvre

A Crisp Riposte

Hummus: Not a Royal Dish Shocker

A Smorgasbord of Delights

Taking the Lid off Tapas

'A dry Martini,' he said. 'One. In a deep champagne goblet.'

'Oui, monsieur.'

'Three measures of Gordon's, one of vodka, half a measure of Kina Lillet. Shake it very well until it's ice-cold, then add a large thin slice of lemon peel. Got it?'

'Certainly, monsieur.' The barman seemed pleased with the idea.

'Gosh, that's certainly a drink,' said Leiter.

Bond laughed. 'When I'm ... er ... concentrating,' he explained, 'I never have more than one drink before dinner. But I do like that one to be large and very strong and very cold and very well-made.'

IAN FLEMING, *Casino Royale*

Eating's Cheating: The Sickly History of the Aperitif

Aperitif comes from the French term for an alcoholic drink that stimulates the appetite. Deriving from the Latin verb *aperire*, 'to open', it was originally a medical treatment based on the doctrine of humourism, current in medicine from classical times up until the nineteenth century. This argued that the human body is made up of four basic substances (humours) and that all illnesses are the result of an excess or deficit of one of these substances, treatable by restoring its balance within the body. So if a patient had a fever, for instance, it meant he had too much blood and needed to be bled. If he had no appetite, it needed to be stimulated with something bitter, to encourage the flow of bile and aid digestion. The medicines prescribed for this were liquors flavoured with strong-tasting herbs and spices. Over time, the medicines' bitterness was dissipated by the addition of more alcohol, and then it wasn't long before the healthy also started developing a taste for them as an appetite-stimulator before a meal.

The strongly herbal taste of drinks such as Dubonnet and vermouth was deliberate: you weren't getting drunk, you were getting better – a view heartily endorsed by myself and Mr Jameson. And drinking an aperitif soon became a social tradition in many parts of Europe, before spreading to the New World. The preferred British and American aperitifs (GIN AND TONIC and MARTINI, respectively) happily picked up on the idea of a medicinal drink before dinner, each beverage including enough strong alcohol to make sure you properly wet your whistle while whetting you appetite (see the box below).

The expressions **wetting your whistle** and **whetting your appetite** are often confused because they sound so similar, but they are in fact very different in meaning. One suggestion for the origin of 'whistle' in 'wet your whistle' is that drinkers at British pubs once had a whistle baked into the handle of their ceramic mugs. Whenever they needed more beer, they would blow the whistle to get served. I'd love to drink in a pub with such attentive service, but sadly neither it, nor this style of drinking vessel, has ever existed: 'whistle' is just a joking reference to your mouth or throat and to the fact that you can't easily whistle when your mouth is dry. Whereas if you are trying to 'whet your appetite', the allusion is to the sharpening of tools on a whetstone (grindstone): 'to whet' simply means 'to sharpen'. Hence 'whetting your appetite' is 'sharpening your appetite'. It is first referred to in Thomas Shadwell's play *The Squire of Alsatia* (1688): 'Let's whett; bring some Wine. Come on; I love a Whett.' Taking the same approach, the slang term for any kind of APERITIF around my way is a **sharpener**.

How Mother's Ruin Became the Sahib's Saviour: The Story of the Gin and Tonic

Now the favourite drink of the British middle and upper classes, **gin** has a rather darker history, as its nickname 'mother's ruin' suggests. Originally made in Holland in the early seventeenth century, it was popularized in Britain by the new Dutch king, William of Orange, when he took the throne in 1689. Back then, gin (its name a mangling of the Dutch *jenever*, meaning 'juniper', the berries of which were used to flavour it) was at first promoted as a powerful medicine for the stomach. But people soon discovered that it offered a far quicker and cheaper way to fall over than drinking beer. And when the government allowed unlicensed gin production, thousands of gin shops, known mockingly as ***gin palaces*** because they were so down at heel, sprang up throughout England.

It's hard to imagine now but, with no controls on gin production in those days, the drink was adulterated with turpentine – cheaper to obtain than juniper berries – and, rather than soothing the stomach, it began to have an increasingly lethal effect on its drinkers. The social degradation it caused is immortalized in William Hogarth's famous engraving *Gin Lane* (1711), which shows a London street in lecherous, drunken chaos, at its centre a woman dropping the baby she is nursing. In deliberate contrast, its companion engraving, *Beer Alley*, created at the same time, is a scene of happy, boozy patriotism. By 1730, the production of gin had increased to six times that of beer and there were real concerns that gin was bringing about a complete moral collapse of Britain's working classes. Hogarth's image was used by campaigners in an attempt to get the lax laws tightened up. The Gin Act of 1736 tried imposing high taxes on the sellers of gin, but when the prices went up there were riots in the streets. The second Gin Act, of 1751, was more successful as it forced distillers to sell only to licensed retailers and brought gin-shops under the jurisdiction of local magistrates.

London's newly regulated recipe soon became a world favourite. So much so that **London dry gin** remains the predominant variety on sale today. And as the British Empire spread across the globe, settlers took gin along with them – it was a lot less bulky than beer – as a taste of England and to blot out homesickness.

Many of these territories, especially India and East Asia, were plagued with malaria, a recurrent, frequently lethal, disease caused by mosquito bites and for which there was only one effective medicine. Back in the sixteenth century, Jesuit missionaries had observed Quechua Indians mixing the ground bark of the Peruvian cinchona or quinine tree with sweetened water to offset the bark's extremely bitter taste and then using it to treat cramps and fever. They had then imported some back to Rome, to deal with the symptoms of a particularly virulent outbreak of malaria in the early seventeenth century, which had accounted for the death of at least one pope and several cardinals. It turned out that the bark didn't just relieve the symptoms, it cured the disease too. And from then on, anyone spending time in a malarial zone was strongly recommended to take a daily dose of quinine.

Indian tonic water (tonic meaning 'cure') was devised to make that process more pleasant. The original recipe was simply a solution of quinine in carbonated water but as it tasted extremely bitter, members of the East India Company stationed abroad started dosing their tonic water with gin, which they would then drink as a *sundowner* – the time of maximum danger from mosquitoes. Soon quaffing this new APERITIF had become such an integral part of their lives (they even brought it back with them to Britain) that they forgot that it had originally been just medicinal.

Shaken Not Stirred: The Martini

You ought to get out of those wet clothes and into a dry Martini.

MAE WEST

The American aperitif of choice is the **Martini** – a mixture of GIN and vermouth, often garnished with an olive. The inclusion of vermouth shows that the drink did at least start as something vaguely medicinal (see APERITIF): the earliest advert (from 1896) shows a wife plying her exhausted husband with a Martini as a restorative.

It's entirely appropriate for such a strong drink that no one can remember who invented the first one or where the name came from. The Americans tell the story of a friendly barman making a specially strengthened pick-me-up for a weary traveller on his way to Martinez, California. The British claim to have named the drink after the Martini-Henry rifle, notorious for kicking like a mule, which was standard army issue during the empire-building 1880s. The Italians, meanwhile, trace the name to the drinks manufacturer Martini & Rossi, who were selling Martini Rosso vermouth from 1863. So, who knows – any or indeed all of these may have contributed towards the name. What is certain, however, is that the first published recipe for the Martini, in Harry Johnson's *New and Improved Illustrated Bartender's Manual* (1888), was American.

Far from being stopped by Prohibition (see CAESAR SALAD), the Martini only grew in popularity in speakeasies all over America. The strong taste of the vermouth masked the rawness of the homemade gin bootleggers brewed up in their bathtubs, and by the time the laws against alcohol were repealed in 1933, it had become the drink of choice for the sophisticated, notably F. Scott Fitzgerald, Dorothy Parker and most of Hollywood.

Ever since the 1930s, the Martini has become increasingly potent, the proportion of vermouth decreasing over time. At one point it made up a third of the drink, now it's closer to a fifth or sixth, with purists suggesting simply waving a firmly closed bottle of vermouth over your glass of icy gin. But the key thing remains that you have to have a strong head to drink more than one. At the height of the Cold War when Russia's premier Nikita Khrushchev was served a particularly potent Martini, he called it 'the USA's most lethal weapon'. So it's hardly surprising it was James Bond's drink of choice, although being Bond he had to make his own adaptations to the recipe (see page 104).

A *Mickey Finn* is a drink that has been drugged, usually to render a person helpless so that a crime can be committed. It is named after the owner of a sleazy Chicago establishment, the Palm Garden Restaurant and Lone Star Saloon, located on Whiskey Row. Taking its name from a scruffy palm in a pot next to the reception desk, the place was a haven for pickpockets and petty thieves, mostly trained by Finn himself. One of Finn's favourite methods was to lace drinks with chloral hydrate (knock-out drops) and then fleece his unconscious victims before dumping them in the street outside. Unsurprisingly, the

Palm Garden was soon closed down, in 1903, although Finn escaped jail and found work as a barman again, where he passed his techniques on to other unscrupulous vagabonds. So don't leave your drink unattended anywhere: you never know who's watching.

The Bloody Mary: Drinking to a Brutal English Queen?

Said to be the perfect hangover cure, a **Bloody Mary** is made up of vodka, tomato juice and various strong seasonings, such as cayenne or BLACK PEPPER and Tabasco or WORCESTERSHIRE SAUCE. It is also said to have been named after the Catholic queen Mary I (1516–58), affectionately remembered as 'Bloody Mary' thanks to her relentless pursuit of Protestant dissenters, of whom nearly three hundred were burned at the stake. Presumably the colour of the tomato juice is thought to resemble the blood she spilled, but the drink's connection with her becomes a little tenuous when you discover that the first reference to a vodka and tomato drink called a Bloody Mary was in Paris in 1921. I doubt the French would be naming a new cocktail after an English queen; in fact, I doubt the average French barman would even know who she was. A more likely candidate in those days would have been the movie star Mary Pickford (1892–1979), after whom another red-coloured cocktail had previously been named.

New York gossip columnist Lucius Beebe made one of the earliest established references to the drink in 1939 when he noted: 'George Jessel's newest pick-me-up which is receiving attention from the town's paragraphers is called a Bloody

Mary: half tomato juice, half vodka.' Nearly three decades later, in 1964, the *New Yorker* printed a story suggesting a French chef called Fernand Petiot had invented the cocktail in all its spicy glory. The magazine quotes Petiot:

> I initiated the Bloody Mary of today. Jessel said he created it, but it was really nothing but vodka and tomato juice when I took it over. I cover the bottom of the shaker with four large dashes of salt, two of black pepper, two of cayenne pepper and a layer of Worcestershire sauce. I then add a dash of lemon juice and some cracked ice, put in two ounces of vodka and two ounces of thick tomato juice, shake, strain, and pour. We serve a hundred to a hundred and fifty Bloody Marys a day here in the King Cole Room [the fashionable cocktail lounge at the St Regis Hotel in Midtown Manhattan] and in the other restaurants and the banquet rooms.

Other accounts back this up, suggesting it was indeed Petiot who invented the drink. And as he was working in Paris back in 1921, perhaps he was the very barman unlikely to have been acquainted with Queen Mary.

Like GIN, the Bloody Mary has also been touted as the perfect healthy breakfast. With this in mind – and strictly for the purposes of researching this book, you understand – I recently sampled twelve of these healthy breakfasts in a row at Johannesburg airport while waiting for a connecting flight, and I have this advice for you, dear reader: don't try it yourself.

Waiter, There's a Mosquito in My Canapé …

Eaten by the French since the eighteenth century, **canapés** traditionally consist of little platforms of pastry, TOAST or crackers with any of a whole variety of more interesting foods perched on top. Like the APERITIF, they are designed to pique the appetite. Generally salty or spicy, to encourage those holding them to drink more, and small enough to be eaten in one bite, canapés are intended to be held in one hand while, most importantly, the drinking hand remains free at all times. Possibly the best-known canapé is the vol-au-vent, a puff pastry case – so light that, according to the original French, it 'flies in the wind' – filled with mushrooms, prawns or other items.

The word 'canapé' has a strange history, curiously unrelated to food. In ancient Greece, a *konops* was a mosquito, while the curtains suspended around a couch to keep them out – an early form of mosquito net – were called a *konopion*. This was then adapted by the Romans as *conopeum*, becoming *canopeum* in medieval Latin and then *canope* in Middle English, as the name for a curtain, leading eventually to the modern word 'canopy'. The French, by contrast, used the word *canapé* – from the same linguistic root – to describe the couch rather than the curtain. Someone must have joked that a piece of toast topped with a savoury food looked like a sofa (*canapé*) covered in cushions and so the word took on the additional meaning.

… And an Outhouse in My Hors d'Oeuvre

Hors d'oeuvres are the grown-up version of CANAPÉS, equally elaborate but rather more substantial. By the turn of the twentieth century, the hors d'oeuvres trolley had become

a familiar feature of grand restaurants all over Europe. Looking not unlike the cover of this book, it would have been laden
with all manner of colourful terrines and moulds, elaborately
decorated pies, salads and tarts. Rather than reading the
menu and deciding what *sounded* good, you could see which
dishes actually *looked* the most appealing and try a little of
several.

When first used, back in 1596, *hors d'oeuvre* (literally 'outside the work' in French) was an architectural term referring to some kind of outbuilding not incorporated into an
architect's main design. By the time it had been adopted
into English, in the early 1700s, it had shifted in meaning to
'something out of the ordinary' but fairly soon acquired its
modern, food-related sense of 'something outside the main
meal'. The expression became a familiar one in Paris at the
beginning of the nineteenth century when the great chefs
formerly employed by the French nobility and now liberated
following the French Revolution opened their own restaurants. Hors d'oeuvres were an ideal way of displaying their
culinary skill and expertise to a whole raft of new customers.
While the French monopoly on fine food over the centuries
can be rather annoying, there is one consolation. The next
time you are served canapés or hors d'oeuvres, just remember that what it really means is that our friends across the
Channel are eating sofas outside their houses.

A Crisp Riposte

On 24 August 1853, George 'Speck' Crum (1822–1914)
was working as head chef at Moon's Lake House in Saratoga Springs, New York, when a customer complained that
his FRENCH FRIES were too thick and not 'as they should
be'. Crum was so annoyed by this remark that he decided to

exaggerate his response by slicing the potatoes as thinly as he possibly could. To his great surprise, the customer was delighted, and **Saratoga Potato Chips**, or **crisps** as we know them in England, proved to be so popular with other diners that Crum was soon able to open his own restaurant with the profits he made from his new recipe.

Hummus: Not a Royal Dish Shocker

Hummus, the dip made from cooked and mashed chickpeas, is very popular in the Near and Middle East. Indeed, the word means 'chickpeas' in Arabic. Chickpeas have been eaten for thousands of years and were a common street dish (see FAST FOOD) in ancient Rome. (According to Plutarch, the famous Roman orator Cicero was named after an ancestor who had a wart on his nose shaped like a chickpea – which is *cicer* in Latin.) The other ingredients of hummus – sesame seeds, garlic, lemon juice and olive oil – come from plants that have also been cultivated since ancient times. No one knows when they were first mixed together to produce the dish but, like the KEBAB, hummus clearly goes back a long way. Thus the legend that it was first prepared in the twelfth century by Richard the Lionheart's princely enemy Saladin seems highly unlikely and a bare-faced attempt to raise the reputation of this ordinary peasant food a notch or two.

A Smorgasbord of Delights

The Swedish have been creating smorgasbords since the Middle Ages. Originally their version of HORS D'OEUVRES, a Swedish **smorgasbord** now consists of a whole variety of dishes to be eaten BUFFET-style. In Norway it is called a *koldtbord*, in Denmark they have their own version, known as a *kolde bord*, while the Finnish call theirs *voileipapoyta*. In each case, the word can be translated into English as 'cold table', the exception being the Swedish term, which loosely translates as 'table [*bord*] of OPEN SANDWICHES [*smörgås*]'.

In Sweden back in the fourteenth century, the upper classes would serve a selection of cold appetizers – always with bread and butter – on a side table, which guests would eat standing up before sitting down to the main meal. By the seventeenth century, the food had moved from the side table to the main table and hot as well as cold dishes were served, so that what had begun as a starter now became a whole meal in itself. Today in Sweden even the grandest meals are still served in this way, including the traditional CHRISTMAS DINNER, the *julbord* (literally 'Yule table').

The smorgasbord arrived in the English-speaking world at the New York World Fair in 1939 when it was presented at the Swedish Pavilion's Three Crowns Restaurant, and soon fashionable restaurants in New York and London were offering their own versions. Now, so firmly entrenched is the word in the English language that it's not just applied to food but used figuratively to mean an array of objects, rather like the **smorgasbord** of entries in this book – please help yourself.

Taking the Lid off Tapas

Many cultures have a rule that you must have a bite to eat every time you have a drink. Spain has taken that idea and developed a whole cuisine around it – **tapas**. Consisting of a wide range of little snacks or appetizers, from juicy olives to spicy chorizo or rings of battered squid, these are now served in select bars or restaurants throughout Spain, Britain and America.

It's possible that they evolved as part of the traditional Spanish working day, which began at first light. At 1.00 p.m., the hottest part of the day, workers would have their main meal, after which they would take a siesta somewhere shady for a few hours to allow their lunch to digest before they returned to work. From the middle of the evening until late at night, they would then socialize, drink wine and graze on various small, easy-to-eat foods.

That's all very likely, but there is, as you might imagine, a better tale to tell. King Alfonso X (1221–84) was a very popular ruler of Castile, León and Galicia. One day, as legend has it, he fell ill and the royal doctor advised him to take small snacks between meals in order to build up his strength. When the king eventually recovered, he continued with this regime, having decided that as eating between meals helped counteract the effects of the wine he was drinking all day, it must be beneficial for him. Reasoning that his subjects would also be drinking wine and might be consuming more than was good for them, he passed a law ruling that wine could not be served in the taverns or inns of his kingdom unless the innkeeper provided a small snack with each glass. To comply with the laws, wine would then be served with a slice of bread, cheese or ham that a drinker could cover his tankard with to keep the flies out of his liquor. When the tankard had been drained, the food was eaten and the process would start all over again, sometimes lasting all night, and so the institution that is *la tapa* was born.

The world's first tapas bar was opened in Seville in 1670, when a local nobleman bought an old convent canteen and dining room and began providing tapas, in their present form, to merchants and traders. El Rinconcillo, as the tapas bar has been known ever since it opened, was bought by ancestors of the present owners in 1860 and remains an integral part of the old city of Seville. The word *tapa* may be translated as 'lid', possibly tracing its origins to King Alfonso's concern for his wine-soaked subjects, his subsequent drinking law and the practice among Spanish workers of covering their wine with food to keep the bugs out of their drinks. Which must mean that while the French are eating their settees (see CANAPÉS), the Spanish are dining on their lids.

Over the years, tapas have become more sophisticated and a vast number of dishes are available. These days many people, especially if they are dining with me, try eating all sorts of food 'tapas' style. The next time you are in a restaurant, and not just a Spanish one, try ordering half a dozen starters and nothing else. It's a great way to share a meal.

7
Soups and Starters

Was Bouillabaisse a Food of the Gods?

Vichyssoise: A Soup by No Other Name

Gazpacho: Together We're Stronger

Who Invented Onion Soup?

Jenny Lind Soup: How the Swedish Nightingale
Inspired a Dish

The Buffet: From Elegant Dining to
Pit-stop Refuelling

Prawn Cocktail: The Sophisticated Snack
that's All about Saying No

Potted Shrimps: A Short History of
Food Preservation

Why Imam Bayildi was a Turk's Delight

Foie Gras: How the Fig Transformed
Liver into a Delicacy

Do you have a kinder, more adaptable friend in the food world than soup? Who soothes you when you are ill? Who refuses to leave you when you are impoverished and stretches its resources to give a hearty sustenance and cheer? Who warms you in the winter and cools you in the summer? Yet who also is capable of doing honor to your richest table and impressing your most demanding guests? Soup does its loyal best, no matter what undignified conditions are imposed upon it. You don't catch steak hanging around when you're poor and sick, do you?

JUDITH MARTIN ('Miss Manners')

Was Bouillabaise a Food of the Gods?

Possibly the most famous fish soup in the world, **bouillabaisse** is really a fish stew, a one-pot meal and the signature dish of Marseilles in the south of France. The story the Marseillais tell is that it was invented by the Roman goddess of love, Venus, who served it to her husband Vulcan to lull him to sleep (presumably French films hadn't been invented by then) so that she could go off and consort with Mars (the protector of the town).

Every decent chef in the world has his or her own variations: the only constant requirement is the freshness of the fish. The type of fish depends on the morning's catch, although a traditional bouillabaisse should contain at least three kinds, including the fearsome-sounding *rascasse* or scorpionfish, so called because of its arsenal of venomous spines. The name of the stew doesn't directly relate to fish but more to the process of cooking it, deriving as it does from the French verbs *bouillir* ('to boil') and *abaisser* ('lower [the heat]'). The dish was developed by Marseilles fishermen, who would put a pot of seawater on to boil by the quayside, adding a few herbs and vegetables and letting it simmer over an open fire while they enjoyed a few glasses of wine in a nearby café and then, at the last moment, popped in any unsold fish, usually the small or misshapen ones.

The first recipe for bouillabaisse was published in 1790 in *La Cuisine de santé* by Jourdain Le Cointe, who called the dish *matelote de poisson* ('mariner-style fish stew') and went on to describe fishermen disembarking along a riverbank, to be met by their wives who already had a pot on the boil for the fish to be added to. Now, that's just about as fresh as you can get.

The French have a similar dish, a slow-cooked meat stew that became popular with the meat traders at London's Smithfield Market. Like bouillabaisse, **pot au feu** (literally, 'pot on the fire') could be made up using any pieces of leftover or unsold merchandise, and was eaten communally. Indeed in Marseilles, its place of origin, bouillabaise is usually made for at least ten people, the idea being the bigger the stew the more varieties of fish can be included and the better the dish.

Vichyssoise: A Soup by No Other Name

Hot leek and potato soup is a staple of the winter cuisine of most north European countries but it took a French chef, Louis Diat (see also SOLE VÉRONIQUE) – sensibly based in New York during the First World War – to turn it into a classic summer dish by serving it cold and sprinkled with chopped chives. Diat, who came from the Bourbonnais, not far from Vichy (hence the name of his creation), was inspired by memories of a hot soup served by his mother when he was a lad. When the Second World War broke out and Vichy was chosen as the new capital of Nazi-governed France, some expat French chefs tried to call the soup *crème gauloise* instead, but unlike the many German-sounding foods rechristened in the previous world war (see BATTENBERG CAKE, FRENCH TOAST and SALISBURY STEAK), this time the name, **vichyssoise**, proved indelible.

Gazpacho: Together We're Stronger

Spain seems such a straightforwardly Catholic country society that it is surprising to discover that between 711 BC (when
General Tariq ibn Ziyad began his campaign to conquer the
peninsula from Morocco) and AD 1492 (when Ferdinand II of
Aragon defeated the last Islamic garrison at Granada) most
of Spain and Portugal was Muslim. It is estimated that by
the year 1200 over 5 million of the region's 7 million inhabitants were naturalized Muslims. Once the Catholics had taken
over again, they were determined to stamp out over 750 years
of Muslim influence and so set up the Spanish Inquisition to
track down anyone continuing to practise Islam (or indeed
any other religion) in secret. The Inquisition was ruthlessly
efficient: between 1540 and 1700, it rounded up 104,000 so-
called heretics, who were then either burned at the stake or
driven from the country altogether.

This policy of zero tolerance fortunately didn't extend
to Moorish architecture, and, rather than being destroyed,
landmark buildings were turned either into churches (the
Mezquita in Córdoba) or royal palaces (the Alhambra in
Granada), even retaining their original names. But probably
the strongest Moorish influence still visible in modern Spain
can be seen in its cuisine, the most famous example being
gazpacho. Made from bread, tomatoes, red peppers, garlic
and olive oil all puréed together and served cold, gazpacho is
the perfect food for the dry heat and desert-like conditions
of Andalucía in southern Spain. Derived from a garlic-based
soup the Moors brought with them from northern Africa, the
name is believed to originate from the Moorish *caspa*, meaning
'residue' or 'fragments', an allusion to the small pieces of
bread and vegetables in the soup. But as it was made in great
quantities for country labourers, who would approach the

communal bowl, dip their bread in and sit back to eat it while another took their turn, this could refer equally well to all the bits of bread that broke off and got left behind in the bowl.

However, the key ingredient of gazpacho, as we'd recognize it today, could have only been added to the recipe after the Moors had been expelled. It feels like it has always been part of our diet, but the tomato wasn't introduced into Europe until the sixteenth century – brought back from South America by Cortez in 1521 – and it wasn't until the early 1600s that it was widely eaten in Spain. By adding it to the original, Moorish ingredients in the soup, the Spanish made gazpacho their own.

Who Invented Onion Soup?

The renowned expert on Mediterranean food Elizabeth David was unimpressed with the 'sodden bread, strings of cheese and half-cooked onion floating about' in a typical 'French' **onion soup**. Made from caramelized onions in a beef stock and traditionally served with croutons and grated Gruyère, the soup has many imitators – some more palatable than others. But arguably the original dish is itself an imitation as the French were by no means the first to come up with it.

Cheap, tasty and easy to grow, onions form the basis of many types of soup the world over, and have done since ancient times. The Persians, for instance, produced their own version of a simple onion soup, thought to date to the time of King Arsaces during his military campaigns of 250 BC against the King of Syria. Onions are also the basic ingredient in Persian *âsh-e-nazri* or **pledge soup**. This is traditionally served by a family seeking support for one of its members – a sick child, for instance, or a son or daughter leaving on a long journey. The soup accompanies prayers for the child's recovery or the traveller's safe return. Other ingredients vary but are donated by relatives, friends and neighbours in equal quantities in order that the rich are not seen to be showing off and the poor are not left feeling inferior. Everyone contributes to the making of the soup, ensuring there is enough for all and plenty left over for distribution to the hungry and homeless. If and when their prayers are answered – the child recovers or the traveller returns safely – then the soup is made every year on the same day as a ritual to give thanks to God.

Both the Persians and the ancient Greeks believed onions provided a man with courage and good fortune and their foot soldiers are known to have lived on a diet of onion soup with dried bread broken into it, beating the French to their croutons by a couple of thousand years.

Jenny Lind Soup: How the Swedish Nightingale Inspired a Dish

Leopold Bloom, hero of James Joyce's stream-of-consciousness novel *Ulysses* (1922), dreams of **Jenny Lind soup** while having lunch at the Ormond Hotel: 'Jenny Lind soup: stock, sage, raw eggs, half pint of cream. For creamy dreamy.' Thick and highly calorific, with all the delicacy of wallpaper paste, the soup is no longer popular in these cholesterol-conscious times, but back in the nineteenth century it was almost as sought after as Jenny Lind herself.

Jenny Lind, the 'Swedish Nightingale', was born in Stockholm in 1820 and died in Malvern, England, in 1887. She was only nine years old when she was overheard singing to her cat by the principal dancer of the Royal Swedish Opera who arranged for her to have an audition at the Royal Theatre School. With the dancer's help, Lind was accepted to study at the school and she began appearing on stage from the age of ten. Aged only eighteen, she debuted as prima donna (first lady) in a performance for the Royal Opera, earning herself thunderous applause and instant acclaim. In the years that followed, she performed throughout Europe, exciting the imagination of audiences and fellow artists alike, including fellow Scandinavian Hans Christian Andersen (1805–75). Three of his fairy tales are said to have been inspired by her, including 'The Nightingale', which in turn gave rise to her famous nickname. He was also one of the many men who fell in love with her, although her feelings for him were purely platonic.

As well as her beautiful voice, Lind was known for her courage – throughout her career she suffered from severe stage fright, which she would have had to repeatedly over-come – and compassion. When not performing, she dedicated much of her time and her profits to good works and helping others.

Indeed it was chiefly for philanthropic reasons that Lind accepted an offer from the legendary showman P. T. Barnum to tour America where, at that time, she was largely unknown. On 9 January 1850, she agreed to a tour of 150 concerts, for which she would be paid £1,000 per show – an unimaginable amount of money in those days. She wasn't being greedy, however, but wanted the money to help fund new schools in Sweden. The publicity Barnum created prior to the tour ensured crowds of over forty thousand people waiting at the dockside just to get a glimpse of the virtuous European star, and the expression 'Lindomania' was coined, before she had even uttered a note. 'Jenny Rage' was soon sweeping America and such was the demand to hear the Nightingale that Barnum was forced to renegotiate his contract with Lind's manager, John Jay, to include a share of the profits, a move that would eventually earn her over £250,000.

Such was the appeal of Jenny Lind and her legendary voice that several objects were named after her, including a locomotive, a ship and a baby's crib. She is immortalized in place names, too, while her portrait appears on a Swedish banknote. But a more unusual memorial to her is the soup that was created specially for her. In later years, whenever she performed (and she always donated the proceeds to charity), she would eat the soup, believing the cream and eggs were soothing to strained vocal cords, and everyone who admired her and wanted to sound like her obsessively ate it too. Lindomaniacs indeed, but definitely preferable to a modern generation of young girls not eating anything at all in order to try and sound like Posh Spice.

The Buffet: From Elegant Dining to Pit-stop Refuelling

The word **buffet** now denotes any sort of meal in which diners serve themselves from a range of dishes, either for a starter or the whole meal. Developed in France in the eighteenth century, in a similar way to the Swedish SMORGASBORD, the food was served on long, specially made cabinets, while drawers in cupboards underneath held the plates, cutlery and, most importantly, the wine. The practice soon spread throughout Europe, becoming popular in England in the second half of the nineteenth century.

It is said that the buffet was named after one Pierre-Alphonse Buffet (1692–1756), a Parisian gentleman, drinker, gambler and general layabout. Like Lord SANDWICH, he also had a passion for cards and may be remembered in the same way. Because Buffet also hated to interrupt his card games with the trivial matter of eating, he ordered his servants to leave dishes on a side table so that he and his guests could help themselves to whatever they wanted whenever they chose. An alternative version of the story suggests that, having staked and lost his dining table in a game of cards, he was forced into using a side table instead, thus inventing the buffet. However, as the only reference I can find to Pierre-Alphonse Buffet is in relation to one or other version of this tale, I smell a French rat.

A buffet is indeed a type of sideboard from which food is served, but sadly there was no card-playing Monsieur Buffet (or not one connected with French cuisine) as the word derives from the Old French for 'stool', *bufet* (not from the similarly pronounced *bouffer*, 'to eat'). The traditional French buffet, laid out with considerable artistic and gastronomic panache, was rather smart, whereas the word has become somewhat devalued in English. No longer aristocrats gracefully grazing but stressed-out workers fighting over the last sandwich (limp and plastic-wrapped) in a cafeteria or train buffet car.

Prawn Cocktail: The Sophisticated Snack that's All about Saying No

Archaeologists sifting through ancient middens (rubbish heaps) – see, it's not all Indiana Jones – have found evidence showing how shellfish of all kinds have been a favourite snack in coastal areas since prehistoric times. What's more, they have been eaten in a spicy sauce for at least two thousand years. Prawns served in a spiced white wine vinegar and egg yolk sauce is an ancient Roman recipe, often attributed to Apicius, the Roman gourmet from the first century AD who wrote the earliest cookbooks. According to legend, Apicius was such a great fan of prawns that when he heard that there were particularly large, luscious ones in Libya, he chartered a ship there on the spot. But so disappointed was he by the first ones brought to him aboard ship that he sailed home immediately, without ever setting foot on shore.

In the 1970s, all sophisticated dinner parties began with **prawn cocktail** (moving on to BEEF WELLINGTON and CHEESECAKE). Although basically an ancient dish, the prawn cocktail as we'd recognize it today is a much more recent creation, deriving from American recipes in the early twentieth century. Incidentally, around the English-speaking world the terms 'shrimp' (see also POTTED SHRIMPS) and 'prawn' are used interchangeably, which can lead to a certain amount of confusion. Americans use 'shrimp' to describe both large and small crustaceans in the Penaeidae and Pandalidae families. The British, on the other hand, use it to describe the smaller variety (the word derives from Middle English *shrimpe*, 'to contract'; hence perhaps its informal meaning of someone who is small in stature) and 'prawn' to describe the larger. So the British dish is an anglicized version of the American **shrimp cocktail**.

A survey of American cookbooks confirms that shellfish in a spicy tomato-based sauce (usually ketchup mixed with HORSERADISH, Tabasco sauce and cayenne pepper – see THOUSAND ISLAND DRESSING) and served in tiny cups as an appetizer was very popular in the early part of the twentieth century. But it was the 1920s and the decade of Prohibition that made the dish wildly fashionable. As alcohol was forbidden by law, there was a real frisson in ordering up a cocktail – even if it was just a few shrimps in a fancy glass. It was a safe way of cocking a snook at authority. **Fruit cocktail**, likewise, was another favourite choice of the rebellious diner. (For other ways in which people coped in the era of Prohibition, see CAESAR SALAD.)

Something that **warms the cockles of your heart** induces a glow of happiness and goodwill. Could a common shellfish, chief ingredient in that favourite cockney dish of **pickled cockles** (see also JELLIED EELS and WHITEBAIT), have any connection with the phrase? In coastal regions of the British Isles, cockles were once a staple part of the diet for many people (hence Molly Malone wheeling her wheelbarrow through Dublin's fair city, crying: 'Cockles and mussels, alive, alive oh!'). As they are roughly heart-shaped, with ribbed shells, it may be that the shape and rib-like veining of the heart reminded surgeons and anatomists of the cockle, but that feels rather tenuous. The more likely reason comes from the medieval Latin term for the ventricles of the heart, *cochleae cordis*. *Cochleae* sounds much like 'cockle', so the phrase may well have started as a doctor's joke, deliberately mangling the Latin. *Cochlea* in Latin is actually the word for a snail; in modern anatomy it is the term used for the inner ear, due to its snail-like structure, and it's likely that the chambers of the heart used to be so called for the same reason. So if this derivation is right, we should really be speaking of warming the snails of one's heart. Which brings us, rather neatly, to that favourite starter of the French – **escargots** with garlic butter. By the way, the French are estimated to eat some 25,000 tonnes of snails each year, equating to around 500 million snails – a statistic guaranteed to warm the heart of many a Gallic restaurateur.

Potted Shrimps: A Short History of Food Preservation

Made ideally with small brown shrimps from Morecambe Bay in Lancashire, **potted shrimps** are the archetypal British starter. The shrimps (see also PRAWN COCKTAIL) are flavoured with mace, cayenne pepper and nutmeg, then placed in small pots and preserved under a thick layer of clarified butter. Like the PORK PIE, they are a fascinating remnant of an old culinary technique. The medieval pie, from which the pork pie derives (see 'A Brief History of the Pie', page 39), was chiefly intended as a method of conserving food rather than presenting it. The thick pastry crust wasn't meant to be eaten but to act as a barrier to harmful substances, and thus the food inside it, having being cooked in a sterile container, remained fresh for a long time. This technique didn't emerge as the result of careful scientific testing, of course, but purely by trial and error. The only design flaw was at the top of the pie where the filling had shrunk away from the pastry during cooking, leaving a gap. This was sealed by pouring boiling (thus sterile) stock or fat in through a hole in the top – which set; hence, for example, the jelly in a pork pie. This presented a reliable way of preserving and transporting food that would otherwise have gone bad very quickly.

Towards the end of the sixteenth century, the pastry began to be replaced with (much more economical and reusable) pots, in which the cooked ingredients were preserved by pouring molten fat on top. Estimates of keeping time ranged from a month to over a year. Three hundred years before the freezer, this predecessor of the tin can became very popular as a means of storing food. It wasn't always foolproof, however. Hannah Glasse's *The Art of Cookery* (see YORKSHIRE PUDDING) has some terrifying tips on how 'to save potted birds that begin to be bad' – basically dipping the birds in boiling water for thirty seconds, adding salt and pepper and then repotting, advice that pretty much guaranteed food poisoning. With the emergence of the tin can (see CHICKEN KIEV), potted food gradually slid out of fashion. Today the only remnants of potting are particular delicacies such as French terrines, with their thick layer of jelly, or potted shrimps with their seal of butter.

Why Imam Bayildi was a Turk's Delight

Imam bayildi – aubergines stuffed with tomato, garlic and onion and simmered in olive oil – is one of Turkey's most popular starters. Curiously, the name has nothing to do with its ingredients but translates as 'the imam fainted'. One of the most important religious positions to be granted in the Arabic world is that of the imam. As leader of a mosque, the imam leads the prayer during Islamic meetings. He may also be regarded as the leader of his community. But what does a religious leader, and a fainting one at that, have to do with a Middle Eastern appetizer?

According to Turkish legend, one day, a long, long time ago, an imam, who was known for his love of food, surprised his friends and family by announcing he was to be married. The lady in question was the daughter of a well-known olive oil merchant and so, as part of her dowry, her father gave the groom twelve great jars of olive oil, each large enough to hold a fully grown man.

One day, soon after the wedding, the young bride, who turned out to be an excellent cook, presented her husband with a special dish of stuffed aubergines cooked in copious amounts of olive oil. The imam was so delighted with the dish that he asked his wife to make it every single day, which she did – until the olive oil ran out, of course. His wife then had the difficult task of informing her husband that they were out of oil and, as the tale concludes, the imam was so shocked that he fainted.

Foie Gras: How the Fig Transformed Liver into a Delicacy

A traditional French delicacy, **foie gras** (literally 'fat liver') is made from the liver of a goose or duck that has been artificially fattened. The technique for producing it is thought to have been developed as long ago as 2500 BC, by the ancient Egyptians. Observing how the livers of migratory geese became enlarged due to overfeeding in preparation for their long flights, they tried force-feeding domestic birds with figs to achieve the same effect. In the tomb of Mereruka – who served as vizier, the second most powerful man in the kingdom, during the sixth dynasty – there are stone carvings of geese being force-fed, showing how the practice was already widespread by 2300 BC.

Goose fattening spread from Egypt to the Mediterranean, where the practice is recorded by Roman commentators. Pliny the Elder, for instance, describes how the gourmet Apicius (see also PRAWN COCKTAIL) tried to apply the method to other animals, too: 'Apicius made a discovery, that we might employ the same artificial method of increasing the size of the liver of a sow, as with that of the goose. It consists in cramming them with dried figs and when they are fat enough, they are drenched with wine mixed with honey, and immediately killed' (*Natural History*, AD 77–9).

The Romans called the resultant dish, made from the fattened liver, *iecur ficatum* or 'fig liver'. These days French geese and ducks are force-fed corn rather than figs, but, interestingly, the French word for liver, *foie*, derives from *ficatum* ('fig'), so closely was animal liver formerly associated with this practice. The French – who are now the main producers in the world (although Hungary comes a close second), with an estimated annual output of around 25,000 tonnes of foie gras – claim the birds grow to enjoy their extra daily ration of corn being pushed down their throats through a funnel. A rather different insight is offered by Charles Gérard, in his *Ancienne Alsace à table*, published in 1877 (at this point animal lovers should look away): 'The goose is nothing, but man has made of it an instrument for the output of a marvellous product, a kind of living hothouse within which there grows the supreme fruit of gastronomy.' It's OK, you can all look back now.

8
Salads and Vegetables

What Did Caesar Do for My Salad?

Sidney Smith: Impassioned Campaigner
and Salad Dresser

From the Waldorf Hotel to Fawlty Towers:
The Descent of a Salad

Coleslaw: Do You Prefer Your Salad Cold
or with Cabbage?

Robert H. Cobb: Salad Maker to the Stars

What are the Right Ingredients for a Nice Salad?

Sauerkraut and the Seaman's Disease

Pease Pudding Hot: What Did Ordinary Folk
Eat in the Middle Ages?

Eggs Florentine and the Wicked Italian Queen
Who Loved Spinach

Did the French Invent Baked Beans?

The Rise and Fall of the Potato

Gratin Dauphinois: A Dish Fit for a Prince ...

... And One that Enticed a Prophet
(Jansson's Temptation)

Colcannon: How a Spoonful of Mash
Could Win You a Husband

The Eggs that were Broken to Make
the First Spanish Omelette

There was an Old Person of Fife,
Who was greatly disgusted with life;
They sang him a ballad,
And fed him on salad,
Which cured that Old Person of Fife.

EDWARD LEAR

What I say is that, if a fellow really likes potatoes, he
must be a pretty decent sort of fellow.

A. A. MILNE

What Did Caesar Do for My Salad?

The name, of course, conjures up a grumpy, toga-clad emperor tucking into a spot of lunch before perhaps throwing a Christian or two to the lions, in the name of entertainment, to keep the people of Rome happy. But instead it turns out that **Caesar salad** is less than a hundred years old and comes from the most unlikely of places, Mexico.

Caesar Cardini (1896–1956) was born in Italy and emigrated to America with his three brothers at the beginning of the First World War. It was the era of Prohibition – also known as the Noble Experiment – when between 1917 and 1933 the sale, manufacture and transportation of alcohol was banned in the United States. The aim was to improve the morality and behaviour of the American people, but in fact it just encouraged a huge rise in organized crime. Realizing what lengths people would go to, just to have a drink or two, Caesar and his brother Alex saw a legal business opportunity and seized hold of it. In 1924, they moved a short distance across the Mexican border, from Los Angeles, and set up a restaurant in Tijuana after the town became a firm favourite for southern Californians looking for a weekend party.

The Cardinis' combination of strong alcohol and tasty Italian food proved to be a winner and their Fourth of July celebrations were so oversubscribed that, according to Caesar's daughter Rosa, her father soon ran out of ingredients to feed his drunken customers. He responded by throwing together a salad of basically whatever he had left in the kitchen: lettuce, croutons, PARMESAN CHEESE, eggs, olive oil, lemon juice,

BLACK PEPPER and WORCESTERSHIRE SAUCE. Perhaps trying to make up for his dish's simplicity, he brought the salad to the table, and with a theatrical flourish, tossed it in front of his customers so that every leaf was covered in the thick dressing.

The story goes that the dish proved so popular with a group of partying Hollywood film stars who had flown in for the weekend that Alex named it 'Aviator salad', in their honour. Later, once their restaurant was established on the ground floor of the Hotel Commercial, the Cardinis could afford to admit the truth and the salad was renamed after Caesar and soon became a firm favourite among the stars of the day, who demanded the dish wherever they travelled in the world.

But while Caesar salad isn't centuries old, it turns out that the Romans were equally enthusiastic about eating raw leaves. Much like their modern counterparts, these salads would have consisted of a selection of leaves, including rocket, watercress, mallow, sorrel, goosefoot, purslane, chicory, beet greens, celery, chervil, basil and other fresh herbs. Our very word derives from the Latin name *salata herba*, literally 'salted herbs', which shows that both Julius Caesar and Caesar Cardini had a similar taste in strongly flavoured dressings. Thanks to his impromptu way of dressing a salad, Caesar Cardini became a rich man and eventually trademarked his famous creation, in 1948. Today the Cardini company remains America's favourite producer of an ever-growing range of oils and dressings.

Sidney Smith: Impassioned Campaigner and Salad Dresser

Sidney Smith (1771–1845) was a writer, publisher and reluctant clergyman who became a hugely popular figure in the early nineteenth century. Although lively and irreverent, he campaigned passionately for many serious things, such as the education of women and the abolition of slavery. His famous lecture tours on moral philosophy earned Smith the respect of politicians and preachers alike, although his intentions were rather more mercenary – once the lectures had achieved their original purpose of providing enough money to furnish his house, he threw the scripts on the fire.

Smith was obliged by circumstances (a law was passed in 1808 forcing all vicars to live within their parishes) to spend most of his time in the wilds of Yorkshire running the farm that came with his vicarage, rather than enjoying his growing celebrity in London exchanging quips with other wits and writing articles for the *Edinburgh Review*. Many of his sayings are still repeated today, but he would be amused to find that he is best remembered for something rather different. For Sidney Smith was also extremely fond of salad, so much so that he translated the recipe for his favourite dressing into a poem:

A RECIPE FOR A SALAD

To make this condiment your poet begs
The pounded yellow of two boiled eggs;
Two boiled potatoes, passed through kitchen sieve,
Smoothness and softness to a salad give.
Let onion atoms lurk within the bowl,
And, half suspected, animate the whole.
Of mordant mustard just a single spoon,

Distrust the condiment that bites too soon;
But deem it not, thou man of herbs, a fault,
To add a double spoon of salt.
Four spoons of oil from Lucca brown,
And twice with vinegar procured from town;
And, lastly, in the flavoured compound toss
A magic soupcion of anchovy sauce.
O, green and glorious! O herbaceous treat!
'Twould tempt the dying anchorite to eat:
Back to the world he'd turn his fleeting soul,
And plunge his fingers in the salad bowl!
Serenely full, the epicure would say,
   'Fate cannot harm me, I have dined to-day.'

The poem was reproduced in Marion Harland's *Common Sense in the Household*, first published in 1871 and making her a household name, you might say. More than 10 million copies of the book were eventually sold, ensuring that the **Sidney Smith salad dressing** caught on throughout America, the words of his poem recited by cooks throughout the land.

From the Waldorf Hotel to Fawlty Towers: The Descent of a Salad

Waldorf salad – chopped apple and celery mixed with grapes and walnuts in a smooth mayonnaise dressing – was created in 1893 at the Waldorf Hotel in New York (now the Waldorf-Astoria Hotel). According to one theory, the iconic salad was originally devised by the Waldorf Lunch System, an early twentieth-century lunchroom chain whose company logo was an apple. But it goes back further than this, the recipe first appearing in 1896 in *The Cook Book by 'Oscar' of the Waldorf*. In what must be one of the earliest Christmas cookbook-type fads, the hotel's maître d', Oscar Tschirky (see also EGGS BENEDICT and THOUSAND ISLAND DRESSING), is credited with persuading his head chef to include his favourite salad on the hotel menu.

Over the years it has become one of America's most popular dishes. In Cole Porter's 'You're the Top', from the musical *Anything Goes*, the singer compares his beloved to all the best things in the world: the smile of the Mona Lisa, the steps of Fred Astaire, Mickey Mouse, Mahatma Gandhi ... and a Waldorf salad. The salad is less popular in Britain, where its most famous cultural moment was in *Fawlty Towers* in 1979. John Cleese's incompetent hotelier spends a whole episode winding up an American guest with his inability to present the salad the guest repeatedly requests. Fawlty ends up asking: 'What is a Waldorf anyway – a walnut that's gone off?'

Coleslaw: Do You Prefer Your Salad Cold or with Cabbage?

Consisting chiefly of shredded cabbage and carrot dressed with mayonnaise, **coleslaw** originated in America in the late seventeenth and early eighteenth centuries, when Dutch immigrants flooded into the country. Indeed, New York was originally called New Amsterdam because of the sheer numbers of Dutch settlers who ended up there. The colonists brought with them their favourite recipe for salad, *koolsla* (from *kool*, 'cabbage', and *sla*, 'salad'), which over the following two centuries became anglicized to 'coleslaw'. But there was initially some confusion as to whether it should indeed be 'coleslaw' or 'cold slaw'. As English became the common language in America, people lost sight of the original derivation of *kool*, believing the word meant 'cool' and hence it must be a 'cold' rather than a 'cabbage' salad. A record from

1794 bears this out, describing 'a piece of sliced cabbage, by Dutchman ycleped [called] cold slaw'. In England, however, where the dish had become popular in the early nineteenth century, the correct form of the term was adopted quite quickly as 'cole' – denoting plants of the *Brassica* genus – was already associated with cabbage.

Robert H. Cobb: Salad Maker to the Stars

Robert H. Cobb – cousin of the baseball legend Ty Cobb, the first player to enter the Hall of Fame in 1936 – was a co-founder of the celebrated Brown Derby chain of restaurants in Los Angeles, California, established in 1926 and synonymous with the Golden Age of Hollywood. The first Brown Derby restaurant, built on Wilshire Boulevard, is actually shaped like a derby hat (a bowler hat, in other words), a design thought to have been inspired by Cobb's business partner, Gloria Swanson's husband Herbert Somborn, in response to being told that a good restaurateur could 'serve food out of a hat and still make a success of it'. The restaurant was an instant success, its quirky shape attracting diners from all over Los Angeles, and soon there was a small chain of Brown Derbys across the city.

What Robert Cobb is chiefly remembered for, however, is his great **Cobb salad**. Late one night, back in 1937 – so the story goes – he was visited by his friend the American showman Sidney Grauman, owner of the legendary Grauman's Chinese Theatre on Hollywood Boulevard. Grauman was feeling peckish and, as the chefs had already left, Cobb offered to rustle something up for him. Rummaging through the fridge, he grabbed some lettuce, tomatoes, avocado, BACON, chicken and Roquefort cheese, chopped them all finely, added a hard-boiled egg and served the resulting dish to his friend. Grauman was so delighted with his midnight snack that he always ordered it when dining in a Brown Derby, and word soon spread throughout Hollywood.

Cobb's wife, however, told a different story: about how her husband had returned hungry from a long and painful trip to the dentist and asked his head chef for something he would be able to eat. The chef chose ingredients he knew his boss enjoyed, chopping them up finely so that he could eat them easily with a swollen mouth, and Cobb loved the resulting salad so much he added it to the menu in all his restaurants. Whichever version of events is right, there's no doubting that the dish can now be found on restaurant menus the world over.

What are the Right Ingredients for a Nice Salad?

As the name suggests, **salade Niçoise** is, quite simply, a salad from Nice, in southern France, and it is made up of locally sourced ingredients – anchovies, garlic, tomatoes, black olives and capers in a vinaigrette dressing. As Nice is a coastal city – and the second most visited in France after Paris – fish feature prominently in its cuisine. Like Marseilles, it is known for its own version of the fish stew BOUILLABAISSE, while anchovies, in particular, appear in several dishes, including the savoury tart *pissaladière* (the word derives from *pissalat*, 'salted fish' – in case you're wondering). Indeed, fish are used to such an extent locally that it has given rise to a saying: 'Fish are born in the sea and die in oil' (olive oil being ubiquitous in Mediterranean cooking). Rumour has it that the dish was developed by the celebrated Russian choreographer George Balanchine (1904–83) while he was based in Monte Carlo, just along the coast from Nice. However, although Balanchine was a great arranger of dancers, it's not known whether he had the same gift with vegetables or indeed fish. The salad is in fact a traditional southern French dish, the only matter for dispute being about exactly which ingredients should be included, potatoes, tuna and green beans being regarded by purists as unwelcome interlopers.

Sauerkraut and the Seaman's Disease

The archetypal German dish, **sauerkraut** means 'pickled cabbage' (literally, 'sour cabbage') and that's exactly what it is. Luckily its history turns out to be rather more complex. As pickling food goes back to at least the third century BC – the ancient Greeks were extremely partial to pickled olives – it has been commonly supposed that sauerkraut is just as ancient. But while, in ancient times, pickles were 'wet' – made by adding ingredients to salted water (brine) – sauerkraut is dry-salted, the salt drawing all the liquid out of the cabbage, which is then preserved and flavoured by fermentation. Although the Romans were very fond of cabbage, crediting it with many health-giving properties, they used the latter process only to make long-lasting cattlefeed rather than anything for their own consumption.

Sauerkraut was first produced in Germany around the sixteenth century, and first mentioned in print a century later. Whoever the absent-minded farmer was who first tried eating it this way, the key upside was that, unlike wet-pickling, this method preserved much of the vitamin C in the cabbage. For a seventeenth-century peasant whose limited diet became even more so in the winter, sauerkraut would have made a vital difference to whether he actually survived until spring. It wasn't until three centuries later, in 1932, that vitamin C was identified as an essential nutrient; what was recognized, however, were the effects of its absence.

First noted by Hippocrates in the fourth century BC, scurvy – caused by insufficient vitamin C in the diet – often killed large numbers of the passengers and crew on long-distance voyages, in which fresh vegetables were generally in short supply. This became a significant issue in Europe from the fifteenth century, the beginning of the Age of Discovery. Magellan, for example, lost 80 per cent of his crew to the disease when crossing the Pacific.

Scurvy first came to public notice in Britain in the 1740s when Commodore George Anson led a squadron on a disastrous mission to the Pacific. He lost all but one of his six ships, and two-thirds of the entire crew (700 survived out of his original complement of 2,000), most to scurvy. Their symptoms were vividly described by the expedition chaplain, Richard Walter, who wrote the official account of the voyage, describing blackened skin, ulcers, difficulty breathing, rictus of the limbs, teeth falling out and an overgrowth of gum tissue that rotted, lending the victim's breath a foul odour. But perhaps worst of all were the delusions and madness sufferers underwent. Walter describes Anson's ships as echoing with the weeping and screaming of those stricken with the disease.

The British navy in its determination to rule the waves became obsessed with trying to stamp out scurvy. The most famous advocate of sauerkraut as a preventative for it was Captain James Cook (1728–79), who took enormous pains to persuade his men to eat what he called 'sour crout'. He would eat it alongside them, deliberately enthusing about how good it was. Cook recognized, as he noted in his journals, the sailors' instinctive distaste for anything 'out of the Common way, although it be ever so much for their own good' and how, by contrast, what 'their Superiors set a Value on ... becomes the finest stuff in the World'.

As a result, only five cases of scurvy were reported by the ship's surgeon during Cook's first voyage and no deaths from it. In his next two voyages, Cook's good management, or luck, persisted, and still no deaths from scurvy were reported. He was consequently hailed by the British as the conqueror of the sea's great plague, his victory reflected by William Bowles in his poem *The Spirit of Discovery* (1804):

> Smile, glowing health! For now no more the
>   wasted seaman sinks,
> With haggard eye and feeble frame diseased;
> No more with tortured longings for the sight
> Of fields and hillocks green, madly he calls.

Lemons have been known since ancient times as a far better preventative of scurvy, but in the eighteenth century they had to be imported and the supplies were extremely unreliable and expensive – unlike the much less romantic cabbage. During the nineteenth century, and in order to combat the disease, a concentrated drink made from lime juice was introduced by the Royal Navy as part of a seaman's daily ration. British sailors became so associated with it that it gave rise to the nickname **Limeys**, still in use today and applied, typically by Americans, to Brits of all kinds, not just seamen. German mariners, by contrast, continued to eat their national dish, earning themselves the nickname **Krauts**. In the early twentieth century, meanwhile, following the outbreak of the

First World War, sauerkraut was briefly rechristened **liberty cabbage** by American manufacturers in a spate of renaming that extended to a number of other foodstuffs (see also BATTENBERG CAKE, FRENCH TOAST and SALISBURY STEAK).

Pease Pudding Hot: What Did Ordinary Folk Eat in the Middle Ages?

It is the humble pea that, for hundreds of years, provided the foundation of the traditional English peasant's diet. Derived from the Latin *pisum*, the word was originally anglicized as 'pease', eventually evolving into 'pea' in the singular. **Pease pudding**, made with yellow split peas and similar in colour and texture to HUMMUS, was part of the everyday diet for generations of country folk. Peas were easy to grow and made ideal food, along with lentils and beans, for one-pot peasant cooking, especially as they could be dried and preserved for long periods.

A pot of yellowish sludge might sound unappetizing, but the lower classes of medieval England actually had a healthier diet than their noble counterparts. Peasant food was largely homegrown: fresh herbs and vegetables from their own plots, nuts and fruit from local trees, some meat (so long as it wasn't hunted – any poaching could result in death or having their hands cut off), wholegrain bread and dairy products. The upper classes, by contrast, disdained most vegetables as they came from the ground and were therefore only fit to feed the poor, and ate only white bread as they considered it more refined (which it was, if only in a literal sense). They ate meat and fish aplenty and, after the Crusades opened up trade further east, liked everything heavily spiced. Needless to say, this led to a whole range of health problems, including skin diseases, rickets and scurvy (see SAUERKRAUT).

In the light of this, the nutrient-laden pea begins to sound a little more glamorous. After being introduced to Britain – probably by the Vikings as it is a traditional Swedish vegetable – peas would regularly be cooked, usually with salted (preserved) bacon, in the form of pease pudding (also known as **pease porridge** or **pease pottage**). And it is still made today: although now rarely mentioned in the south of England, it remains popular in the north, where, like that other culinary favourite, **mushy peas**, it can be purchased in tinned form. Two centuries ago, pease pudding was still such a part of the English way of life that children would sing about it in a nursery rhyme, originally published in 1760 in John Newberry's *Mother Goose's Melody*:

> Pease porridge hot, pease porridge cold,
> Pease porridge in the pot, nine days old;
> Some like it hot, some like it cold,
> Some like it in the pot, nine days old.

Eggs Florentine and the Wicked Italian Queen Who Loved Spinach

The adjective Florentine simply means 'in the manner of the city of Florence'. Applied to food, it refers to something cooked on a bed of spinach – such as **veal florentine** or, most typically, **eggs florentine** (see also EGGS BENEDICT).

As a noun, florentine, in a culinary context, originally meant a kind of pie, either savoury or sweet, such as the Bedford-shire **apple florentine**, an apple pie made with the unusual addition of ale and formerly a Christmas treat. Today, **florentine** as a noun refers only to a type of biscuit, made with nuts and dried fruit and coated with chocolate on one side.

Cooking spinach in the Florentine style can be traced back to one Florentine in particular, someone who had a huge effect on the culture of Renaissance Europe. Catherine de Médicis was born in Florence in 1519. Both her parents died within weeks of her birth (her father from syphilis and possibly her mother too, infected by her husband), but her lonely child-hood only made Catherine stronger. She came from a pow-erful family, favoured by the Pope, yet the Medicis weren't quite royalty – they had clawed their way into power through ability and sheer ambition. And Catherine was no excep-tion. Aged only fourteen, she married Henri, the dauphin of France (see GRATIN DAUPHINOIS), and when his father, François I, died in 1547 she became Queen of France.

Her marriage was an unhappy one, however, as Henri pre-ferred his mistress, Diane de Poitiers, heaping favours upon her and condemning his wife to a life of virtual seclusion. As a result, Catherine didn't became truly powerful until thirteen years later, following Henri's death, when she took over as regent on behalf of their ten-year-old son, François. When he died in 1560, she ruled on behalf of their second son, Charles, and then in 1574 on behalf of their last-born, Henri. Catherine was a fighter and she almost outlived them all as Henri was murdered less than a year after her own death in 1589. She was notorious for her political manoeu-vring and for her persecution of the Protestant Huguenots, whom she had formerly supported, in particular for autho-rizing the St Bartholomew's Day Massacre of 1572, in which thousands of Huguenots were either butchered or forced into exile abroad (see HOLLANDAISE SAUCE, MORNAY SAUCE and SALLY LUNN BUN). Huguenot writers later accused her of adopting the cynical tactics of Machiavelli (1469–1527), another hugely influential Florentine, to fell all her enemies at one blow.

Nostalgic for Italy, Catherine longed for a taste of her home town and so imported chefs from Florence. Known as 'Madame Serpent' for her tendency to dispatch wayward courtiers with a dose of poison, she no doubt felt safer with members of her own retinue in charge of the royal kitchens. But she also made many innovations – she is credited with introducing table etiquette and the fork to France, for instance (see also 'From Fine Sauces to Haute Cuisine', page 185) – and among the various Italian dishes produced by her chefs was a way of cooking her favourite vegetable, spinach, which so caught on that it became known as spinach *à la florentine* and then just *florentine*, spinach being implicit. The aura of sophistication and exoticism surrounding the word clearly attracted later cooks, who would apply 'florentine' (minus the spinach) to any special celebratory pie, recalling as they did a city that had produced such cultured and talented, if wicked, individuals – and no doubt recognizing that every good dish needs a touch of something sinful.

Did the French Invent Baked Beans?

Anyone who's seen the classic scene in Mel Brooks's comic western *Blazing Saddles*, where the cowboys sit around the campfire eating **baked beans** and farting copiously, will be convinced it is an American dish through and through. Supporting this is the theory of some food historians that baked beans are based on a Native American dish consisting of beans cooked with bear fat and maple syrup. The French, on the other hand, maintain that the dish can be traced to their classic bean stew, **cassoulet**, which they say they introduced to the Americans while fighting alongside them during the Revolutionary War of 1775–83 (see FRENCH FRIES and TEA). But, given that the haricot beans integral to the American recipe are native to the US and that most cultures have independently developed their own recipe for bean stews, that seems a pretty tenuous claim to me.

What is certain is that America has made the baked bean its own. The name of the dish is a reminder of how it was traditionally cooked – baked in a ceramic or cast-iron pot. Bean-hole cooking, as practised in logging camps in the north-eastern states, used a stone-lined fire pit in which the bean pot would be buried overnight to cook. Historically, America's baked bean 'capital' was Boston, where beans slow-baked in molasses were so popular the city was nicknamed 'Beantown'.

With the invention of the tin (see also POTTED SHRIMPS), canned beans were among the first convenience foods. During the American Civil War in the 1860s, the US army was fed on canned salt pork and beans with stewed tomatoes. Henry Heinz launched his baked beans in the US in 1895 and brought them to the UK nine years later. Beans promptly became a staple of the British diet. Originally the product contained a small piece of pork, but Second World War rationing put an end to that and pork has never been replaced, although some brands do include small pork sausages, harking back to the original recipe.

The expression *full of beans* is regularly applied to anyone behaving in a lively and energetic manner. A similar expression, *feeling his oats* – evoking the friskiness of a recently fed horse – provides a clue to the origin of the first phrase. The Romans are recorded to have used beans as fodder for their horses – known accordingly as 'horse beans'. Hence any well-fed and energetic horse was regarded as 'full of beans'.

The Rise and Fall of the Potato

As with the tomato (see GAZPACHO), it's hard to imagine a time when the **potato** wasn't a fundamental ingredient in British cooking, but this root vegetable – the most versatile of all – wasn't introduced into Europe until the sixteenth century. At first many Europeans were suspicious of the potato, believing it to contain harmful poisons. To be fair, there was some justification as it is from the same family as deadly nightshade, which is poisonous raw. In 1748, the French Parliament actually banned cultivation of the crop, believing it to cause leprosy, among other things, while during the 1770s, a period of recurrent famines, wagonloads of potatoes sent by Frederick the Great of Prussia were rejected by starving peasants, but attitudes soon began to change, thanks to the efforts of one man.

PARMENTIER: CHAMPION OF THE POTATO

Antoine-Augustin Parmentier (1737–1813) was an army chemist who was captured no less than five times by Prussian forces during the Seven Years' War (1756–63). In captivity, Parmentier and his fellow prisoners of war were forced to survive on a diet of potatoes and so, with plenty of time on his hands, the scientist began a detailed study of this unpopular food. When the Academy of Besançon later sponsored a competition to find a 'food capable of reducing the calamities of famine', Parmentier submitted his paper, 'The Chemical Explanation of the Potato', and won first prize.

Parmentier then spent the rest of his life promoting the humble spud throughout Europe as a cheap, nutritious and reliable crop, and in 1785 finally managed to persuade Louis XVI (1754–93) to encourage cultivation in France. The king allowed him to plant one hundred acres on royal land, close to Paris, and Parmentier engaged a heavily armed guard to protect the crop. This strange move aroused the curiosity of local farmers, who became desperate to know more about this obviously valuable crop, and as word spread among the puzzled population, Parmentier delivered what turned out to be his masterstroke. He dismissed the armed guard and, as he anticipated, the French flocked into the fields, dug up the potatoes and replanted them in their own farms, smallholdings and gardens.

The habit of growing potatoes then quickly spread throughout the continent, such that by the time of the onset of the French Revolution in 1789, they were a staple in the diet of every French family, including that of the soon-to-be-headless king and his queen, Marie Antoinette, who were both known for their love of potatoes. (So much so in the case of Marie Antoinette that she even wore a headdress of potato flowers at a fancy-dress ball.) And for this, the name of Antoine-Augustin Parmentier has become synonymous with the potato in France. Indeed, many potato-based recipes are called after him – including **hachis Parmentier**, a form of French COTTAGE or SHEPHERD'S PIE – so the next time you pick up a bag of Parmentier potatoes at the supermarket you will know exactly who he was.

HOW THE POTATO KILLED A MILLION PEOPLE

But one European country had already cottoned on to the benefit of the potato: Ireland. Sir Walter Raleigh (1552–1618), the British explorer known for his expeditions to the Americas and for throwing his best cloak across a puddle so Elizabeth I could walk across it, had introduced potatoes to Ireland, planting them at his Irish estate at Myrtle Grove, Youghal, near Cork. Legend has it that he then invited the local gentry to a banquet featuring potatoes in every course. Unfortunately, his cooks, who knew nothing about the vegetable, tossed out the tubers, bringing to the table a poisonous dish of boiled stems and leaves instead, which promptly made his noble guests extremely ill.

Unlike in France, where the potato worked its way from the top of society down, in Ireland its popularity grew from the bottom up. Ireland's rain-soaked climate meant that few crops prospered and before the seventeenth century its peasants depended very heavily on oats. Offering two-to-four times the calories of grain per acre, and much simpler to cook, potatoes rapidly took over as the country's main crop. The Irish became known for their expertise in cooking them: the favourite street snack of eighteenth-century London was the **baked potato**, preferably cooked and sold by an Irishman, although its popularity was eclipsed in the nineteenth century by another Irish potato speciality, the chip (see FISH AND CHIPS and FRENCH FRIES).

The problem was that the Irish put all their eggs (or rather potatoes) in one basket. Depending so heavily on a single crop meant that one bad harvest represented a catastrophe. And when one bad harvest turned into four, people started dying in their thousands. At the height of the famine (around 1845), at least 1 million people died of starvation, leaving many poverty-stricken families with no choice but to emigrate. Towns became deserted and many businesses closed: with no customers, shop owners were forced to leave too. Over 1.5 million people sailed for North America and Australia, and within a few years Ireland's population had dropped by half, from around 9 million to little more than 4 million. And it was all because of the potato.

Gratin Dauphinois: A Dish Fit for a Prince ...

Until I started doing my research, I had assumed that this delicious dish of creamy, garlicky sliced potatoes was called 'dauphinois' because it was created for a prince. Dauphin was the traditional title given to the heir apparent to the French throne – it is also the French word for 'dolphin', the animal appearing on the dauphin's coat of arms. I thought it might well be a case of finding out which prince had been the biggest fan of the humble spud before Madame Guillotine put paid to the French royal family in January 1793. But the answer lies further back in history, long before the royal title came into existence. Dauphiné was a former French province located in the south-east of the country, its name deriving from the dolphin insignia of one of its rulers. The province functioned as an independent state from 1040 until its annexation into the kingdom of France in 1349. A condition of its integration was that the heir to the French throne would henceforth be known as the dauphin and would represent the interests of this historically rebellious area – the direct equivalent of Britain's Prince of Wales. **Gratin dauphinois** is the key dish of this mountainous region, now, like the former province, shared with the rest of France.

The word *gratin*, applied to a topping of breadcrumbs and cheese, evolved from the French word *gratter*, meaning 'to scrape', as in 'scrapings' or leftovers, in this case of cheese and bread. It also provides the root of the English word 'to grate'. Used figuratively, **gratin** indicates the very best of something and the crème de la crème of Parisian society are known as **le gratin** – literally, the upper crust.

... And One that Enticed a Prophet
(Jansson's Temptation)

This Swedish version of GRATIN DAUPHINOIS (the addition of anchovies gives the dish a salty kick) is traditionally served at Christmas throughout Scandinavia. It goes by the intriguing name of **Jansson's temptation**. Needless to say, there are various theories about who was the actual Jansson and how he came to be tempted. It is claimed, for instance, that he was Pelle Janzon (1844–89), an opera singer popular in the late ninetennth century, who was on a perpetual diet because the one thing that he couldn't resist was the calorific potato dish he'd grown up with.

But the suggestion I prefer is that the dish is named after Erik Jansson, a nineteenth-century religious zealot and self-appointed prophet. Jansson regarded the Swedish clergy and establishment as corrupt and was highly vociferous about it. The dislike was mutual and Jansson and his followers were persecuted until forced to emigrate. Like the Puritans on the *Mayflower*, Jansson and his disciples rejected the sinful Europe they had grown up in and wanted to establish a New Jerusalem in America.

Claiming to be the new Messiah, Jansson declared: 'I am come in Christ's place to bring grace. Whoever despises me despises God.' Having arrived in America, he founded a colony in Illinois called Bishop Hill, where he and his followers lived a simple life stripped of hedonism and adhering to strict codes of dress and behaviour, including food. According to Swedish legend, one day, although adamantly opposed to the pleasures of the flesh, Jansson found himself so sorely tempted by the dish that would bear his name that he threw over his principles to eat some – in secret, of course. And then he was caught in the act by a disillusioned follower.

Colcannon: How a Spoonful of Mash Could Win You a Husband

Colcannon is a traditional Irish dish made of mashed potatoes mixed with cabbage. Simple fare, in other words, sometimes flavoured with cream, butter, garlic or bacon, although such luxuries were rarely available during harsher times. The name of the dish comes from the Gaelic *cál ceannann*, meaning 'white cabbage', although there is evidence to suggest that 'cannon' evolved from the Older Irish *cainnenn*, translated variously as onion, garlic or leek.

Other countries have similar versions of the dish. In England, for instance, leftover potatoes and vegetables (often from the SUNDAY ROAST), plus a bit of cold meat, are chopped up and shallow-fried as **bubble and squeak** – the name deriving from the sound the ingredients make when being heated. In Scotland, shredded onion and cabbage are mixed with mashed potatoes and baked with a topping of cheese into the splendidly named **rumbledethumps**, suggesting particularly vigorous cooking – or a rather bad-tempered chef.

In Ireland, a ring or a small coin would traditionally be hidden in a dish of colcannon and the lucky girl who found it in her helping would be the next to receive a marriage proposal. Following another custom, unmarried girls would

hang a sock filled with spoonfuls of colcannon above the front
door on the night of Halloween, in the belief that the next
man to pass through the door would be their future husband
– making that a popular evening for village idiots across the
land. But a word of warning: if somebody invites you to their
house at Halloween and you see a bulging sock outside the
front door, make sure you know what their daughter looks
like before you ring the bell.

The Eggs that were Broken to Make
the First Spanish Omelette

Known in Spain as *tortilla de patatas* (round potato cake),
Spanish omelette is made up of fried potatoes mixed with
beaten eggs and sometimes onion. Using basic ingredients
that were easy to forage, the dish was historically popular
with soldiers on the move. Indeed, legend has it that it was
created by one particular soldier, the Carlist general Tómas
de Zumalacárregui y de Imaz (1788–1835).

Carlism – a political movement in support of the Infante
Carlos of Spain (1788–1855), regarded by traditional royal-
ists as the rightful, male heir to the Spanish throne – was the
cause of a series of civil wars in Spain during the nineteenth
century and beyond. In the first Carlist uprising following the death of King Ferdinand VII in 1833, and the disputed accession of his infant daughter Isabella, Zumalacárregui took command of the troops supporting Don Carlos
and, through a series of successful battles, gained possession of much of the country supporting Isabella. During the
Siege of Bilbao in 1835, which resulted in the death of the
doughty commander and the failure of the uprising, it is said
that Zumalacárregui happened upon a remote farmhouse
and demanded food from the farmer's wife. All the terrified
woman had at her disposal was a potato, some eggs and an

onion, which she cooked together and served to the general. According to the story, Zumalacárregui was so pleased with the resultant dish that he ordered his army chefs to make it regularly for the entire force, and so the Spanish omelette was born.

The word 'omelette' is of course French rather than Spanish, and has been used since the middle of the sixteenth century, probably modified from the Latin word *lamella*, meaning a small thin plate. The first printed reference to the word in English was in Randle Cotgrave's *Dictionary of the French and English Tongues*, published in 1611. This includes an entry for 'Homelette ... an Omelet, or Pancake of eggs'. Meanwhile, *Le Pâtissier françois* (1653) by French master chef François Pierre de la Varenne – author of three groundbreaking books that form the basis of modern French cuisine (see also 'From Fine Sauces to Haute Cuisine', page 185) – lists several omelette recipes; it is thought the translation of the book into English in 1660 led to the dish becoming popular in Britain. The expression **You can't make an omelette without breaking eggs** is a common English idiom used to indicate how sacrifices have to be made in order to achieve anything of any use or importance. A sentiment General de Zumalacárregui y de Imaz would surely have agreed with.

9
The Fish Course

Lobster Thermidor: A Luxury Dish with
a Revolutionary History

How Whitebait Transformed MPs
into Commoners

John Dory: An Odd-looking Fish that Tastes Divine

Pickled Herring: Delicacy of the Powerful
and the Hung-over

Culinary Espionage à la Diamond Jim

What was the Inspiration for Sole Véronique?

Why Paella, Historically Speaking,
Shouldn't be in this Chapter

The Salmon Dish that Returns from the Grave

Sushi: The Sour Dish that Became a Fast Food

Why Sashimi is Not for the Squeamish

'Oh, as to the whiting,' said the Mock Turtle, 'they – you've seen them, of course?'

'Yes,' said Alice, 'I've often seen them at dinn–' she checked herself hastily.

'I don't know where Dinn may be,' said the Mock Turtle; 'but, if you've seen them so often, of course you know what they're like?'

'I believe so,' Alice replied thoughtfully. 'They have their tails in their mouths – and they're all over crumbs.'

LEWIS CARROLL, *Alice's Adventures in Wonderland*

Lobster Thermidor: A Luxury Dish with a Revolutionary History

Consisting of lobster meat mixed with egg yolks and brandy, served in a lobster shell, often with cheese on top, **lobster Thermidor** is an extremely expensive dish, eaten mostly by the wealthy and privileged. So you may be surprised to learn that its name derives from a period in French history when wealth and privilege were very much under attack.

The French Revolution (1789–99) arose out of a strong feeling of discontent among the working people, fuelled by widespread famine and the near bankruptcy of the nation following a series of ruinous wars. As the revolutionaries saw it, the ruling classes of France had had all the power and all the money for far too long; they were determined to establish a new world order that would change everything, even down to the way things were measured. A simpler, standardized method would be adopted, in which everything would be in multiples of ten. And so the metric system came into being, first taken up by France and now, of course, employed internationally. Rather less successful was the attempt to apply the same system to the way in which time was recorded. Each day was divided into ten hours each consisting of 100 minutes. Each month now lasted three weeks and the weeks were each ten days long, while their old, elitist names (July and August were named after Roman emperors, Julian and Augustus) were replaced by utilitarian words referring to the weather or nature, such as Pluviôse, Ventôse and Floréal ('Rainy', 'Foggy' and 'Flowery'). Thermidor, from the Greek *thermos* or 'hot', was, as the name suggests, a summer month, lasting from 20 July to 18 August in the old terminology.

The problem arose when these ideas didn't end up working in practice, the ideals of the newly established Republic – liberty, equality and fraternity – little more than empty rhetoric. After the execution of the French king, in 1793, there were food riots and civil unrest and the Republicans imposed what came to be known as the Reign of Terror. Maximilien Robespierre (1758–94) was the guiding force behind it, believing the Terror to be wholly necessary as a means of keeping France on the straight and narrow by rooting out so-called traitors. Revolutionary France rapidly turned into a paranoid dictatorship: anyone who stepped out of line or disagreed with the increasingly unstable leadership was summarily executed. On 9 Thermidor, Year II (27 July 1794), disaffected members of the National Convention, the Republican government, arrested Robespierre and executed him without trial. The phrase 'coup de Thermidor' refers to this event and, by extension, 'Thermidor' has come to indicate the 'cooling off' phase in any revolution, when power slips from the hands of the original revolutionary leadership and radicals are replaced by a more conservative regime, sometimes to the point where the political pendulum may swing back to its pre-revolutionary position.

So how did it come to be applied to a dish? According to one theory, lobster Thermidor was created by a French chef in honour of Napoleon Bonaparte (1769–1821) – the perfect example, you might say, of how far the political pendulum may swing back, for Napoleon not only ruled France like a king but crowned himself emperor in 1804. It is said that his chef suggested 'lobster Napoleon' but the diminutive Frenchman insisted the dish should be associated instead with the coup de Thermidor. As the recipe didn't appear in print until the 1890s, however, it seems unlikely a full one hundred years would have passed before anybody recorded it. It is also unlikely that a man as vain and egotistical as Napoleon would decline the honour of having a dish named after him, and even less likely that he would call it after a point in recent history marking the downfall of a power-crazed dictator.

A more plausible story suggests that the dish was created at the Café de Paris to mark the opening night of a new play by Victorien Sardou (1831–1908) at the Comédie Française theatre in January 1891. A few years earlier, in 1887, Sardou's play *La Tosca*, on which the celebrated opera by Puccini is based, had made him famous. In honour of Sardou, the chef at the Café de Paris, Tony Girod, created a lobster dish that he named after the new play. *Thermidor* dramatized Robespierre's downfall and the difficulties of maintaining revolutionary ideals in the face of reality: unfortunately, like the Republican month it was named after, it was not a success, and if it weren't for Tony Girod's (rather more digestible) cheesy lobster dish, it would be completely forgotten today.

A whole new kettle of fish or *a different kettle of fish* is one of our more unusual idioms, although its meaning is straightforward – 'another matter altogether' or 'a different situation entirely'. Some research has suggested that the word 'kettle' in this case is a corruption of the Old English *kiddle*, which was a grille set across a river to catch passing fish. A fisherman might return to find poachers had helped themselves to the catch and left only weed and debris in the 'kettle'. Consequently, he might well claim that this was a 'different kettle of fish' to the one he was hoping for. However, a more likely origin can be found north of the border, where it was common for families and friends to spend the day feast-ing and socializing (see PICNIC) on the banks of a river. The main dish would consist of salmon, freshly caught in the river and cooked in a 'kettle' or cauldron – a rather larger version of the fish kettle you might use at home to poach a salmon. For this reason, the outings were known across Scotland as a 'kettle of fish' and, owing to the unpredictability of the weather and behaviour of the guests, one kettle of fish (day out) could be very differ-ent from another. One of the earliest recorded references can be found in Sir Walter Scott's novel *St Ronan's Well* (1823), which includes the line: 'As the whole company go to the waterside today to eat a kettle of fish, there will be no risk of interruption.'

How Whitebait Transformed MPs into Commoners

Whitebait are tiny silver-white fish, thought in the past to be a separate species but in fact simply the fry (babies) of vari-ous fish, mostly herring (see also KIPPER, PICKLED HERRING and RED HERRING). Whitebait are traditionally deep-fried and eaten whole, accompanied with slices of brown bread and butter. The dish was commonly eaten by ordinary people living along the Thames because whitebait were abundant, providing a cheap and nourishing meal. Whitebait appeared on English menus from the early 1600s, although the little fish had been popular with Londoners for quite some time before that. But then the dish suddenly moved upmarket (away from other working-class favourites like JELLIED EELS and PICKLED COCKLES) – all thanks to an invitation to lunch during the late eighteenth century.

Sir Robert Preston (1740–1832), MP for Dover, had a cottage on the banks of Dagenham Reach, 'an idyllic sort of place'. At the end of May, Preston used to invite his friend George Rose, secretary to the Treasury, down for a day of whitebait, wine and free-ranging conversation. In 1782, Rose brought his friend William Pitt the Younger (1759–1806), who had been promoted to the government by Lord Shelburne (see BOODLE'S ORANGE FOOL) earlier that year. While enjoying a simple lunch in charming surroundings, the three politicians mulled over the weighty issues of the day, in particular the threat of revolution hanging over Europe. They had such a good time and the discussions away from the packed and frenetic House of Commons were so useful that they decided to turn this into an annual event.

All kinds of momentous things occurred over the forthcoming year, including the declaration of American independence from Britain, but one of the most unusual was that Pitt became the youngest prime minister in history, at the age of just twenty-four (a record he still holds today). Despite the pressing matters of state, the young leader was keen to replicate the informal get-together of the previous year and so took his entire ministerial cabinet to Dagenham for a meal of the local whitebait. The only problem was that it took such a long time to get to Preston's cottage, so the following year the group of ministers settled at much nearer Greenwich, establishing an annual tradition that became known as the Ministerial Whitebait Dinner.

Over the years, following its relocation to Greenwich, the meal became one of the most renowned events of the nineteenth century. People travelled eight hundred miles just to witness it. Crammed into the taverns were leading figures from the major parties, all enjoying the same food as the people who were gawping at them. Of course the politicians were mostly washing their whitebait down with champagne rather than ale, but they were still there in the flesh, behaving like ordinary people – and could be approached by ordinary people. The Ministerial Whitebait Dinner may well be one of the reasons why when the French working classes rebelled in 1789 the English didn't follow suit. Unlike the unreachable French aristocracy, the English knew their politicians were (relatively speaking) normal people. The Whitebait Dinner was an affirmation of the British constitution before the majority of the electorate even had the vote.

John Dory: An Odd-looking Fish that Tastes Divine

Pesce bolito con maionese is one of Venice's key dishes, although you'd never guess it from the direct translation of its name – 'boiled fish with MAYONNAISE'. But then the Venetians are famous for their subtle wit and their ability to hide treasures away from prying eyes: it was they who invented double-column book-keeping, after all. The title of the dish appears non-specific, but the *pesce* in question has to be **John Dory**, one of the most prized species of edible fish.

This has been the case since ancient times when John Dory was considered sacred to the king of the gods, hence its species name *Zeus faber*. When Christianity took over, the fish was claimed for St Peter, leader of the Apostles. The story goes that, at Christ's bidding, Peter caught the strange-looking, thin yellow fish and took a coin from its mouth to pay a tax collector, his fingers leaving the indelible and distinctive black spots that mark the fish on either flank.

To this day, the Pope is described as the direct descendant of Peter and he wears the Fisherman's Ring, a signet ring depicting the saint and used to seal official documents, in honour of the man who caught John Dory in the Sea of

Galilee. The unlikeliness of a seawater fish (the John Dory) being caught in a freshwater sea was presumably not going to spoil a good tale for the early Gospel writers. In France the fish is called *Saint Pierre* and in Spain *pez de San Pedro*, while in Britain and throughout her former colonies the fish has simply been called John Dory, possibly a mangling of the French *jaune doré* ('golden yellow'), the name given it by French Canadian fishermen after the colour of its scales.

The expression ***red herring*** is used to describe something that provides a false or misleading clue, often in a detective story. In the eighteenth and nineteenth centuries, herring was one of the most widely caught fish in the seas around Britain. In the days before refrigeration, it would have been preserved by salting and smoking (see KIPPER) to ensure it was still edible by the time it arrived at market towns inland. The smoking process would turn the herring a deep, brownish-red colour, as well as giving the fish its characteristically pungent taste and smell. To find out how **red herring** came to be used figuratively, we need to turn to the early 1800s and to hunting or, more accurately, hunt saboteurs. The modern fox lover has a long history, for on hunt days the strong-smelling fish would be dragged by saboteurs along the hunt route and away from the fox. This confused the hounds, which followed the scent of the red herring rather than that of the fox, allowing it to scurry off to safety. So effective was this tactic that the expression soon passed into common English usage.

Pickled Herring: Delicacy of the
Powerful and the Hung-over

Herring has been a staple food in Europe since 3000 BC. First recorded in the eighth century, the word herring means 'army' – because of the vast shoals in which they used to travel. Jane Grigson in *The Fish Book* (1973) writes about one shoal, measured in 1877, that covered an area that would have stretched from Marble Arch to the London docks in one direction and up to Euston Station in the other. Unfortunately, overfishing has diminished these armies to the size of small guerrilla forces, but their legacy lives on in the number of herring recipes that abound in European cuisine (see WHITEBAIT). The preservation of herring so that it could be eaten all year long was an important aspect of that and, aside from smoking (see KIPPER and RED HERRING), a favourite method of preservation was pickling.

THE CAT'S BREAKFAST THAT
ISN'T A DOG'S DINNER

The best-known **pickled herring** dish today is the **rollmop**. Its name originates from the German words *rollen*, meaning 'to roll', and *Mops*, a 'pug dog' – a rollmop from the side does look a little like the circular, squashed-up face of a pug. Consisting of herring fillet rolled around a piece of gherkin and neatly fixed with small wooden skewers, rollmops were a specialty of Berlin. Although they are eaten at any time of the day, rollmops are most commonly served as a German hangover cure known as *Katerfrühstück* – literally the 'cat's breakfast' (a tom cat's breakfast, to be precise – the male of the species traditionally being in likelier need of the cure). Pickled fish seems rather unappealing for a head and stomach that are feeling a little fragile but as these snacks were readily available in German pubs, it may well be that they were eaten alongside the first drink of the day: the cat's breakfast accompanying the hair of the dog (see below).

The phrase **the hair of the dog** is a contraction of 'the hair of the dog that bit you'. Early English medical theory suggested rubbing the hair of a particular dog into the wound caused by its bite, in the belief this would heal the wound – a crude form of homeopathy, you might say, following the idea that like cures like. The phrase was used in many different contexts until settling down as a hangover remedy. These days a few more drinks the morning after a night of heavy drinking is said to cure the effects of a hangover and is known as 'the hair of the dog'.

THE HERRING THAT CHANGED THE FACE OF EUROPE

In the nineteenth century, the same pickled herring fillets, supplied flat and without gherkins, had a rather more glamorous reputation around the world. For they were named after the Prussian hero who changed the course of European history. Born in 1815, the year of the Battle of Waterloo, Otto Eduard Leopold von Bismarck was brought up in a Europe that had been thrown into chaos by the Napoleonic Wars and in which Germany was no more than a scattered collection

of quarrelsome states. An outspoken royalist and a natural
public speaker, Bismarck was elected to Parliament in 1847,
his chief ambition to make his native Prussia a stable country.
When revolution broke out the following year – 1848, the
Year of Revolution, which saw political upheaval throughout
Europe – he tried to raise an army of peasant workers from
his own family's extensive estates to march on Berlin in support of the king.

And after the Crimean War of the mid 1850s, in which
Prussia had been sidelined by other participating nations,
Bismarck was determined to create a unified German nation
that would not so easily be ignored. In 1862, and now prime
minister of Prussia, he made a rousing speech to the Prussian Chamber of Deputies, concluding with the now famous
words: 'The great questions of the time will not be resolved
by speeches and majority decisions, but by iron and blood.'
This speech helped turn the tide and within five years, the
northern German states were combined under King Wilhelm
II as president and Bismarck as chancellor. He then used his
position to bring together the remaining states and establish a
united German Empire in 1871, earning himself a reputation
as the 'Iron Chancellor', a role he maintained until his resig-
nation in 1890 (at the age of seventy-five) following repeated
clashes with the king over foreign policy. Even in retirement
Bismarck continued to warn the king, famously commenting
on one occasion: 'One day the great European war will come
out of some damn foolish thing in the Balkans.' He warned
that this catastrophe, as he called it, would come twenty years
after his departure, predicting with prophetic accuracy the
date of the outbreak of the First World War. Bismarck was
also right about its cause: in the event, 15 million people died
as a result of an insignificant quarrel in the Balkans – exactly
as he had predicted.

During his lifetime, Bismarck was respected as a powerful

diplomat, using military force only as a last resort, as borne out by his words: 'Anyone who has ever looked into the glazed eyes of a soldier dying on the battlefield will think hard before starting a war.' His dry wit was much appreciated by the German people and many quotations of his have been recorded, including 'Politics is the art of the possible', 'Laws are like sausages; it is better not to see them being made' and (on Americans) 'They have contrived to be surrounded on two sides by weak neighbours and on the other two sides by fish'.

In 1853, Johann Wiechmann opened a fish-processing factory, the first on the German Baltic coast, and sent his hero Bismarck a barrel of pickled fish as a birthday present. The Iron Chancellor surprised the young businessman by sending a handwritten thank-you letter in return. When Bismarck established a unified Germany in 1871, Wiechmann again sent Bismarck another barrel, this time with a letter asking the chancellor if he would give permission for the company to sell the product using the name **Bismarck herring**. Wiechmann was soon in possession of a reply confirming the chancellor's agreement and, with permission granted, the now world-famous Bismarck herring from Stralsund began appearing all over Europe.

Culinary Espionage à la Diamond Jim

Nicolas Marguery (1834–1910) was a culinary legend. His restaurant, Au Petit Marguery, was one of the most popular in Paris during the nineteenth century, the great and the good of French society regularly filling his dining room. In fact they still do, enjoying surroundings that have hardly changed since the famous chef was there, creating dish after dish in his busy kitchens, almost 150 years ago.

Nicolas Marguery's cooking, particularly his **sole Marguery** – sole served in a sauce of white wine and fish stock blended with egg yolks and butter (see also SOLE VÉRONIQUE) – was renowned throughout Europe and America. French cuisine was the world leader and its chefs jealously guarded the recipes of their signature dishes. Sole Marguery was one such dish and the story of how it emigrated from France to America is an intriguing one, full of subterfuge, audacity and a level of commitment that is hard to imagine.

As the immigrants who introduced the HAMBURGER and the HOT DOG to New York settled throughout America, so the economy expanded, mainly through the growing railway network. Jim Brady (1856–1917), a salesman for the Manning, Maxwell and Moore Railroad Company, was part of this. And he was highly successful: the sums that he made selling railway tracks throughout America and across the world were so immense that he began to invest in diamonds and other precious stones, earning himself the nickname Diamond Jim.

A larger-than-life character, Brady also had a prodigious appetite. He was rumoured to consume a gallon of orange juice, steak, potatoes, bread, flapjacks, muffins, eggs and pork chops – just for breakfast. A mid-morning snack might be three dozen oysters and clams, followed by lunch of another three dozen oysters, three stuffed crabs, four lobsters, a joint of beef and a salad. During the afternoon, Jim would down six sodas and a seafood snack before taking a nap, and then came dinner: thirty-six oysters, six lobsters, two bowls of green turtle soup, steak, vegetables and a pastry platter. But it didn't end there: after a customary trip to the theatre, where he would eat two pounds of glacé fruits, Jim then rounded off his day with a supper of half a dozen game birds and a couple of large beers.

And this was Diamond Jim's intake every single day. His friend the restaurateur Charles Rector, owner of Rector's

Restaurant on Broadway, New York, would import several barrels of extra-large oysters from Baltimore every day, just for Jim. It's hardly surprising, therefore, that Rector once described the railway magnate as 'the best twenty-five customers I have ever had'.

One afternoon, during a marathon eating session with friends, Diamond Jim began telling the group about the exquisite sole Marguery he had been served at Au Petit Marguery during a recent business trip to Paris. Unable to explain the recipe to Rector, he teased his friend that he might have to find another restaurant where he could eat sole Marguery. Rector on the spot resolved to be the first restaurant in New York to serve the dish and set about obtaining the recipe, by fair means or foul. So he summoned his son, George, from Cornell University and sent him to Paris to obtain the recipe.

The young man arrived in Paris fully aware he could not walk into the restaurant as a complete unknown and ask for it, so he applied for a job as dish washer to see what he could learn from the kitchen staff. It soon became obvious that he would discover nothing from the chefs, who carefully guarded their recipes from all the menials in the kitchen, so George applied for a job as an apprentice chef.

It took him over two years of hard work to become senior enough to have the recipe for the legendary Marguery sauce explained to him, and as soon as it was he resigned, catching the boat back to New York. It is said that both his father and Diamond Jim Brady were waiting for him at the dockside as the ship drew in, with George shouting to them from the deck: 'I got it!' The young chef was sent straight into the kitchen to prepare sole Marguery and, as legend has it, when Diamond Jim tasted the dish he declared: 'If you poured this sauce over a Turkish towel, I believe I could eat all of it!' And that, dear reader, is why the land of the free has a

French-inspired dish going by the name of **sole Marguery
à la Diamond Jim**.

Jim Brady died in his sleep in 1910 and only then did doctors discover he had an unusually large stomach, almost six times the size of a normal man's. George Rector went on to take over his father's restaurant business. He also wrote cookbooks and cookery columns for the newspapers, as well as hosting a radio show called *Dine with George Rector*. He is said to have literally dined out on the story of how he had claimed Marguery sauce for America for the rest of his life.

What was the Inspiration for Sole Véronique?

Another classic dish made with sole (see also SOLE MARGUERY) – this time gently poached and served in a white-wine sauce to which seedless green grapes have been added – is **sole Véronique**. As with so many classic dishes, there is disagreement about who originally came up with it. Some say that it was the great chef Auguste Escoffier (see PEACH MELBA and POIRE BELLE HÉLÈNE), who had accepted an invitation in 1890 from the impresario Richard D'Oyly Carte (1844–1901) to take over the kitchen of his new luxury hotel, the Savoy. D'Oyly Carte also ran the next-door Savoy Theatre – subsequently celebrated for its staging of the operettas of Gilbert and Sullivan – and it was he who built the Royal English Opera House (now the Palace Theatre), where the comic opera *La Basoche*, by French composer André Messager (1853–1929), was one of the first works to be put on. The opera went down well but it was Messager's *Véronique*, staged in London from 1898 and running for 496 performances, that took the capital by storm. It is said that, to mark the occasion of the opera's opening night, Escoffier created a dish in honour of the composer – a friend and fellow countryman – calling it sole Véronique.

Louis Diat, creator of VICHYSSOISE SOUP, had a different story, however. He believed that the inventor was one Monsieur Malley, a chef at the Paris Ritz (where Escoffier set up the kitchens in 1898). A special party was planned and Malley, in an imaginative twist to a classic dish, decided to add grapes to the sauce for the fish course. He gave instructions to a trusted under-chef and went out, as usual, for the afternoon. When he returned, he found the young man so excited that he could hardly work: his wife had just presented him with a baby girl, their first child. Monsieur Malley asked what they would name the child. 'Véronique' came the reply. '*Alors*,' said the chef de cuisine, 'we'll call the new dish *filets de sole Véronique*.' And so it is called to this day.

Why Paella, Historically Speaking, Shouldn't be in this Chapter

Today this archetypal Spanish dish is best eaten by the sea: its juicy yellow rice packed with prawns and chunks of garlic cod, chicken and chorizo. But **paella** was originally labourers' fare, cooked over an open fire in the fields of Valencia and eaten directly from the pan as a communal meal. The cooks used ingredients that were close to hand. Snails were the most commonly used meat as they were easily scavenged; rabbit or duck would be added otherwise and occasionally chicken. Even today, a paella made in the traditional Valencian style includes no seafood, although Valencians living by the sea – who would have used fish instead of meat – might beg to disagree.

The dish has a long history. Alan Davidson, in *The Penguin Companion to Food* (2002), describes it as symbolizing the union of two important cultures: the Roman, which gave us the special utensil in which it is cooked, and the Arab, which introduced that staple of Eastern cooking to Europe – rice.

The name derives from the Latin word for a special kind of deep concave pan, *patella* – which is also, incidentally, the medical name for the kneecap (which does look quite like a pan resting face down). As time went on, the design of the patella/paella became flatter, adapting to the types of fires it was being cooked over. The Arabs (see GAZPACHO) traditionally cooked special communal dishes based on rice, often flavoured with saffron, at family and religious feasts. (It was the Arab engineers' mastery of irrigation that meant rice could be grown much closer to Europe and led to it becoming a staple ingredient there.) Later, as rice became a much more everyday food, it was combined with pulses and vegetables and dried cod, especially during Lent when meat was forbidden.

This was picked up on in Valencia where, from the eighteenth century, rice, flavoured with saffron, was cooked in the open air in a paella pan. In the nineteenth century, with improvements in transport and general living standards, family outings to the countryside rapidly grew in popularity and the making and eating of paella became an essential part of the fiesta. The dish soon caught on throughout Spain, with seafood being added to the original Valencian recipe, giving rise to seafood and mixed paella. Like GRAVLAX and BARBECUES, the cooking of paella has always been seen as a male activity and there is even a special etiquette about eating from the communal pan: everyone takes his or her wooden spoon and draws a triangular wedge in the rice, marking it out in a kind of culinary round table.

The Salmon Dish that Returns
from the Grave

Gravlax or **gravad lax** is a popular Scandinavian dish commonly served as an appetizer as part of the traditional SMORGASBORD. Freshly caught salmon is skinned and boned, cut along its length and seasoned with salt, pepper and sugar. One fillet is placed in a shallow bowl, skin side down, and seasoned with fresh dill, the second fillet laid on top, followed by a plate or board and a heavy weight. The salmon is then left in a cool place for three days or so. Every twelve hours, the fillets are turned and basted with the juices that have collected. In Scandinavia the making of gravlax is seen as a traditionally male activity (on a par with PAELLA or a BARBECUE), stemming from the original, and rather unusual, way of preparing it.

Its earliest mention in print is from 1348, in the form of a name, Olafuer Gravlax, a man from Jämtland in Sweden. His surname, following a practice that was common at the time, indicated his profession – that is, he made the dish for a living, which suggests that gravlax must have already been in existence for some time. Fishermen like Olafuer would bone and fillet the salmon they caught, wrap it in birch bark and then bury it for 4–6 days in the brine-soaked sand just above the high-tide line. This short-term burial resulted in a fermentation that softened the flesh, giving it a tangy taste and rendering it edible while still essentially raw. The Scandinavian word for 'hole in the ground', or 'grave', is *grav*, while *lax* simply means 'salmon'. Although the dish is no longer prepared in this way, the name is still with us and 'salmon from the grave' continues to haunt menus the world over.

Sushi: The Sour Dish that Became
a Fast Food

It's a common fallacy to believe that **sushi** is always made
with raw fish. This is to confuse the dish with SASHIMI, as
rice is the main ingredient in sushi and the kind of fish traditionally used isn't raw but fermented. Every country with
a coastline has come up with its own method of preserving
freshly caught fish, whether salting, smoking or pickling (see
BOMBAY DUCK, GRAVLAX, KIPPER and PICKLED HERRING).
In South-east Asia, cleaned, gutted and salted fish were kept
between layers of rice whose natural fermentation helped
preserve it. In Japan this method was called *nare-zushi* (sushi
or *zushi* translates as 'it's sour' – from the taste of the vinegar
produced by the fermenting rice); after a couple of months
of fermentation, the rice was discarded and the fish was ready
to eat. By the fourteenth century, the Japanese had started
eating the rice alongside the fish in a dish called *seisei-sushi*
that became extremely popular. The only downside was the
delicacy's pungent smell, which has been described as a cross
between blue cheese, fish and rice vinegar, and so a quicker
method of preserving the fish was devised, marinating it in
rice vinegar alone.

How this turned into the version of the dish we are most
familiar with today, **nigiri-sushi**, was down to one man,
Yohei Hanaya, a greengrocer's son, born in 1799 deep in the
Japanese countryside. When he moved to Tokyo in 1818,
the only job he could find was working as a FAST FOOD vendor. Yohei was determined to be successful and struggled for
some time to find the perfect recipe to appeal to the sophisticated palate of the people of Tokyo. Adapting the recipe for
seisei-sushi, he used cooked rice in a vinegar dressing which
he compressed into sticky, finger-shaped rolls (*nigiri* means

'squeezed'), placing a slice of marinated fish on top of each one. Word soon spread of this new type of sushi that could be eaten with one's hands wherever and whenever one liked and Yohei became very rich.

Why Sashimi is Not for the Squeamish

A Japanese dish of raw fish, **sashimi** consists of slices of very fresh fish. The word comes from *sashi*, meaning 'to pierce', and *mi*, 'flesh'. It's thought that this might derive from the traditional method of dispatching the fish, by piercing its brain with a sharp spike, killing it instantly. The fish is then placed immediately in ice, ensuring that it remains fresh for several days. In some restaurants in Japan a diner can choose their own sashimi from a tank full of live fish. The chosen fish is hooked out of the tank, carved into bite-sized pieces and eaten, all within the space of a few minutes. Traditionally sashimi is regarded as the most important part of a meal, hence only the best-quality fish is used, the type of fish depending on the season. Presented with great elegance, sashimi is often served on a bed of white radish with wasabi paste and soy sauce, although the dish has many variations.

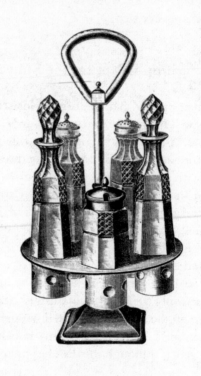

10
Sauces and Seasonings

From Fine Sauces to Haute Cuisine:
The Evolution of French Cooking

Mayonnaise: The Sauce the British
Found Hard to Swallow

Store-cupboard Classic from the Thousand Islands

Pepper: The Black Gold of Former Times

How a Sprinkling of Salt Keeps the Devil at Bay

Béchamel: Return to the Mother Sauce

The United Nation of Mornay

Béarnaise: A Mother Sauce Begets a Child

The Accidental Birth of Beurre Blanc

Hollandaise: Sauce of the Huguenots

The Sauce Created in Honour of the Prince Consort

Worcestershire Sauce: Who were
Mr Lee and Mr Perrins?

From Pickled Fish to Tomatoes: The Strange
Story of Ketchup

What Does the HP in HP Sauce Stand For?

SAUCE, n. The one infallible sign of civilization and
enlightenment. A people with no sauces has one thousand vices; a people with one sauce has only nine hundred and ninety-nine. For every sauce invented and
accepted a vice is renounced and forgiven.

AMBROSE BIERCE, *The Devil's Dictionary*

From Fine Sauces to Haute Cuisine: The Evolution of French Cooking

The word **sauce** is from Old French, based in turn on the Latin *salsus*, meaning 'salted'. In the days before refrigeration, meat, including fish and seafood, didn't stay fresh for long. Strong-tasting sauces were therefore used to mask the flavour, in much the same way as we'd put a throw over an ugly or burst sofa. And they go back a long way in culinary history. The Romans, for instance, were obsessed by a potent fish sauce called 'garum', made by crushing the intestines of various fish, including mackerel, tuna and eel, and fermenting them in brine to produce a multi-purpose condiment – a kind of precursor to WORCESTERSHIRE SAUCE. Like olive oil, the best garum was skimmed off the top of the rotting liquid and sold to the rich, while the dregs (called 'allec') were snapped up by the poor to flavour their staple dish of PORRIDGE. Garum was also used as a medicine for many ailments, including dog bites (see also the box on page 171), dysentery and ulcers, and as a digestive aid to ease chronic diarrhoea and to treat constipation. As time went by and cooking became more sophisticated, sauces became a more integral part of cooking. No longer just the culinary equivalent of a throw over your burst sofa, they now blended with a dish. In the form of a marinade (see KEBAB), for instance, they tenderized meat, while as the liquid in a casserole or stew, they provided a liquor for the cooking, adding flavour and ensuring the other ingredients in the dish didn't dry out.

When Catherine de Médicis arrived at the French court

in 1519, she was only fourteen years of age and wielded little influence. But when, in 1547, she finally became queen, she invited some of the finest chefs from her home town of Florence (see EGGS FLORENTINE), paving the way for a complete change in French cooking, for the chefs brought with them new ingredients and culinary techniques unknown outside Italy up until that point. Among the skills the Florentine chefs taught their hosts was how to uses spices and herbs to enhance a meal instead of disguising the taste, while butter and flour replaced stale bread as a thickening agent for stews.

Soon the French were outstripping their teachers, incorporating Italian techniques into an increasingly sophisticated cuisine of their own. Sauces took pride of place: split into five 'mother' types on which all others were based (see BÉCHAMEL SAUCE for more on this), they laid the foundation for a whole range of new and subtle-flavoured dishes. Food presentation also changed, with sweet and savoury dishes being served as separate courses rather than together, and vegetables being presented as side dishes.

All this culminated, a century later, in a seminal cookbook, *Le Cuisinier françois*, written and published in 1651 by master chef François Pierre de la Varenne (1618–78) and one of the founding textbooks of modern French cuisine (see also SPANISH OMELETTE). It is clear, from the book, that by then chefs no longer favoured strong spices – which had featured in upper-class cooking since the Middle Ages (see PEASE PUDDING) – replacing them in savoury dishes with lighter, locally grown herbs, including parsley, tarragon, bay leaves and sage. *Le Cuisinier françois* became an instant bestseller, its influence spreading beyond France to the rest of Europe, changing attitudes towards cookery and its presentation and providing recipes for many dishes, including sauces, that can be found on menus to this day.

Needless to say, it was only the upper echelons of society

who benefited from such groundbreaking cuisine. The peasant classes continued to live off much simpler fare, or, if they were a little less fortunate, they starved. Then, at the end of the eighteenth century, came that great event that rocked the whole of France, shaking up the lives of rich and poor alike – the French Revolution (see LOBSTER THERMIDOR). While the uprising was good news for the majority of the population, it clearly wasn't much fun for the nobility, for whom, thanks to Madame Guillotine, the finer points of dining etiquette were now no longer a priority. Nor was it much easier for anybody who had worked in the great chateaux and palaces, including the cooks and kitchen staff, who now had to look elsewhere for employment.

As a result, a number of them set themselves up in some of the many grand buildings of Paris that had been 'liberated', in the hope that people would need feeding and be able to pay or barter for it. So began a different kind of revolution – a gastronomic one this time. Within a few years, these restaurants had become highly fashionable and full of an entirely new class of people, who were hooked on and prepared to pay for a sophisticated style of cooking previously accessible only to the nobility and known, therefore, as **haute** (high-class) **cuisine**.

Mayonnaise: The Sauce the British Found Hard to Swallow

This famous cold white sauce, found in refrigerators the world over, is a simple mixture of olive oil, lemon juice or vinegar, and egg yolk. Its name may in fact derive from this last ingredient. According to *Larousse Gastronomique* (1961 edition), **mayonnaise** 'is a popular corruption of *moyeunaise*, evolving from the Old French word *moyeu*, meaning egg yolk'. Other theories abound, however, including one linked to Charles de Lorraine, Duke of Mayenne (1554–1611), who was so fond of a particular white sauce ('Mayennaise'), and spent so long eating a portion of chicken covered in it, that he lost the Battle of Arques in 1589 during the French Wars of Religion. A far more likely reason is that he ran away after being confronted by 4,000 British troops sent to reinforce British ranks facing the opposing French army.

I have also found references to an Irish general called MacMahon, who claimed he first created the sauce, originally called 'MacMahonnaise' (and presumably the ideal accompaniment for a Big Mac), and there are suggestions that it derives from 'Bayonnaise' after the city of Bayonne. However, it is far more likely that the now ubiquitous condiment originates from the town of Mahon, the capital of the Balearic Island of Minorca, and from an incident that reflects far less well on the British.

Minorca has been conquered several times throughout its history, most notably by the Carthaginian general Mago (243–203 BC), brother of Hannibal and legendary founder of Port Mahon, but in 1756 it was occupied by the British, who had become rather lazy about maintaining their defences. The principal protection of the island was the responsibility of Admiral John Byng (1704–57) with his fleet of thirteen British ships. But due to a major tactical error, the fleet was decimated and the French were able to land 15,000 troops at Mahon under the leadership of the duc de Richelieu (1696–1788), a gentleman celebrated for his insistence on dining in the nude – which may well have led to his particularly enthusiastic championing of a new sauce that enhanced the flavour of cold foods (a much safer choice for the naked male diner) … but I'm getting ahead of myself here.

The British garrison of 3,000 men surrendered the island to the French on 28 May and Byng returned to Gibraltar, where he was tried by court martial for incompetence and subsequently shot. Commenting on the trial in his satirical novella *Candide* (1759), French philosopher Voltaire famously wrote: 'The British shoot an admiral every so often *pour encourager les autres* [to encourage the others].' Adding to British mortification, the invasion of Port Mahon on 19 April was so successful that the French didn't suffer a single fatality and Richelieu threw a lavish feast in celebration.

Legend has it that the duke's chef, when preparing the victory banquet, realized to his horror that he didn't have any cream to make the rich sauce he needed. In desperation he followed the recipe for a local sauce, **aioli** – popular in many Mediterranean countries – but omitting the industrial quantities of garlic essential to it. To his great relief, the result was a success; indeed, the duke liked it so much that he took the recipe back to France with him, calling it 'Mahonnaise' in memory of his great victory over the British at Port Mahon. The use of mayonnaise as a dressing and as an ingredient for other sauces spread quickly throughout France following the duc de Richelieu's triumphant return to his homeland, where he dramatized and elaborated on the story of how the sauce was invented under his inspiration. The British, understandably enough, grumpily avoided mayonnaise for almost a century before finally succumbing. Introduced to Britain in 1841, according to the *Oxford English Dictionary*, it has been a regular feature of our cuisine ever since.

Store-cupboard Classic from the Thousand Islands

The exotically named Thousand Islands are a cluster of islands (there are 1,793 in total) in the Saint Lawrence River on the border between America and Canada. Every July and

August, when New York turns into a humid oven, city dwell-
ers traditionally escape to the islands, where many of the
houses are owned by these vacationers. Around the turn of
the twentieth century, a well-known Thousand Island fisherman, George LaLonde Junior, was teaching a prominent
New York actress, May Irwin (1862–1938), to fish. One evening, following a fishing expedition, LaLonde's wife Sophia
served one of her 'shore dinners': the popular actress was
particularly impressed with the salad dressing, made from
mayonnaise and TOMATO KETCHUP mixed with finally
chopped green olives, pickles, onions and hard-boiled eggs.
Impressive as it was – and rather like the recipe concocted by
the duc de Richelieu's chef (see MAYONNAISE) – the dressing was essentially made with whatever came to hand. On
these islands at that time, with little access to fresh ingredients, dishes had to be prepared using store-cupboard basics.
May Irwin asked for the recipe and immediately passed it on
to her friend and fellow Thousand Island vacationer George
C. Boldt (1851–1916). Boldt, owner of the Waldorf Hotel
in New York, was equally impressed with the sauce, asking
his maître d', Oscar Tschirky (see also EGGS BENEDICT and
WALDORF SALAD), to refine it and introduce it to the diners
at the hotel. Today **Thousand Island dressing** is internationally known and has itself become a store-cupboard basic,
sold in a jar in supermarkets throughout the world.

Pepper: The Black Gold of Former Times

One of the oldest-known spices on the planet, **black pepper**
has been used as a flavouring for over seven thousand years.
A much prized spice, it was frequently used for bartering
instead of money. In AD 408, the Visigoths, a barbarian
Germanic tribe led by Alaric the First, rebelled against the

Romans. It was the first time in almost eight hundred years that the Romans had lost a major military conflict and the stakes were high. Alaric succeeded in pushing the Roman army back to Rome and then laid siege to the city. As winter approached, disease and starvation spread and the Senate, in desperation, tried to broker a deal, offering gold and black pepper in exchange for the liberation of the city. Alaric the First accepted the terms, thereby ensuring that pepper – at the time, equal in value to gold – would thereafter be known as the spice for which Rome, the heart of the greatest empire in history, had been traded.

Throughout the centuries that followed, pepper continued to be highly valued. The earliest reference to black peppercorns in England, for instance, can be found in the statute books of King Ethelred (978–1016) in which it is recorded that ships delivering to Billingsgate must pay a toll of a ten-pound sack of pepper at Easter and at Christmas. Peppercorns have a symbolic monetary value even today, enshrined in the English legal system. According to English law, every legal contract requires that each party gives something of value to the other. If not, then the contract is considered not to be binding and cannot be enforced. For example, when you sell your house, the other party gives you money for it, hence something of value is exchanged by each party, either a house or money. For the contract to be valid it is not necessary, however, for the items being exchanged to be equal in value, but an exchange must take place, even if something of very little value is offered in return for something of far greater worth. In such cases, a token sum may be given, historically measured in peppercorns. Hence a landlord wishing to let a property essentially for free must set up a contract with the leaseholder for a nominal sum, referred to as a ***peppercorn rent***. Likewise, if a company has debts amounting to more than its overall worth, a new owner can obtain the business for no money at all, so long as they agree to take over the debt, but the contract between the two parties would not be legally binding if the buyer did not offer something nominal in exchange. This, by law, is known as a ***peppercorn payment*** and is exactly how Ken Bates managed to acquire Chelsea Football Club during the 1980s for just £1, a ***peppercorn***. Obviously they use cash these days, but a single pound or dollar payment is still known as the 'peppercorn'.

Pepper can also be regarded as a chief motivating factor in the Great Age of Discovery, which began during the late fifteenth century and continued into the early 1600s. European explorers, especially the Spanish and Portuguese, who were, by then, free of Moorish domination (see GAZPACHO), chartered ships to seek out new territories, establishing in the process trade links with previously unknown cultures. The shipping lanes between Europe and Asia soon became known as spice trade routes and for centuries black pepper was the principal commodity. During the mid sixteenth century, for example, the price of pepper served as the basis for all European business at Antwerp in Belgium, in much the same way as the price of oil affects world trade today. Indeed, it was the passion for pepper, and the search for a new source of the valuable condiment (see CHILLI PEPPER), that led to the King and Queen of Spain financing a certain voyage by one Christopher Columbus, who set out to find an old spice and instead discovered a new world.

How a Sprinkling of Salt Keeps the Devil at Bay

Salt is one of the most basic food seasonings. Before the introduction of the tin can and the refrigerator, it was also the chief means of preserving food (for other methods, see POTTED SHRIMPS) and, like BLACK PEPPER, highly valued as a result (see also the box on page 195). Its value was symbolic too: the mineral was regarded as an auspicious substance by many religions and is still used in religious ceremonies today. In the Christian faith, holy water is said to derive from the ancient practice among the Egyptians, Greeks and Romans of invoking the gods with offerings of salt and water. Meanwhile, the Bible frequently mentions salt, most famously in the reference to Lot's wife being turned into a pillar of salt for her disobedience, and in the words of Christ to his followers, whom he calls the 'salt of the earth' (Matthew 5:13).

Numerous superstitions are associated with it as well. During the Middle Ages, it was thought to neutralize the power of witchcraft. Anybody affected by a curse would be advised to sprinkle salt into an open fire every morning for nine consecutive days with the words: 'Salt, salt, I drop thee into the fire and may the person who has bewitched me neither eat, drink or sleep until the spell is broken.' On the tenth morning, it was believed, the curse would be lifted. It was also believed that if a dead man's hand was placed on a plate of salt overnight, this would provide a cure for chilblains – providing you didn't mind having your feet rubbed by a salty, dead hand, that is. Belief in the curative powers of salt was so strong that it was thought that a bag of hot salt could cure toothache or earache and, if placed in a baby's crib, would protect an infant against illness and disease. In the north of England there is a legend claiming that during the Great Plague, which decimated London in 1665, every single employee of a former salt works escaped infection.

The most commonly known superstition connected with salt is that a person who spills it should take a pinch and throw it over their left shoulder. This was thought to blind the devil – lurking, it was believed, behind your left shoulder – so that he wouldn't notice the spillage and heap misfortune upon you. It's also why you should never stand behind a busy chef, unless you want to be showered with salt. The superstition appears to be religious in origin, dating back to the Last Supper when Jesus dined with his twelve Apostles and announced one of them would betray him to the Roman authorities. According to some accounts, Judas spilt a cellar of salt at the table and removed the offending mess by scooping it up and tossing it over his shoulder, a historic event said to have been depicted by Leonardo da Vinci in his painting *The Last Supper* (1498), although Judas must have disposed of the salt as I can't see it anywhere.

As an auspicious, luck-bringing substance, salt was used as an early form of confetti, thrown over a newly wedded couple, or sprinkled on the ground after the bearer of bad news had left, to ensure he didn't return. It was also considered unlucky for a fisherman to set out to sea without a bag of salt in his boat. From ancient times until the Middle Ages, newborn babies were rubbed with salt to ward off evil spirits, a practice referred to in the Old Testament, in Ezekiel 15:8: 'And as for thy nativity, in the day thou wast born thy navel was not cut, neither wast thou washed in water to supple thee; thou wast not salted at all.' It was also used to mark the end of a person's life: in Wales, for instance, a plate of bread and salt would be placed on a coffin prior to burial, in the belief that the salt would soak up the dead person's sins. A local sin-eater would then consume the bread and salt, absolving the sins of the deceased and allowing them to rest in peace.

SALT features in many of our most common idioms. ***Rubbing salt into the wound***, for instance, is to make a person's shame, or pain in an emotional sense, even worse than it already is. A frequently suggested source for the expression is nautical in origin. Once an errant sailor had been punished by flogging, his comrades would rub preserving salt into his wounds, making them much more painful but healing the injuries a good deal faster than if they had been left untreated. This may very well be the origin of the phrase, but for another possible source, and an earlier one at that, we need to turn to an associated idiom.

If someone is ***not worth their salt***, they are regarded as not very good at their job or a particular task. During the days of the Roman Empire, salt was an expensive commodity and soldiers were paid partly in salt, which they carried with them in leather pouches. This form of payment was known as a *salarium*, from the Latin word *sal*, meaning 'salt'. Hence to be not worth one's salt would mean being not worth paying (in salt). It is thus easy to see how the English word ***salary*** also originates from the word *sal* (salt). Any Roman who had been injured in battle would have to rub part of his salt (i.e. his wages) into the wound to help the healing process.

Adding salt to food has given rise to another common idiom, ***take with a pinch of salt***. In the same way that a pinch of salt can make otherwise plain food more interesting and palatable, a metaphorical pinch of salt will help us to accept something we are being told that we might otherwise doubt.

Béchamel: Return to the Mother Sauce

Béchamel, one of the five so-called 'mother' sauces of French cuisine (the others being **velouté** and **espagnole** – each made using stock and thickened with flour and butter – HOLLANDAISE and **tomato**), is widely used in European and American cookery. A smooth, white sauce made with milk and thickened with flour and butter, béchamel is usually served with white meats, eggs or vegetables. The question of its origin has long been the subject of debate, as noted by the New York food critic Raymond Solokov:

> Gastronomic literature is filled with tedious pages and trifling disputes and Béchamel has inspired more than its fair share of this piffle. People will argue about whether the correct spelling should not be *béchamelle* or if not the Italian version *balsamella* from the Romagna region is the original of the best known and easiest mother sauce. In such matters prejudice will always rule, for there is no evidence one way or the other. We can only point to the appearance of a sauce called Béchamel during the reign of Louis XIV of France. And, as so often, the original sauce bore only a slight resemblance to the modern version …

Following this lead, there was indeed a Marquis Louis de Béchamel (1630–1703), a rich financier and a member of the court of Louis XIV. In 1685, Béchamel took on the honorary position of chief steward to the king. This was a position of power, giving valuable access to the king (see MAIDS OF HONOUR), but it also entailed great responsibility, ensuring that Louis XIV – a highly cultivated man, known as the 'Sun King' for his sophistication and love of culture – was happy with his food. The marquis is said to have invented the sauce when trying to come up with a new way of serving and eating dried cod. It is more likely to have been created by one of the chefs who reported to Béchamel and who dedicated it to him as a compliment or in return for a favour after it was served to the king and became a firm royal favourite.

This prompted some jealousy along the way. The duc d'Escars is recorded as commenting: 'That fellow Béchamel has all the luck. I was serving breast of chicken *à la crème* more than twenty years before he was born, but I have never had the honour of giving my name to even the most modest sauce.' You've probably never heard of the duc d'Escars either, which is hardly surprising. As the great chef Auguste Escoffier (see PEACH MELBA, POIRE BELLE HÉLÈNE and SOLE VÉRONIQUE) correctly noted in his memoirs: 'After all, if it wasn't for his divine sauce the marquis de Béchamel would have been forgotten long ago.' And Escoffier wasn't often wrong when it came to food.

The United Nation of Mornay

A prime example of a mother sauce (see BÉCHAMEL) being used as a base for something new is **Mornay sauce**. Many suggest that this sauce – where two types of grated cheese, usually Gruyère and PARMESAN, are added to béchamel – was called after Philippe, duc de Mornay (1549–1623), a prominent French Protestant writer. But, as he pre-dated Louis de Béchamel, de Mornay cannot have invented the sauce himself: it's far more likely that it was inspired by his life and achievements.

At the outbreak of the French Wars of Religion (1562–98) between the Catholics and the Protestants (known as Huguenots – see also HOLLANDAISE SAUCE and SALLY LUNN

BUN), de Mornay joined the army, although a convenient fall from his horse meant that he avoided direct military action. Warned by a Catholic friend, he also managed to escape the St Bartholomew's Day Massacre, a brutal campaign of mob violence and assassinations that took place in 1572 (see EGGS FLORENTINE). De Mornay spent the rest of his life devoting himself to furthering the Huguenot cause wherever possible, becoming known as one of its leading supporters, while his influence on European religion and politics is well documented. He was the right-hand man of the Protestant Henri de Navarre (see BÉARNAISE SAUCE), who converted to Catholicism for purely political reasons on gaining the French throne, declaring: 'Paris is well worth a Mass.' Once safely in power, however, he passed the Edict of Nantes, which, in recognizing Protestantism in France, marked the end of the Wars of Religion and restored peace to the nation. This sauce could be described as a microcosm of de Mornay's ideal France, with its two different, strong-tasting cheeses symbolizing the Protestants and Catholics living together in harmonious union.

Béarnaise: A Mother Sauce Begets a Child

And from the king's adviser (see MORNAY SAUCE) to the king himself ... Henri IV (1553–1610), one of the few French kings to be granted the title of 'Great', was a revolutionary monarch. Instead of waging costly wars to suppress opposing nobles, as all his predecessors had, Henri simply paid them off. He is often quoted as saying: 'If God spares me, I will ensure that there is no working man in my kingdom who does not have the means to have a chicken in the pot every Sunday!' An attitude that was highly unusual for someone of his standing, demonstrating how well he understood the plight of the French worker or peasant farmer. Never before had a French ruler really considered the welfare of his subjects, nor would one again until the French Revolution. Meanwhile, the peace that Henri restored to France following decades of religious war ushered in a period of relative prosperity that would have helped put a chicken in every peasant's pot.

After he was stabbed by a Catholic fanatic, the French people mourned their monarch, whom they had nicknamed Le Béarnais after his birthplace, Béarn, a former province in the Pyrenees in south-west France. Statues were raised, portraits painted and books written in honour of Le Béarnais. But the sauce that bears his name wasn't invented until the nineteenth century when chef Jules Colette, working at a restaurant named after the king, Le Pavillon Henri IV, invented his own, extremely delicious version of HOLLANDAISE SAUCE. **Béarnaise sauce** – an emulsion of egg yolks and clarified butter, flavoured with herbs – rapidly became as popular as its royal namesake, so much so that every chef at the smart Parisian restaurant tried to claim it as their own.

The Accidental Birth of Beurre Blanc

Another famous sauce, **beurre blanc** ('white butter') apparently evolved from a mistake made by French chef Madame Clémence Lefeuvre towards the end of the nineteenth century while she was working in the kitchens of the marquis de Goulaine. On one occasion, the story goes, intending to make BÉARNAISE SAUCE for a pike dish, Lefeuvre ran out of eggs at the crucial moment and had to quickly improvise, using wine and lemon juice instead. Legend has it that her new sauce became so popular she opened her own restaurant, La Buvette de la Marine, on the banks of the Loire River near Nantes, on the strength of it with beurre blanc as her signature sauce.

Hollandaise: Sauce of the Huguenots

An emulsion of egg yolk and butter, seasoned with lemon juice, **hollandaise sauce** would appear, from its name, to come from Holland, but the recipe is not an obviously Dutch one. Like so many other dishes, it has a strong connection to the French Huguenots (see also BÉARNAISE SAUCE, EGGS FLORENTINE and SALLY LUNN BUN), a Protestant minority in a country dominated by the Catholic Church. Subjected to religious persecution from the sixteenth century, they were forced to emigrate and by the end of the seventeenth century – when Louis XIV revoked the Edict of Nantes (see MORNAY SAUCE) – roughly 200,000 Huguenots had been driven from France. They sought refuge in the Protestant countries of northern Europe, including England, Germany and the Netherlands, gradually returning to France when it was safe to do so. Huguenots returning from Holland brought back with them a sauce that they had developed during their time away. Very like MAYONNAISE, it was made using melted butter rather than olive oil, which would have been difficult to obtain so far north.

Hollandaise is thought to have been originally called **sauce Isigny**, after the butter-producing town of Isigny-sur-Mer in Normandy, the butter and cream capital of France. When butter production ceased in the region during the First World War, a new source had to be found and so it was imported from Holland. Hence it was from around this time, according to one theory, that sauce Isigny became known as hollandaise sauce. Which sounds a little unlikely, however, as the Dutch association with the sauce had been established well before then. There is, for instance, a recipe for *sauce à la hollandoise* in the 1758 edition of François Marin's *Les Dons de Cormus*. Likewise, Mrs Beeton, in her *Book of Household Management* (1861), refers to a 'Dutch sauce, for fish', as well as a variant,

'Green sauce, or Hollandaise verte'. Probably both names, hollandaise and sauce Isigny, existed side by side until the former eventually won through as the name familiar to cooks the world over.

The Sauce Created in Honour of the Prince Consort

A 'child' of VELOUTÉ, **Albert sauce** is thickened with cream and egg yolks and flavoured with HORSERADISH. A feature of traditional British cuisine, the sauce is particularly good with braised or roast beef. (I happen to be a real fan and not just because we share a name.)

Some say that the sauce is German in origin, invented by one Albrecht (Albert) Pfalzgraf, who wrote a gastronomic work in 1554 which included cooking techniques and recipes. Others claim the sauce was developed in honour of Thérèse Vernet (1805–46), a French actress who became the idol of Paris during her career as 'Madame Albert'. Much more convincing, however, is option three, that it was named after the short-lived and much loved husband of Queen Victoria, Albert of Saxe-Coburg-Gotha (1819–61), the prince consort. Despite influencing sweeping reforms throughout the country, in education and welfare, and promoting British trade and industry by hosting the Great Exhibition in 1851 – using the profits to establish the Victoria and Albert Museum – Albert never really enjoyed any popularity with the British public, largely it seems, because he was German.

However, after his death at the age of just forty-two, leaving the queen in mourning for the rest of her life, the British began to honour the prince in all sorts of ways. The Albert Memorial, Albert Hall and Albert Bridge, for instance, are among the many monuments built in his honour. A less conventional memento is the Prince Albert piercing, on a part of the body exclusive to the male gender (yes, you know where I mean), said to have been pioneered by the prince to ensure he always looked magnificent in his tight breeches. It is quite possible that royal chefs wished to honour his memory too, creating the sauce in sympathy for the grieving queen and to encourage her to eat her SUNDAY ROAST. A gravy boat produced by Royal Albert Ltd (later to become Royal Doulton) and called the Royal Albert is perhaps further evidence that the Albert in question is the prince.

Worcestershire Sauce: Who were Mr Lee and Mr Perrins?

In the 1830s, in the cellar below a chemist's shop in Worcester called Lea & Perrins, a barrel of spiced vinegar – made according to an Indian recipe for a customer but never collected as it had been considered undrinkable – sat for some years. Clearing out the cellar, the chemists were about to throw away the barrel but fortunately tasted it first, finding, to their astonishment, that the mixture had nicely matured. And so **Worcestershire sauce** was born. The exact ingredients of the recipe are jealously guarded, but they include soy sauce and anchovies, which is why the mixture started fermenting. Worcestershire sauce is thus a modern, and rather more palatable, version of the Roman fish sauce **garum** (see 'From Fine Sauces to Haute Cuisine', page 185). In 1838, the first distinctively labelled bottles of 'Lea & Perrins Worcestershire Sauce' were released to the general public, and Mr Lea and Mr Perrins subsequently made their fortune from the distinctive-tasting condiment. The sauce remains hugely popular around the world to this day, especially in China and Japan, where it is praised for enhancing *umami* – the fifth basic taste, or 'savouriness', considered fundamental to their cuisine.

From Pickled Fish to Tomatoes: The Strange Story of Ketchup

Ketchup, as a condiment, far pre-dates the sauce in the form we know it today. For centuries, the Chinese have been enjoying a spicy, pickled fish sauce made with anchovies, walnuts, mushrooms and kidney beans, and known as *ke-tsiap*. The Indonesians made their own version, which they called *kecap*. Seventeenth-century British seamen brought *kecap* home with them and it rapidly caught on, the word evolving, Chinese whisper fashion, into 'catchup' and then, by 1711, into 'ketchup'. The first ketchup recipe, printed in 1727 in Eliza Smith's *The Compleat Housewife*, called for anchovies, shallots, vinegar, white wine, sweet spices (including cloves, ginger, mace and nutmeg), BLACK PEPPER and lemon peel. At this point, it was still a fish-based sauce, therefore, not unlike WORCESTERSHIRE SAUCE.

It was the Americans who introduced the tomato to the sauce, the first recipe for **tomato ketchup** being published in 1801 by Sandy Addison. In 1837, Americans selling tomato ketchup in Britain were encouraged to rename it 'tomato chutney' in order to draw attention to the difference between their product and the mushroom ketchup popular there. Then the American ketchup boom happened and the British mushroom ketchup was left behind in the rush: by 1900, there were over a hundred manufacturers of ketchup in the US. But when Henry Heinz (see also BAKED BEANS) added tomato ketchup to his line of pickled products in 1872, his recipe became and remains the market leader. A large part of its initial success lay in its cunning advertising, pointing out that Heinz ketchup could free the family cooks from the laborious tyranny of making their own tomato sauce: 'Blessed relief for Mother and the other women in the household!'

What Does the HP in HP Sauce Stand For?

Rather as football and rugby were once the same game until they were formally separated in 1863, today's bottle of **brown sauce** was once KETCHUP – a British-made ketchup of earlier times. It sits proudly alongside tomato ketchup on the tables of most British cafés and is a distinctively British preference. People who haven't been brought up with it can find the strong tang of tamarind (also present in WORCES-TERSHIRE SAUCE) a little off-putting. The original recipe for **HP Sauce** – today's best-loved brand of brown sauce – was invented and developed by Frederick Gibson Garton, a Nottingham grocer who registered the name 'H.P. Sauce' in 1896. Garton called the sauce HP because he had heard that a restaurant in the Houses of Parliament had begun serving it. For many years, the label on the bottle has sported a picture of the Houses of Parliament. So it's somewhat ironic that Houses of Parliament Sauce, the epitome of traditional British taste, is now owned by an American company (Heinz) and manufactured in the Netherlands.

11
The Meat Course

The Dark Story Behind Steak Diane

Rag Pudding and Kate and Sidney Pie

Kleftiko: What Do You Cook for a Bandit
who Steals Everything?

Favourite Dish of the Iron Duke

Frozen Food from Siberia: How Beef Stroganoff
Came About

Haggis: A Covert Symbol of Rebellion?

Irish Stew and Its Cousins Across the Sea

Was Steak Tartare the Original Food on the Hoof?

Why Chicken Kiev Rules Supreme

Chicken Marengo: Napoleon's
Culinary Good Luck Charm

Bangers and Mash: Exploding Food
from the Trenches

Faggots: The Perfect Snack for a Burning

How Goulash Helped Overthrow Oppression

How Does Meat Become Jerky?

What is the Difference between Shepherd's
and Cottage Pie?

Man is a carnivorous production,
And must have meals, at least one meal a day;
He cannot live, like woodcocks, upon suction,
But, like the shark and tiger, must have prey;
Although his anatomical construction
Bears vegetables, in a grumbling way,
Your labouring people think beyond all question,
Beef, veal, and mutton better for digestion.

LORD BYRON, *Don Juan*

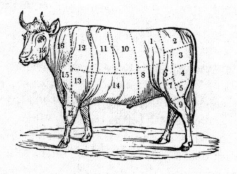

The Dark Story Behind Steak Diane

Diana ('Diane' to the French) was the Roman goddess of virginity and the moon. She was also goddess of the hunt and since Roman times certain game dishes have been dedicated to her. In France, joints of venison *à la Diane* were sautéed and served with a sharp-tasting sauce to complement the sweetness of the meat. The earliest mention of **sauce Diane** in print wasn't until the twentieth century, however, when a recipe for it appeared in *Le Guide culinaire* by Auguste Escoffier in 1907 (see also PEACH MELBA, POIRE BELLE HÉLÈNE and SOLE VÉRONIQUE). Described as a *sauce poivrade* (pepper sauce), this was finished with whipped cream and pieces of hard-boiled egg white and truffle cut in small crescent shapes in honour of the goddess.

After the Second World War, when thousands of American GIs returned home after being stationed in France, **steak Diane** (as the dish was called by then, although consisting of beef rather than venison and served with a different sauce) began to find its way on to the menus of many big city restaurants. In New York during the 1950s and 1960s, a number of top hotels created versions of steak Diane as their signature dish, each claiming to have invented it. None of them had, of course, but they all had their own unique variations. Further afield, at the Copacabana Palace Hotel in Rio de Janeiro, Brazil, presenting the dish was made into a theatrical spectacle. The steak was hammered until it was very thin and then, on a small gas burner by the diner's table, quickly fried in butter, brandy poured over and the pan flamboyantly set aflame. The tableside chef, presumably wearing a fireproof hat, would then finish the sauce with more butter, chives and a splash of sherry.

But there is a more macabre aspect to this dish, one that diners would probably prefer not to contemplate as they cut into their juicy steaks. As goddess of the hunt, Diana was a popular subject for painters from the Renaissance onwards. According to Roman myth – and in a scene famously painted by the great Venetian artist Titian (*c*.1473/90–1575) – Actaeon, out hunting in the forest, accidentally came across Diana while she was bathing in a secluded pool. As no mortal was allowed to see her naked, the furious goddess immediately turned him into a stag in punishment. The hunter became the hunted and when his own pack of hounds caught up with him, they tore him apart and ate him. Hence mythologically speaking, at least, Actaeon was the original steak Diane.

Rag Pudding and Kate and Sidney Pie

Steak and kidney provide the main ingredient for two traditional British dishes, a pudding and a pie – one made with a suet crust, enclosing the whole dish, and the other with a lid of shortcrust or puff pastry. But which was the first to arrive on the scene? The pudding, it would seem. Suet – the fat used for making the pastry – is obtained from around the kidney of a cow or sheep. Hence it must have seemed logical to pop the offal in with the meat, and so **steak and kidney pudding** was born, known to have been well established by the middle of the eighteenth century.

A similar dish, **rag pudding**, comes from Oldham in Lancashire. If that sounds a little indigestible, then I should add that the name derives from the way of cooking it, rather than the contents, which consist of a rather tastier mix of minced meat and onions wrapped in suet pastry. Before the advent of the ceramic basin, boiling puddings – suet or otherwise – in a cloth was the sole means of cooking them, taking over from boiling them in an animal's stomach lining (see CHRISTMAS PUDDING). And as Lancashire, in the middle of the nineteenth century, was the centre of the flourishing cotton trade, scraps or offcuts of cloth would have been plentiful. It needed to be a clean cloth, however, as Hannah Glasse, author of *The Art of Cookery* (see YORKSHIRE PUDDING), stresses to her readers: 'In boiled Puddings, take great Care the Bag or Cloth be very clean, and not soapy, and dipped in hot water, and then well flowered.' So not a scrap plucked straight from the factory floor.

But what about that close relative of the pudding, **steak and kidney pie**? Meat pies have long been a part of the English way of life; indeed, hot meat pies were known to have been hawked around London from the fifteenth century onwards. By the nineteenth century, they and those who ate them had clearly become a bit of a national stereotype, as commented on by the French novelist J.-K. Huysmans in *À Rebours* ('Against Nature'), published in 1884: 'robust English women with boyish faces, large teeth, ruddy apple cheeks, long hands and legs … attacked, with genuine ardour, a rumpsteak pie, a warm meat dish cooked in mushroom sauce and covered with a crust.'

Mushrooms accompany the steak in this particular pie (see also BEEF WELLINGTON) and it seems that kidneys weren't a common addition until the following century. Offal, being cheap, was probably added to help eke out the more expensive beef, as much as for the contrast in texture. Now considered the most classic of meat dishes, **Kate and Sidney pie** – as it's known in cockney rhyming slang, together with the rather more alarming **snake and pygmy** – has become a firm favourite and something of a national institution.

The expression **as easy as pie**, meaning very easy indeed, is a curious one. Why should a pie be easy, after all? It seems that the ease of the pie is in the eating rather than the making of it, as in the similar expression **nice as pie**. Both originate in nineteenth-century America, where likening something to a particular pie is also archetypally American – **as American as apple pie**, in fact.

Something described as **pie in the sky**, another phrase from America, is essentially a good idea but unlikely to amount to anything in reality. The phrase comes from a trade union parody of the hymn 'The Sweet By and By' that was often sung during the years of the Great Depression early in the twentieth century. The song was entitled 'The Preacher and the Slave' and its chorus, goes like this:

> You will eat, bye and bye
> In that glorious land above the sky;
> Work and pray, live on hay,
> You'll get pie in the sky when you die.

And somehow that passed over into wider use, but don't ask how.

Moving back across the Atlantic, **to have a finger in every pie** is an expression commonly used to describe a person who has an interest in many things, especially business-related. It would be easier to understand if the phrase read 'a finger in *making* every pie', which would rid us of the image of somebody going around poking their finger into other people's peach crumble, thereby suggesting an interfering meddler. The expression has been in use for over four hundred years and is applied

> to anybody with wide and varied business interests. It
> is also used by some people to describe themselves in
> an attempt to appear mysterious and interesting when
> in fact they've probably never had their finger in any-
> body's pie.

Kleftiko: What Do You Cook for a Bandit who Steals Everything?

Greece has an ancient culinary history. Going back several thousand years, it has influenced the cuisine of numerous other countries. **Kleftiko** (or **klephtiko**) is one of its historic dishes, its name referring to the klephts, a gang of Greek bandits living in the mountains from the fifteenth century.

After the fall of Constantinople in 1453, most of Greece was absorbed by the Ottoman Empire. Any surviving Greek troops unwilling to join the Ottoman army or serve in the private army of a local nobleman had to fend for themselves. Many therefore chose to escape to the mountains – which being inaccessible weren't under Ottoman rule – and join the klephts, swelling their ranks to thousands. Regarding themselves as heroic freedom fighters, they were nonetheless forced to live like criminals on what they managed to steal. (*Klepht* is also the root of the word 'kleptomaniac', used to describe a person who has a constant urge to steal.)

Having fled for the best possible reasons, because they were keen to maintain their Greek identity and Orthodox Christianity, the klephts soon became a much feared group, preying on local peasants and only leaving their hideouts to raid villages or ambush travelling merchants in the mountain passes. As they knew the land much better than the Ottoman soldiers sent to capture them, the klephts were always one step ahead. The best clue to where they were hiding was the smoke from their fires, giving their pursuers a chance to catch them by surprise as they were enjoying their stolen food. The canny klephts soon solved that problem, however, by inventing the cooking method for the dish that still bears their name to this day. Kleftiko, literally 'stolen meat' (by association with the klephts), is a dish of lamb marinated in garlic and lemon juice and cooked on the bone for a long period at very low temperature. The klephts would seal their kleftiko pots in fire pits that were then covered over, allowing no smoke to escape. This enabled the bandits to spend the day pillaging and looting, secure in the knowledge that the Ottomans wouldn't be waiting for them on their return and they could tuck into their pots of illicit lamb, slow-cooked to perfection.

Favourite Dish of the Iron Duke

The Iron Duke, who beat Napoleon at the Battle of Waterloo, was the British hero who has given his name to a range of items, including numerous streets and pubs, a rubber boot and a truly delicious way of cooking beef fillet in pastry.

Arthur Wellesley, 1st Duke of Wellington (1769–1852), was a brilliant and daring soldier who pursued successful military campaigns in India, Spain, Belgium and the Netherlands. He was happiest enjoying a Spartan existence, staying in tents alongside his soldiers. He was so indifferent to what he ate – food was just fuel – and the cooking conditions were so basic, that he had a very high turnover of chefs. But then, according to the legend, one chef came up with the duke's ideal dish: one that he then insisted on serving at every formal dinner he was to hold for the rest of his long life.

It was the fashion at the time to bake joints of meat in pastry so they would remain moist. Like his men, Wellington preferred beef to any other meat and, to add extra flavour, his cook added a creamy mushroom paste to the fillet before wrapping it in pastry. The resulting dish was tender and delicious: the duke approved, the chef felt appreciated and the recipe for Beef Wellington was soon picked up by keen cooks all over the world.

Apart from the French, that is, who cannot bring themselves to honour the man who crushed their little leader at Waterloo in 1815: their version of the dish has added truffles and pâté de FOIE GRAS and simply is known as *filet de boeuf en croûte*. Indeed, an alternative theory is that during the Napoleonic Wars, when England was constantly at odds with France, a patriotic British chef changed the title of what was basically a French dish in order to give it an English name, one honouring the man who would decimate their enemy. Yet another theory suggests that the dish, wrapped in well-browned pastry, so resembled one of Wellington's long military boots that it was called after the celebrated wearer of them.

Frozen Food from Siberia: How Beef Stroganoff Came About

It will surprise few people to learn that **beef stroganoff**, a favourite winter dish, was developed deep in the Siberian Plains of Russia. Created by sautéing thinly sliced pieces of beef with onions, mushrooms and paprika and then stirring in sour cream, the dish is credited to the chef of one of Russia's most colourful families of its imperial past, the Stroganovs. Unlike the egalitarian French, who tended to name a dish after the man who created it, regardless of his status, the Russian dynasties usually took the credit if one of their kitchen workers made a success of a new idea.

The Stroganov in question credited with the dish bearing his family name is Count Paul Sergeyevich (1823–1911), a prominent nineteenth-century Russian diplomat, well known across Europe and a close confidant of the Tsar. But it turns out that he was taking credit for a dish invented for one of his ancestors, another Paul Stroganov, Pavel (Paul) Alexandrovich (1772–1817) – a diplomat, like his descendant, and a lieutenant-general serving in the Napoleonic Wars between 1811 and 1815.

Legend has it that when his infantry battalion was stationed in the bleak Siberian wastelands, his chef discovered that their solidly frozen meat ration was easier to cope with when it had been cut up and then stored in thin strips, rather than larger cuts that needed to be thawed properly before they could be cooked. Other ingredients available in the wilderness out there were wild mushrooms and onions, presumably plenty of SALT and as much milk, or cream, as they could squeeze out of the local cows and goats. The recipe for the subsequent creation soon became a family favourite and was popularized by successive Stroganovs, including the younger Count Paul.

Beef stroganoff became fashionable in England when the recipe was first published in Ambrose Heath's *Good Food* in 1932 and it travelled across the water to America when GIs returning after the Second World War took home with them Count Stroganov's dish of sautéed beef, served Siberian-style.

Haggis: A Covert Symbol of Rebellion?

No book about food would be complete without this great Scottish favourite. The original recipe for **haggis** consists of the heart, lungs and liver of a sheep minced with onion, oatmeal and suet, stuffed into the animal's stomach lining and simmered for three hours. And when served with mashed potato and turnips, or tatties and neeps as gastronomes north of the border call them, it becomes the Scottish national dish.

Some believe haggis first arrived in Scotland with the Vikings around AD 800 and that the word itself evolved from the Old Norse *haggva*, which loosely translates as 'to chop up', although the idea of serving an animal's offal wrapped in its stomach lining or intestines was hardly unique to the Vikings or the people they invaded. It's essentially how sausages are made (see BANGERS AND MASH), after all. Nose-to-tail eating was a pragmatic product of the hand-to-mouth existence of life in the past: nothing edible could be wasted. The French have a similar dish, **andouillette**, originally served for the coronation of Louis II at Troyes in September 878, and, delving further back in time, the Romans were known to have made a haggis-like dish of animal intestines stuffed with entrails. There is even a section in Homer's *Odyssey* (*c*.800 BC) comparing its hero, Odysseus, to someone roasting a 'stomach full of fat and blood' over a blazing fire.

There is, however, very little evidence that the offal pudding called haggis is purely Scottish in origin. The first known written recipe for 'hegese', as it was termed, is in a Lancashire cookery book, *Liber Cure Cocorum* ('The Art of Cookery'), dating from around 1430. It was certainly a common English food during the early seventeenth century, as Gervase Markham noted in his 1615 cookbook *The English*

Housewife: 'Oatmeal mixed with blood and the liver of either sheep, calf or swine, makes the pudding called a haggas or haggus, of whose goodness it is in vain to boast because there is hardly to be found a man that does not affect them.'

What is more interesting is why the Scots proudly claim haggis as their national dish: it's linked with their favourite poet, Robert Burns (1759–96). The son of a Scottish farmer, Burns began writing poetry as a teenager. His early works (written in Scottish dialect) were dedicated to various local beauties and his roving eye led to an increasingly bad reputation, which was only compounded when two local girls fell pregnant. The young farm labourer was under great financial stress with no means to support a single family, never mind two. On 27 November 1786, he set out for Edinburgh, with his manuscripts under his arm, principally to find out if he had anything worth publishing.

When his collection was bought and published to great critical acclaim, the young man instantly became part of the Edinburgh social elite, accepting invitations from academics, writers, artists and aristocrats. Consequently Robert Burns's lifestyle varied little until his death at the age of thirty-seven in 1796, still dominated by his preoccupation with women, to whom he dedicated much of his poetry. He also knew how to enjoy a party: his poem 'Auld Lang Syne' is still sung all round the world at midnight on New Year's Eve, despite the fact that only a tiny fraction of those singing it, even in Scotland, have a clue what the words mean. Such is his importance as a poet that the anniversary of his birth is celebrated on 25 January every year by Scots around the world.

The format of Burns Night has become a tradition. The centrepiece consists of a vast haggis that is brought in, to the wailing of bagpipes, and toasted with Scotch whisky by all there, while Burns's 'Address to a Haggis' is read out. It's a comic poem that lists the many virtues of haggis, insisting how wrong so-called sophisticates are to look down on it, as it's the true food of Scotland and properly sustaining, unlike fancy foreign dishes, which would make even a pig sick. But behind the humour is a serious purpose. Burns was writing shortly after the failure of the Jacobite Risings (1688–1746) against the English, who had in punishment stamped down on all things Scottish (the wearing of tartan, for instance, was punishable by seven years in prison). To Burns and his Scottish followers, it was crucial to celebrate all the aspects of Scottish life and culture in case they ceased to exist altogether. Because Burns wrote in a strong dialect that was opaque to non-Scots, his English readers missed the openly rebellious message of 'Address to a Haggis'. Here's a translation of one of the verses:

> But take note of the strong haggis-fed Scot,
> The trembling earth resounds his tread.
> Clasped in his large fist a blade,
> `He'll make it whistle;
> And legs and arms and heads he will cut off,
> Like the tops of thistles.

Note to American readers: ignore what the Scots tell you; haggis is not a small furry animal that lives in the Highlands and has one set of legs that are shorter than the other, enabling it to run nimbly along the steep slopes of the Scottish mountains.

Irish Stew and Its Cousins Across the Sea

Irish stew, celebrated as the national dish of Ireland, should be made just with neck of mutton (mature sheep), potatoes, onions and water, according to purists. In Ireland, only the older sheep were eaten as the younger animals, although more tender, were too useful as a source of milk and wool. For the non-purist, additional ingredients might include carrots, turnips and pearl barley, or, when circumstances were straitened, pretty much anything that came to hand. The genius of the recipe is that its slow cooking (see also KLEFTIKO) is the perfect way to make the tough joints of mutton tasty and delicious. Traditionally, Irish stew would have been cooked for many hours over an open fire. It's status as a national dish, and a filling one at that, has been acknowledged for centuries, as exemplified by these lines from an English broadsheet ballad from around 1800: 'Then hurray for an Irish Stew / That will stick to your belly like glue.'

But Irish stew is not unique. Over the sea, in Britain, various regions have a similar dish. **Scotch broth**, for instance, uses lamb or mutton, pearl barley, carrots and turnips. **Lancashire hotpot** is essentially the same: lamb or mutton and potatoes all cooked together, very slowly, in a large pot. In the port of Liverpool, famous for having many Irish immigrants, a similar dish, called *lapskaus* – the Norwegian word for 'stew' – was imported by Scandinavian sailors during the eighteenth century. The name of the dish was corrupted to 'lobs course', 'lobscouse' and finally **scouse**, the word – like other diet-based national nicknames, such as Limey and Kraut (see SAUERKRAUT) – becoming associated with the good folk of Liverpool. A 'pan of scouse' became a common part of the diet in working-class areas of the city, while **blind scouse** is the version made without meat. Made with lamb or mutton, onions, carrots and as many potatoes as will fit in the pot, the dish is cooked slowly, to tenderize cheap cuts of meat, just like its more celebrated cousin, the traditional Irish stew.

Was Steak Tartare the Original
Food on the Hoof?

Steak tartare is made from minced, ground or finely chopped meat – chiefly beef but also venison and, in some countries, horsemeat. Sometimes it is cut into strips and beaten until flat, then marinated, chilled and served raw, often with an equally raw egg yolk on top. It's most likely that the dish gets its name from **tartare sauce** – made with MAYONNAISE mixed with finely chopped onions, cucumber and capers – served with steak in French restaurants early in the twentieth century. Originally called *steak à l'américaine*, the recipe then evolved into the dish as we know it today.

There is, however, a much more entertaining suggestion for its origin: that the dish comes from the Tartars themselves – the nomadic people of the Central Asian steppes. Renowned horsemen, their name, Tatar or Tartar, derives from the Turkish or Persian *Tätär*, meaning a mounted courier or messenger, although some etymologists maintain that the 'r' was added by the Romans, who associated the savage riders with Tartarus, their name for Hell.

Fiercest among the Tartars was their famed leader, the emperor of all emperors, Genghis Khan (*c.*1167–1227), who invaded and conquered two-thirds of the known world – stretching from the Pacific to the River Volga – with his army of Mongol horsemen. Constantly on the move, his men had to eat on the hoof – quite literally. Famous for staying in their saddles for very long periods as they rode towards yet another land in need of conquering, the Mongols discovered that if they carried their meat ration wedged under their saddles, by the end of the day the toughest piece of steak would be tenderized enough to eat. Sometimes they would chop up and flatten this meat into little patties, which tasted better warm off the horse's flank than if the rider had stopped to build a camp fire to cook his food.

By the time the emperor's grandson, Khublai Khan (1215–94), finally conquered Moscow, they had introduced their tenderized meat rations to the locals, who named it steak Tartar, which, for them, meant 'steak of the violent invaders'. Over the years, chefs from Russia and further afield developed the dish and diners no longer need to ride over rugged terrain for several days with it wrapped around their horses before eating it.

It's a great story, but according to some historians there's no reference to such a practice in medieval records, neither in the Middle or the Far East. Their theory is that the story most likely arose from an existing practice by the Central Asian nomads for putting pieces of meat on their horses' backs. But the reason they did it was to lubricate and soothe their mounts' sores, much as we would put a raw steak on a black eye. Which isn't to say that they wouldn't have eaten it afterwards.

Why Chicken Kiev Rules Supreme

Possibly the most famous chicken recipe in the world, what we know as **chicken Kiev** was originally an Italian dish called *pollo sorpresa*, or 'chicken surprise'. The surprise is the molten garlic butter that jets out of the breadcrumb-covered chicken breast once you stick a fork in it. The French version of this – acknowledging the fact that the whole point of a surprise is that you don't know it's coming – is known as *suprême de volaille*, 'best chicken' (although it can also refer to chicken breast cooked in a rich white sauce). It was the French version that gave the world the taste for the dish, and it was all due to Napoleon (1769–1821). A keen military campaigner, he famously remarked that 'an army marches on its stomach', offering a prize of 12,000 francs to anyone who could devise a method of preserving food to help keep troops on the move. After fourteen or so years of experiment, it was Nicolas Appert (1749–1841) who won the prize, in January 1810, for his technique of preserving food in sealed bottles.

It is said that one of the first foods he managed to preserve in this way was his version of **chicken supreme** and as a result the dish was exported around Europe at a speed never previously known. His book *L'Art de conserver les substances animales et végétales* ('The Art of Preserving Meat and Vegetables') was published the same year, the first cookbook on modern preservation methods. Within ten years, canning had evolved, based on the technique established by Appert, who was known thereafter as the 'father of canning' (see also POTTED SHRIMPS) and his technique as 'appertization'.

But how did chicken supreme became chicken Kiev? According to the Russian food historian William Pokhlebkin – his surname deriving from *pokhlebka*, or 'stew', the underground nickname adopted by his father during the 1917 Revolution – the Russian version of the recipe was invented in the Moscow Merchants' Club in the early twentieth century. This was at a time when Communist Russia rejected everything outside its borders and only Russian names were tolerated. The canny chef at the club renamed the dish chicken Kiev and it became hugely popular as a result. The twentieth century also saw a huge wave of Russian immigrants escaping persecution in their homeland. Many travelled to America and restaurants, particularly on the east coast of America, began to call chicken supreme chicken Kiev to attract new customers familiar with the dish from their native land. It was during the two world wars that the new name would have migrated back to Europe. In 1976, chicken Kiev made history by becoming the first ready meal produced and sold by Marks & Spencer, another step in a different revolution – the conquest of the kitchen by FAST FOOD.

In an ironic footnote to the overall story, despite Nicolas Appert's success in inventing a process directly leading to the mass production of tin cans, it would be nearly fifty years before another inventor came up with the can opener. Now, that's worth thinking about for a moment.

Chicken Marengo: Napoleon's Culinary Good Luck Charm

Chicken Marengo is a popular Italian dish originally created on 14 June 1800 to mark one of the key events in European history. In early 1800, Napoleon was elected First Consul of France, the most powerful position in the new republic. His first act was to cross the Alps and enter Italy, where French troops had previously been driven out by the Austrian army. It was here, as his forces pitched camp on the Marengo plain near the city of Alessandria, that a surprise attack by the Austrians left the French in disarray, although Bonaparte was quick to react, calling in reinforcements and reversing the initiative with a decisive counter-attack, driving the Austrians back and eventually out of Italy altogether.

This famous victory, known as the Battle of Marengo, further enhanced Bonaparte's political and military reputation in Paris and sealed the success of his campaign in Italy. Once the battle was over, legend has it, Napoleon was famished and ordered his Swiss chef, a man called Dunand, to prepare a meal for him. But Dunand had lost his food wagons during the initial surprise advance and had to improvise with ingredients he found in a local village, which is why we have the unusual combination of chicken, crayfish, eggs and TOAST (originally made from the soldiers' bread ration) all on the same plate. The superstitious Napoleon loved the dish so much that he ordered it to be served on the eve of every battle, believing it would bring him luck and a successful outcome. It is not known whether he continued to demand chicken Marengo during his long exile on the Isle of Elba – he may have lost faith in its efficacy by then – although the dish remains a regular feature on European menus to this day.

Bangers and Mash: Exploding Food from the Trenches

No book about the history and origin of food would be complete without the staple English fare of **bangers and mash**. A simple **sausage** and potato dish, it is second only in the hearts and minds of the English people to FISH AND CHIPS (see also HOT DOG). The 'mash' part of the name is easy to work out, but where does 'bangers' come from?

The sausage, one of the oldest types of processed food in history, can be traced back to ancient times. The Greek philosopher and author Epicharmus (540–450 BC), considered to be the first comedy playwright, wrote a comedy called *Orya* ('The Sausage'), with lots of ribald references to its shape, while the epic poet Homer (*c*.850 BC) makes reference to a type of blood sausage in the *Odyssey*. Originally made from offal stuffed into lengths of animal intestine, sausages are a little more sophisticated these days, unless you are a fan of **black pudding** or HAGGIS, both harking back to earlier times. In Britain today, sausages are made from all sorts of meat, including pork, beef, lamb, venison and chicken, and a vast range of herbs and spices. Sometimes meat is omitted altogether, as in the **Glamorgan sausage**, made with cheese and leeks.

British pork sausages, similar to those of France and Italy, began to be mass-produced during the nineteenth century.

The Victorians, sceptical of what was actually in a sausage, nicknamed them 'Little Bags of Mystery', an expression that seems to have evolved around 1850, based on the suspicion that they were filled with horsemeat. Following the outbreak of the First World War in 1914, food shortages and rationing led to a reduction in the amount of meat in a sausage, from whatever animal. Instead producers packed them out with scraps, cereal and water, which caused them to pop and hiss when cooked over an open fire on a shovel in the trenches of northern Europe. As a result, the Tommies nicknamed them 'bangers' and the phrase 'bangers and mash' caught on, already well established by 1919 when soldiers were returning to their old lives.

Faggots: The Perfect Snack for a Burning

Today *faggot* is derogatory American slang for a homosexual, obscuring its far longer-standing use as the name of a popular British dish. A **faggot**, falling somewhere between a sausage and a meatball, is prepared with meat offcuts, chopped up and mixed with offal, breadcrumbs and onions and usually served with gravy.

The word itself derives from a much older one, meaning 'bundle of sticks'. Faggots were standard in size: a 'short' faggot consisted of a two-foot bundle of sticks each three feet long, while the sticks in a 'long' faggot were four feet in length. The word itself comes from Old French *fagot*, deriving in turn from the Greek *phakelos*, from which 'fascism' also originates. Reference to faggots in medieval documents is generally in a rather barbaric context – piled up to burn wrongdoers at the stake. There was even a 'Fire and Faggot Parliament', set up in 1414 during the reign of Henry V in an attempt to curb the Lollards, followers of the reforming theologian John Wycliffe (*c.*1330–84). Campaigning for political and religious freedom and for the Bible to be written in English, the Lollards were seen as heretics and many fell victim to the Parliament's gruesome form of punishment.

It's hard to believe now, but burnings were once the reality TV of the Middle Ages and people would flock in their thousands to see a good execution. Faggots (as in the food) were so called because they were made with scraps or the 'faggot ends' of meat. They also provided a quick and hot refuelling, as faggots did to a fire. At a burning, opportunistic food vendors shouted about the merits of their faggots and the crowds snacked on their own harmless version while waiting for the real ones to be lit. Ironically, it was faggots burning in the oven of a bakery on Pudding Lane that later started the Great Fire of London in 1666.

As time went on, more sophisticated dishes took the urban fancy and faggots were exiled to the countryside: they remain particularly popular in the Black Country, near Birmingham. They came back into favour during the Second World War – when food rationing ensured that no scraps were wasted – and more recently, with the fashion for serving traditional British dishes. But a word of warning: if you are in America and about to order lunch, don't ask for the house faggots. You may be misunderstood.

How Goulash Helped Overthrow Oppression

Ostensibly just another beef stew, **goulash** has more to it than meets the eye, for it turns out to have been both the earliest example of the stock cube and an expression of national identity. The dish can be traced back as far as the ninth century, to the cattle ranchers of the proudly independent Magyar tribes living in the Great Plain of Hungary. Before travelling great distances with their flocks, they would slowly casserole diced meat with onions and spices, cooking it until all the liquid was absorbed and then drying it in the sun before storing it away in bags made from the stomach lining of a sheep. This portable food would then be unpacked at night, popped into a pan of water and boiled up into a soup or stew. In Hungary the dish is called *pörkölt*, and it is still served both as a soup and as a stew, depending on how much water is added: the rest of the world knows it as 'goulash', deriving from the Hungarian word *gulyás*, meaning 'cowboy' or 'cattle herder'.

Goulash remained a peasant dish until the end of the eighteenth century and a rise in national awareness throughout the country. As part of the Austro-Hungarian Empire, Hungary was under the rule of the Austrian Hapsburg emperors, who at that time were intent upon homogenizing their territories. Fearing that their national heritage was under threat, Hungarians eagerly embraced anything that expressed their cultural identity. It became imperative to protect the Hungarian tongue (German had become the national language) and every aspect of the traditional Hungarian way of life, including its gastronomy. Hence goulash became highly fashionable, the dish that had until then been eaten only by herdsmen now served in castles and palaces. Like HAGGIS for the Scots, goulash became a symbol of Hungarian identity in the face of oppression. The dish's growing popularity was helped by the introduction of paprika around this time, a smoky flavouring made from dried red peppers that has become Hungary's signature spice and an essential ingredient of goulash as we know it today.

After the Second World War, Hungary fell again under the control of another oppressive regime, the USSR, and a Stalinist system, political and economic, was imposed upon the country despite growing dissent and protest. In October 1956, a spontaneous revolt took place, starting as a student demonstration and spreading nationwide. The government fell and the revolt continued to spread until the Soviets sent in troops to suppress it. Thousands were arrested, the rebel leader was executed and a puppet government installed. Ten years of severe repression followed but, by 1966, this had gradually given way to attempts at economic reform. It marked the beginning of what is sometimes called **goulash communism**, deriving from the notion that the stew, like the politics of a country, is made up of a mixture of ingredients. In Hungary, goulash communism represented a discreet attempt by the government to introduce elements of capitalism without acknowledging that there had been any deviation from a socialist economy, in the knowledge that any open dissent from the Soviet system would be brutally put down. This gradually paved the way for independence, which was formally declared in 1989. So you can see how having a national dish can be vital for a country's survival, sustaining its people in both a literal and a symbolic way.

How Does Meat Become Jerky?

Developed by the Quechua tribes of the Andes in South America, *charqui* (literally 'dried meat') was a traditional way of curing meat – usually llama, horse or beef – so that it could be stored for long periods, making it an ideal food for travellers. The technique was picked up by European settlers, who would lay thin strips of beef to dry in the sun, or beside a fire, and then use it on their long journeys across the continent. They called it **jerky** and it remains popular to this day, albeit in a highly processed form. The Quechua word also transferred, via the slave trade, to the Caribbean and to Jamaica in particular, where **jerk** describes a traditional way of grilling meat over a hardwood fire – originally on a framework of sticks (see BARBECUE) and now in a steel drum known as a 'jerk pan' – in which meat or fish are rubbed with a special mixture of spices known as **Jamaican jerk spice**.

What is the Difference between Shepherd's and Cottage Pie?

Europe's growing enthusiasm for the potato (see 'The Rise and Fall of the Potato', page 152) and, crucially, its high yield in a small space meant that by the beginning of the eighteenth century every smallholder and peasant was growing their own in whatever bits of land they could find. The combination of 'meat and potatoes', with its perfect balance of protein and carbohydrate, soon became the epitome of a square meal for the working man, so much so that it started to be used figuratively, to mean the fundamental part or basis of something. And that meant that, despite their more primitive cooking arrangements, peasants could now make their own version of the pies that had become such a feature of noble banquets. Instead of the inedible huff paste (see 'A Brief History of the Pie', page 39), however, every bit of these pragmatic dishes was intended to be eaten, including the topping of cooked potato (either mashed or sliced) that replaced the pastry.

The addition of potato also helped eke out the remains of the SUNDAY ROAST for further meals. And once mincing machines became common in the 1870s, ordinary folk, cottagers and shepherds alike, could shred the meat for their potato pies.

COTTAGE PIE

First mentioned in 1791, **cottage pie** is a simple minced-beef dish bulked out with onions and other vegetables. The cottagers themselves were farm labourers who survived on a basic diet of potatoes and whatever scraps and offcuts they could salvage from previous meals. The name may well have emerged as a joking reference to the roofs of rural cottages: the top layer of potato browned in the oven giving the pie its own thatched roof, as it were. In a similar way, COTTAGE CHEESE was so called because it, too, was made by farm labourers in their homes, using any milk left over after making butter and as a speedy and cheap alternative to hard cheese.

SHEPHERD'S PIE

A later version, made, as the name suggests, with lamb instead of beef, is **shepherd's pie**. Not mentioned until the 1870s, the dish would have evolved in exactly the same way, chiefly in the north of England and in Scotland, where sheep provided the main source of income for highland farmers. Minced lamb and potatoes were cheap and readily available, becoming the staple diet of land workers in these areas.

Both names have since been used almost interchangeably, regardless of whether the principal ingredient is beef or lamb, although many British cooks insist on differentiating between them. In America, cottage pie is now called for obvious reasons **cowboy's pie**. Canada and Australia appear to be less fussy (perhaps due to the decided lack of thatched cottages), happy to go with 'shepherd's pie' for both dishes.

12
Indian Takeaway

Exploring for Peppercorns and Discovering Chillies

How Indian Cuisine Conquered Britain:
The Story of Curry

A Drink that Can Knock You Out

Pick Up a Poppadom

Vindaloo: A Portuguese Dish in Indian Guise

What is Birmingham's Contribution
to World Cuisine?

Coronation Chicken and Its
Distinguished Predecessors

Kedgeree: From Humble Staple to Breakfast Classic

Chutney: Essential Accompaniment
to an Indian Meal

Tale of the Raj: The Invention of
Mulligatawny Soup

Bombay Duck and Fishy Goings-on in Officialdom

'A chilli,' said Rebecca, gasping. 'Oh, yes!' She thought a chilli was something cool, as its name imported, and was served with some. 'How fresh and green they look,' she said, and put one into her mouth. It was hotter than the curry; flesh and blood could bear it no longer. She laid down her fork. 'Water, for Heaven's sake, water!' she cried.

WILLIAM MAKEPEACE THACKERAY, *Vanity Fair*

Exploring for Peppercorns and
Discovering Chillies

In medieval Europe BLACK PEPPER was the king of the spices, essential to cooking and used by the rich and privileged. Pepper was always expensive but when the Ottomans captured Constantinople in 1453, the easiest trade route to the East was blocked and its price began to spiral out of control, going up by 400 per cent between 1496 and 1505 alone. Hence it became imperative to find a new route to the East, in particular India and the Spice Islands. Christopher Columbus (c.1451–1506) decided to take a different approach: when he set sail in 1492, he was convinced that if he simply kept heading west he would find a new source of pepper and a passage to the East. This was based, of course, on the notion that the world is round, an untested theory at the time. Perceived wisdom of the day insisted the earth was flat, and people waited confidently for news that Columbus had sailed off the edge and into infinity. To many of his sailors such a fate was, quite literally, just over the horizon.

Landing in the islands of the Caribbean, he was convinced that he had reached the East by going the other way round the globe, especially when he noticed how the inhabitants ate their food very heavily seasoned with hot spices. In particular they used a vegetable they called *ají*. This was the first time a European had come across a **chilli pepper**. Columbus was so sure that this was a type of the pepper that he and the backers of his voyage were so keen to find (he had no idea what kind of plant he was looking for, after all) that he named it 'pepper of the Indies'. Although he had actually discovered both chillies and America, Columbus remained sure until the end of his life that he had succeeded in his original aims. And that's why the chilli has been called a pepper ever since. America, on the other hand, wasn't named after its reluctant discoverer but another explorer, Amerigo Vespucci (1454–1512), who was the first to identify the New World of North and South America and realize it wasn't Asia after all.

A few years later, the Portuguese explorer Vasco da Gama (*c.*1460/1469–1524) discovered the elusive route to India; the Portuguese (see VINDALOO) promptly seized control of the pepper trade and became the richest nation in the world. They also introduced the chilli pepper to India in return, and within thirty years at least three different types were growing along the Malabar Coast (today's Goa and Kerala). The Indians then started exporting the dried spice to Europe in such vast quantities that within a few years it was believed to have originated in India.

How Indian Cuisine Conquered Britain: The Story of Curry

Britain's oldest cookbook, dating back to the fourteenth century and the kitchens of Richard II, is called *The Forme of Cury* and its recipes include all kinds of spices from the East, such as nutmeg, cardamom, ginger and BLACK PEPPER. But two centuries before Vasco da Gama found a safe sea route to India (see CHILLI PEPPER), 'cury' didn't relate to spices but was merely the Middle English word for cooking. The word we know comes from India and is derived from the Tamil *kari*, meaning a sauce or relish for rice. Its first appearance in print was in a seventeenth-century Portuguese cookery book, which included a recipe for *karil*, a dish very similar to what we would recognize today as **curry**. The fact that the foreign term has been adopted so completely that it has blotted out the memory of the older word is a vivid indication of how important curry has become in Western cuisine.

Legends abound when it comes to explaining how the squeamish Brits developed a taste for this exotic dish. One that tries to grab the word back for the British recounts the tale of a nineteenth-century soldier, Sir George Curry, who served with the East India Company before becoming a general in the Indian army. Curry, we are told, was the first Briton to develop a liking for the highly spiced local food and tried, on several occasions, to introduce it to the English foot soldiers under his command, causing widespread revolt and mutiny. Starved into submission, the men eventually caved in, however, and then found they had developed quite a liking for it.

Yet as *The Forme of Cury* shows, the British have always had a predilection for highly spiced food. And in the days before the tin can (see CHICKEN KIEV and POTTED SHRIMPS), when the only food remaining from home would be weevil-ridden SHIP'S BISCUIT, soldiers would have had no choice but to eat locally. Meanwhile, as the influence of the British in India grew, so did the interest in Indian food back in Britain, leading to the publishing of recipes and the commercial creation of curry powder in 1780. In fact the recipe that turned into WORCESTERSHIRE SAUCE consisted of a curry powder added to vinegar. The first appearance of curry on a menu was in 1773, while the first establishment dedicated to Indian cuisine was the Hindostanee Coffee House at 34 George Street, London, set up in 1809.

Indian cuisine as we know it today is actually a ragbag of different culinary styles – an amalgam of the most appealing aspects of the cuisines of successive waves of invaders and traders to the Indian subcontinent. The Mongolians brought their hotpot cooking (see BALTI) and Chinese traders introduced the stir-frying and the sweet-and-sour sauces that feature in many curries. From the Persians (the Mughals) came rich creamy **korma**, with dried fruit and nuts. The **biryani** (literally, 'fried food'), consisting of rice and meat layered together, is also a Persian-derived dish. While the **tandoori** – from tandoor, the traditional clay oven used for cooking the food in – came originally from the Middle East. Its name derives from the Babylonian word *tinuru*, meaning 'fire'; Hebrew and Arabic then made it *tannur*, evolving into *tandur* in Turkey and Central Asia, and *tandoor* in India and Pakistan.

Europeans trading with India took home many spices, along with lavish fabrics and precious stones, but they exchanged other items in return. Through these traders, potatoes, chillies and tomatoes were introduced to the subcontinent. Although some Indians were initially suspicious of tomatoes (see also GAZPACHO), seeing them as bloodlike, they were soon adopted into the nation's cuisine. Some aspects of European cooking were also incorporated (see VINDALOO). The British contributed the least of all to Indian cuisine, although they did make KETCHUP, soup (MULLIGATAWNY) and milky TEA (*chai*) very popular throughout the subcontinent. It was the Indian invasion of British cuisine that had the most resounding impact, turning curry into a national dish.

A Drink that Can Knock You Out

Punch, beloved of parties and PICNICS (not to mention carol singers – see WASSAIL), is a drink to be avoided at all costs. Some hosts seem to regard it as their duty to make it using the strongest alcohol available. A big mistake, as it usually ends up tasting like it should be poured into the engine of a rusty tractor. Punch feels like a British drink through and through, but it's not. During the early 1600s, as English explorers first made their way to the Indian subcontinent, one of their discoveries was a popular local drink consisting of five different ingredients: water, fruit juice, spirits, sugar and spices. The Hindi word for five is *panch* – from the Persian *panj*, from which the English numeral '5' is also derived – and this is how the drink became known when it was served back in England at social gatherings. Unfortunately, in my experience, some people seem to delight in including paint stripper, paraffin and white spirit, which is not the idea at all.

Pick Up a Poppadom

Hobson-Jobson (the opinionated Anglo-Indian dictionary originally published in 1886 and updated in 1903 – see the box on page 318) describes the **poppadom** as 'a kind of thin scone or wafer, made of any kind of pulse or lentil flour, seasoned with asafoetida and fried in oil, and in West India baked crisp, and often eaten at European tables as an accompaniment to curry'. To which it adds: 'It is not bad, even to a novice.' In the West poppadoms tend to be eaten as an appetizer with CHUTNEYS and drinks, while in India they are served with the main meal. The word – rendered in many different ways, including **pappadum**, **appalum** and **papad** – derives from the Tamil (south Indian) *paruppu*, 'lentil', and *atam*, a cooked cake. Each region of India has its own variety, some plain and others highly spiced. Sometimes bicarbonate of soda is added, ensuring that when fried a poppadom bubbles up and pops, leading to its nickname of 'popper' and 'popper cake' (see also BANGERS AND MASH for explosive food of another kind). In India they have fun with the word too, which features in a popular Hindi tongue twister: '*Kachaa paapad, pakaa papad*' ('Raw papad, fried/roasted papad').

Vindaloo: A Portuguese Dish in Indian Guise

In Britain a **vindaloo** is assumed to be the very hottest curry and often ordered after closing time by the lagered-up as a trial of strength usually sorely regretted the following morning. The recipe for proper vindaloo comes from Goa, on the west coast of India. The correct spelling of its name, *vindalho*, gives away the ingredients of the main dish, once a Portuguese pork casserole (*carne de vinha d'alhos*), seasoned with *alhos* ('garlic') and *vinho* ('wine'), the latter acting as a preservative that allowed the stew to be eaten over several days. The type of meat shows the strength of the Portuguese influence, as the eating of pork is against both the Hindu and Muslim religions.

The earliest Portuguese settlers in Goa became infamous among fellow European visitors for the degree to which they had become assimilated: they observed many of the same customs and wore the same light clothes as the Goans, bathed at least once a day, a habit not practised by Europeans at the time, married locally and happily ate the local food. Their enduring gift to their colony was the CHILLI PEPPER (seen as a botanical oddity in Portugal), which was soon growing everywhere and was added by the locals in copious amounts to their food and especially to their interpretation of Portuguese pork stew, so much so that the dish soon became almost unrecognizable – as integrated into Goan cuisine as the Portuguese settlers had become integrated into Goa.

To butter someone up is to flatter them with the aim of gaining something to your advantage. Some suggest the expression derives from the smooth way butter spreads on to bread, to make it more palatable. And it seems a perfectly plausible explanation, until you visit the Hindu temple in Madurai, Tamil Nadu, that is, supposedly the largest temple in the world. Here guides speak of the ancient custom of throwing butterballs of ghee (the clarified butter used as the basis of all Indian cooking) at statues of the gods, a method of seeking favour termed 'buttering up the gods'. Another custom, Buddhist this time, may also contribute to the origin of the phrase. During celebrations for the Tibetan New Year, the lamas at all the monasteries create sculptures or 'butter flowers' out of coloured butter. These are then traditionally displayed on the fifteenth day of the Tibetan lunar year following a religious ceremony the previous evening. The tradition of creating butter sculptures, presented as offerings to statues of the Buddha, can be traced to the Tang Dynasty (AD 618–907) and the belief that such offerings would bring peace and happiness for the full lunar year. This tradition was known as ***buttering up the Buddha***. (For more on the Buddha and food, see PORRIDGE.)

What is Birmingham's Contribution to World Cuisine?

The **balti** is proudly assumed to be a CURRY that was invented in the UK. It is in fact surprisingly modern, in the sense that there was no such thing as a 'balti' prior to the 1980s.

Now one of the most popular curry dishes in the world, balti incorporates a particular, regional style of cooking unknown in Europe until only a few decades ago when a couple of young immigrants from Baltistan – an area in northern Kashmir on the border between China and India – opened their first restaurant in Birmingham, England. Using techniques they had learned from home, they created a new type of curry, calling it balti both after their home region and the metal cooking pot used by every mother and housewife in Baltistan. Known also as a karahi, the balti pan is a heavy, round-bottomed, wok-like dish with two handles. The curry is both cooked and served in it, turning former expediency, in which your cooking pot by necessity doubled up as your plate, into an exotic restaurant prop. (And as *balti* is also the Hindi word for 'bucket', the pan's uses probably didn't stop there.) It's a rough-and-ready peasant-style meal, the Kasmiri equivalent of IRISH STEW or GOULASH. Traditionally, it is also eaten without rice or cutlery: naan bread is used to scoop up the food, using the right hand only. The first balti restaurants were basic workers' cafés, where the lack of fancy side orders and washing up made them much easier to run, and within ten years almost every Indian restaurant in Britain was offering their own increasingly sophisticated version of the dish.

Pat Chapman in his fascinating book on the balti, *Curry Club Balti Curry Cookbook* (1997), points out that its origins are wide-ranging and owe as much to Tibet and China – with its wok-like pot and slight resemblance to the spicy cooking of Szechuan – as to Kashmir, with its aromatic spices and taste of Persia and the Mughal emperors. Balti cooking retains these traditional elements while also encompassing other popular styles of curry never heard of in Baltistan. Hence the diners at a Birmingham balti house have about as much in common with a Balti or Pashtun tribesman as an alien from outer space. Indeed, many of the balti-house owners and staff are probably no more likely to have been to Baltistan than their customers.

Coronation Chicken and
Its Distinguished Predecessors

This is a dish that has very little to do with India but a lot to do with the English determination to tame CURRY. The combination of cold chicken with MAYONNAISE, curry powder and apricots, otherwise known as **coronation chicken**, was suggested by society florist Constance Spry and created by Rosemary Hume for Elizabeth II's coronation banquet in 1953. The pair, who ran the Domestic Science School in London, had been invited to create a special dish for a coronation luncheon attended by all the Commonwealth heads of state – not an easy task when your kitchen is over thirty miles from the dining room and you have over 350 world leaders to cater for.

But Rosemary Hume was equal to the challenge and served a spicy chicken salad, which earned the praise of the great and the good from around the globe. Commoners like you and me were also enjoying the dish as the recipe for it had been published in the national newspapers a week earlier. Yet it appears not to have been an original recipe after all but based on an earlier dish, albeit with equally grand credentials. Served for the Silver Jubilee celebrations of Queen Elizabeth's grandfather King George V in 1935, this was called, somewhat unsurprisingly, **jubilee chicken**.

And it doesn't stop there. Further investigation reveals that a niece of Rosemary Hume, Griselda Barton, once confirmed that her aunt had been inspired by a recipe from Mrs de Salis's *Savouries à la mode*, published in 1903 and containing a recipe for chicken with curry and apricot butter. This was apparently a favourite sandwich filling of Queen Adelaide, wife of William IV, who reigned between 1830 and 1837, making this antecedent of the two later dishes at least a hundred years old by the time of George V's jubilee.

Kedgeree: From Humble Staple to Breakfast Classic

A traditional dish of rice and lentils or rice and beans, *kitchari* (meaning a mixture, usually of two grains) can be traced back to the early fourteenth century, when it was a staple part of the Indian diet. Brought back to England by returning British colonials, the dish evolved into something much more lavish, including flaked fish (usually smoked haddock), hard-boiled eggs, parsley and curry powder. Served for breakfast (often as part of the FULL ENGLISH BREAKFAST), it might use fish and rice left over from a meal the day before. In other words, **kedgeree**, the classic of the Victorian breakfast BUFFET, is little more than Indian BUBBLE AND SQUEAK – not that there is anything wrong with that.

Chutney: Essential Accompaniment to an Indian Meal

No Indian meal would be complete without **chutney**, lime and mango being the most popular varieties. Boiled-down fruits preserved with vinegar and sugar and mixed with spices have been popular in India for centuries, and by the beginning of the sixteenth century, as European explorers opened up trade with India (see CHILLI PEPPER), these exotic preserves were being imported to northern Europe as luxury goods. The Hindu word for these spicy accompaniments to a main dish is *catni*, pronounced 'chat-ni', which serves as the root for the word we use today when asking for something in which to dip our POPPADOMS.

Tale of the Raj: The Invention of Mulligatawny Soup

One food that is not a traditional Indian favourite is soup. Although not an authentic Indian dish, **mulligatawny** stands as a vivid reminder of the days the British got their feet under the table in the Indian subcontinent. And it was all due to trade.

Initially dealing in spices, cotton and opium, the East India Company rapidly became so successful that it had to protect its trade routes and personnel with private militias. It even bought territory in India to give itself a base in the part of the world where it conducted most of its business. At the time, India was made up of many states and kingdoms and Company employees soon found themselves getting involved in local politics. With uprisings and power struggles all over the land, it was left to them to restore order and protect their business interests. Under the leadership of Robert Clive (1725–74), rebellions were crushed and great battles were won, including those at Calcutta (of Black Hole fame) in February 1757 and at Plessey four months later. As a result, the East India Company came to rule whole swathes of India, exercising military power and assuming administrative functions, to the exclusion, gradually, of its commercial pursuits. Eventually Queen Victoria's government absorbed the Company and India became an official part of the British Empire.

With Britain now controlling much of the country under the banner of the British Raj (deriving from the Hindi word *raj*, meaning 'reign'), order was re-established and law enforced using a new court system. As British expatriates integrated into the Indian way of life, an Anglo-Indian society began to form, with both cultures adapting to each other, absorbing each other's customs. Mulligatawny arose out of this as an ingenious adaptation necessitated by the British requirement for soup as a separate first course, a concept previously unknown in India. Its name a corruption of the Tamil *milagu-tannir* 'pepper-water', the spicy meat soup became so popular with the British stationed there that officials in the Madras Presidency were nicknamed 'mulls' after it. (Likewise, officials in Bombay were called 'ducks' – see BOMBAY DUCK.) Mulligatawny was introduced to the British by Eliza Acton through her recipe book *Modern Cookery for Private Families*, first published in 1845, and has remained one of the most popular soups across the Commonwealth ever since.

Bombay Duck and Fishy Goings-on in Officialdom

Many cuisines rely heavily on small, strong-tasting preserved fish to add flavour to their meals. In the West we tend to salt these (anchovies) or to putrefy them into a sauce (see WORCESTERSHIRE SAUCE), but while fish sauce is an integral part of Far Eastern cooking, it's never taken on in India. Their favourite fishy flavouring is called **Bombay duck**, which, somewhat contrarily, isn't a duck but a lizardfish. Known in India as a bummalo or bombil, this small fish is caught in great numbers along the west coast of India. Once dried and preserved, it remains edible for a very long time and is commonly used in CURRY or prepared as a pickle. It is also notorious for its extremely pungent smell once it has been dried – not that this deters aficionados (if you'll excuse the pun), who regard it as a delicacy.

But where does it get its name from? According to one story, it was coined by the celebrated Clive of India (1725–74) after trying some (and promptly spitting it out) during his conquest of Bengal. Meanwhile, another theory suggests that the train compartments of the *Bombay Dak* (in English, the *Bombay Mail*) were so packed with the strong-smelling delicacy – commonly transported by rail during the British Raj – that British expats began to refer to the peculiar smell of their newspapers and letters as 'Bombay Dak', a name which then transferred to the fish itself.

By 1997, imports of the fish to Britain had reached no less than twelve tonnes per year before the European Commission, in their infinite wisdom, banned the product on the grounds that it was not produced in the EC-approved canning and freezing facilities. This was despite their admission that they had no evidence against Bombay duck, nor was there any record of bacterial contamination or cases of food poisoning associated with the fish. This caused a furious backlash and a 'Save the Bombay Duck' campaign, leading to the Indian High Commission approaching the EC and pointing out that the very essence of Bombay duck was to be dried in the open air, not frozen. Eventually regulations were relaxed and the fish only had to be packed in an EC-approved factory; it could still be dried in the traditional way. Soon a Birmingham wholesaler discovered a packing source in Mumbai and Bombay duck was once again back on the menu all over Britain. That's a relief because, with feelings running so high, things could have become nasty.

13
Italian Takeaway

From Marco Polo to Spaghetti Trees:
The Origins of Pasta

Bolognese: The Sauce or the School of Art?

Carbonara: A Very Revolutionary Pasta Sauce

Pesto: A Sauce Made with Elbow Grease

How Fettuccine Alfredo Became a Star Turn

Pizza: How a Dish from Naples
Conquered the World

The trouble with eating Italian food is that two or three days later you're hungry again.

GEORGE MILLER

From Marco Polo to Spaghetti Trees: The Origins of Pasta

One of the great food myths is that when Marco Polo returned from the court of Kublai Khan in 1295, he brought **pasta** back to Italy with him. But the Italians had been eating it long before that: a list of the possessions of a dead man, Ponzio Bastone, drawn up in 1279, includes 'a basket of dried macaroni', indicating that pasta was already a well-established and valued foodstuff years before Marco Polo returned from his epic journey to the East. While many cultures have since antiquity eaten some sort of noodle-like food composed of grain, pasta is made from a particular type of wheat – durum wheat semolina, with a high gluten content – which was unknown in China, where noodles were traditionally made using millet or rice. Another distinguishing feature of pasta is its malleability, which has resulted in the extraordinary range of shapes and sizes that characterize this food.

The truth is that it's difficult to pinpoint when and where pasta was invented. For a start, the name – meaning 'dough' and akin to our word 'paste' – has only been in common use since the end of the Second World War. Before that, it would have been known by the names of individual types of pasta rather than this generic term, but they all were forms of the same thing. And it goes back a long way. Alan Davidson, in *The Penguin Companion to Food* (2002), describes an Etruscan relief from 400 BC that shows a set of perfect pasta-making tools. The Romans had their own kind of pasta dish (see LASAGNE for more on this) and a text of 1154 describes people in Palermo, Sicily – where durum wheat, the basic ingredient of modern pasta, had been introduced by the Arabs in the seventh century – making strings of dough that they were already exporting all round the world. By 1351, Boccaccio was writing in the *Decameron* of a fantastical mythical land whose inhabitants rolled macaroni down mountains made of grated cheese. And by the sixteenth century, thanks to Catherine de Médicis and her introduction of Italian cooking to France (see EGGS FLORENTINE and 'From Fine Sauces to Haute Cuisine', page 185), pasta began to catch on throughout Europe.

Pasta has been integral to Italy's national identity ever since. When Mussolini's enemies rumoured that he was planning to ban the consumption of pasta because he felt it was responsible for the low state of the Italian people, there were riots and protests. (The reverse was true, in fact: Mussolini regarded it as so important that he wanted to dedicate more land to growing wheat and turn Italy into a self-sufficient producer.) The only outspoken critics of pasta were the Futurists, the artistic movement of the early twentieth century that despised tradition of any kind, including Italy's national dish, which it denounced as 'a symbol of oppressive dullness, plodding deliberation and fat-bellied conceit'. Somewhat unsurprisingly, the movement didn't last long – its supporters would have been too hungry to keep it going.

There are more than six hundred different types of pasta, in every conceivable shape and with exotic names to match. Here's a little more on the six most interesting varieties:

SPAGHETTI

Spaghetti (see also SPAGHETTI BOLOGNESE) is thought to account for over two-thirds of the annual pasta consumption around the world, although it only became popular during the late nineteenth century when the introduction of factories with powerful extrusion presses meant that it could be mass-produced. Prior to this, it would have been made by hand, a time-consuming and complicated process. The word *spaghetti* translates as 'thin strings'. Hence when Galileo Galilei (1564–1642) wrote that he had 'attached two balls to spaghetti' for one of his experiments, this didn't necessarily mean he had been playing with his food. The Italians only started associating the word with thin strips of pasta in the early nineteenth century; it's first recorded use is from 1836, and it would be another fifty years before it became common parlance elsewhere in Europe. Since then, spaghetti's profile has risen so high that it is regarded as the defining type of pasta and, aside from PIZZA, the food most associated with Italy. So much so that, during the 1960s, Americans even began calling their low-budget cowboy films – produced and directed by Italians and shot in Spain or Italy – *spaghetti westerns*.

Spaghetti didn't take off in Britain until the latter half of the twentieth century. Indeed, it was still uncommon as recently as 1957, when the BBC were famously able to convince the public that it was grown on spaghetti trees. Richard Dimbleby's so-called documentary had viewers convinced to such an extent that many were inquiring where they could buy their own spaghetti bush. That is until the BBC pointed out the date of their broadcast, 1 April, and people realized they had been subjected to what is now considered one of the great April Fools' Day pranks of all time.

VERMICELLI

Vermicelli, essentially extra-fine spaghetti, is most notable for the meaning of its name: 'little worms'. An even thinner type is called **capelli d'angelo**, which translates as 'angel's hair'. A recipe for vermicelli first appeared in a very specialized cookbook, *De arte coquinaria per vermicelli e maccaroni siciliani* ('The Art of Cooking Sicilian Vermicelli and Macaroni'), written in the fifteenth century by Martino da Como, highly respected for his culinary knowledge and possibly the world's first 'celebrity' chef.

RAVIOLI AND TORTELLINI

Consisting of a filling between two thin layers of pasta, **ravioli** were first mentioned in the fourteenth century, in the writings of Francesco di Marco, a merchant of Prato, and in *The Forme of Cury* (see CURRY), where they appear as 'rauioles'. But the type of stuffed pasta that has most caught the Italian imagination is **tortellini** (from *tortello*, 'small cake'). Originating from the Italian towns of Bologna and Modena, the foodstuff has a number of legends explaining how it was invented. According to one of these, Lucrezia Borgia (1480–1519), the FLORENTINE beauty and infamous poisoner, was staying at a small inn in Modena. The innkeeper was so captivated by her that he couldn't resist the urge to peek into her room through the keyhole, to try and see her naked. But from his vantage point and in the dim candlelight, he could only make out her navel. Even so, according to the story, this was enough to send him into an ecstasy that inspired him to create tortellini – with its distinctive umbilical shape – that very evening. A more widely accepted explanation is that tortellini is based on the shape of a turtle, in an attempt to replicate the famous symbol of Modena, many of whose buildings bear the turtle motif.

MACARONI

Macaroni, a tubular form of pasta, was probably one of the first pastas to be made. While its name is believed by some etymologists to derive from the Italian *ammaccare*, meaning 'to crush', the *Oxford English Dictionary* suggests that it comes from the Greek *makaria*, 'food made from barley', which is also the root of 'macaroon' (although, as its chief ingredient is ground almonds, that might seem to point to the first derivation). Macaroni was so popular in former times that its name was used as a generic term for pasta. In England during the eighteenth century, the word was also used as a pejorative term for a fop or dandy – typically, fashionable young men who had been to Italy on the Grand Tour and returned full of continental affectation in their speech and dress. The item most associated with the *macaroni* was an immensely tall white wig whose powdered curls might be thought to resemble tubular pasta.

LASAGNE

The oldest pasta of all is **lasagne**. It's suggested that the word may derive from the Roman *lasanum*, meaning a cooking pot, a term that was subsequently applied to the dish. Or that it might come from the Greek *laganon* (*lagana* in the plural), a flat sheet of pasta cut into strips. Indeed, Horace, writing in the first century BC, talks of *lagana*, fine sheets of dough that were fried and consumed as an everyday food. Likewise, an early cookbook, from the fifth century, describes a dish called *lagana* that consisted of layers of dough with meat stuffing and which could perhaps be the ancestor of the modern dish. It certainly seems to have been established by the thirteenth century: Marco Polo, in his writings on the Orient, mentions eating a 'lasagne' made using flour from the breadfruit, implying that he was already familiar with the more conventional version of the dish, made from wheat flour.

The first cookbook to appear in print – Platina's *De honesta voluptate et valetudine* ('On honourable pleasure and health'), published in 1474 – gives the instruction that a certain type of PASTA should be cooked for the amount of time it takes to say three paternosters. That is a remarkably short time even for fresh pasta and shows how, even then, the Italians preferred their pasta chewy or **al dente**. In Italian this means 'to the tooth' or 'to the bite', indicating that the cook should pop a piece of the pasta in their mouth and, if it still offers some resistance when bitten, then it is cooked to perfection. Leave it in the pan much longer and it will become overly soft and lose its texture. Leave it in for too short a time and it will stick to the teeth when chewed; not so much 'to the tooth' as 'on the tooth' and definitely undercooked.

Bolognese: The Sauce or the School of Art?

Ask anybody in the little town of Bologna about **spaghetti bolognese** and they will insist there is no such thing. Ironically enough, they much prefer tagliatelli or LASAGNE. However, to the rest of the pasta-loving world the 'sauce from Bologna' (bolognese) – typically made with minced beef and chopped vegetables in a TOMATO SAUCE (although authentic recipes use stock and wine and no tomato) – is famously mixed with SPAGHETTI and sprinkled with PARMESAN CHEESE. In

Bologna, they call the sauce *ragù alla bolognese*, *ragù* coming from the French word *ragoût*, meaning 'stew'.

The people of Bologna themselves are far prouder of the Bolognese Artists, a group of painters who emerged from the Bologna School of Painting and who so dominated the cultural scene from 1582 until 1700 that Bologna rivalled Rome and Florence as the centre of the Italian arts. Consisting of Annibale Carracci, his brother Agostino and their cousin Ludovico, the Carracci, as they were collectively known, led the group of painters into what became known as the great century of Bolognese painting. The talent the Carracci fostered around the world through their tuition has secured their place in history, although I imagine most people will be more familiar with the town's spaghetti sauce than they are with its painters.

Carbonara: A Very Revolutionary Pasta Sauce

Second only to SPAGHETTI BOLOGNESE, **spaghetti carbonara** – the sauce made with BACON, eggs, garlic and BLACK PEPPER – must be one of the most popular pasta dishes of them all. The name *carbonara* derives from the Italian word for 'charcoal', which has led to the theory that the dish was first devised as a hearty meal for the charcoal burners working in the forests around Rome. An alternative suggestion is that the copious amounts of black pepper added to the dish look like flakes of charcoal, and hence the name.

There is a more interesting theory, however, one that also revolves around the connection with charcoal. The Carbonari (literally 'charcoal men') were a group of freedom fighters who formed a secret society in Naples around 1808 with the sole intention of overthrowing the foreign government imposed by Napoleon in 1805, when the upstart Frenchman declared himself King of Italy. Using coded language based on the occupation of charcoal burning, they would meet in forest huts that they called 'places of selling charcoal', while many of their rituals were drawn from the Freemasons of Italy and France. After Napoleon's final defeat at Waterloo in 1815, Austria once again became the dominant power in Italy, successfully crushing uprisings by leading members of the Carbonari, notably in 1821 and 1831.

Carbonari members Giuseppe Mazzini (1805–72) and Garibaldi (see GARIBALDI BISCUIT) fought both political and military campaigns throughout their lives and are remembered as the leading figures of the Italian Risorgimento (resurgence), a movement intent upon Italian unification. It was Mazzini who, in 1831, believing the Carbonaris' influence to be waning, formed a new secret society, La Giovine Italia (Young Italy), which rose to become the most significant revolutionary group in Europe, paving the way for the unification of Italy in 1861.

There is, however, no record of the Carbonaris' preferred sauce for pasta, or whether it was made using bacon and eggs. Indeed, there is no record of the dish until after the Second World War, when it was taken back to America by troops stationed in Italy, leading to *spaghetti alla carbonara* becoming hugely popular in the States. Some say that it was the soldiers themselves who invented the dish, handing over their ration of bacon and eggs to local Italian chefs, who transformed the ingredients into the famous sauce.

Pesto: A Sauce Made with Elbow Grease

Originating in Genoa and typically consisting of a mixture of basil, garlic, pine nuts, grated cheese and olive oil, **pesto** is most commonly served with pasta. The derivation of the word, from the Italian *pestare*, 'to crush' or 'to pound', reveals how the dish is prepared: by grinding the ingredients together, traditionally using a pestle and mortar. Interestingly, 'pestle' has a similar root, from the Old French *pestel*, taken in turn from the Latin *pistillum*, which derives from *pinsere*, 'to pound'. It shares this derivation with **pistou**, the Provençal version of pesto, made in the same way and using all the same ingredients except pine nuts. The earliest reference to a dish resembling pesto (or pistou) can be found in Roman textbooks and a cheese spread called *moretum*, to which basil would have been added following the Roman conquest of north Africa, where the herb is believed to have originated. Now, of course, no Italian dish would be complete without a scattering of fresh basil leaves.

How Fettuccine Alfredo Became a Star Turn

This dish, of **fettuccine** tossed with PARMESAN CHEESE and butter, is said to have been created in 1914 by Alfredo di Lelio at his restaurant, Alfredo alla Scrofa, in Rome. He made it for his pregnant wife who was suffering badly from morning sickness and finding it difficult to keep most things down. In America chefs also add prawns, garlic and green vegetables (high in folic acid, incidentally), such as broccoli or parsley. **Fettuccine Alfredo** soon became the restaurant's signature dish and popular with American tourists after the First World War.

Di Lelio's restaurant became world famous in 1927 when Douglas Fairbanks, the most recognized film star on the planet at the time, booked a table while on honeymoon with Mary Pickford. The restaurateur made such a performance of serving his fettuccini Alfredo to the couple that they fell in love with it. To show their appreciation, Fairbanks returned the following day with a golden spoon and fork, which he presented to the restaurant, along with a framed photograph of themselves that di Lelio proudly hung on the wall. On returning to America, Fairbanks and Pickford served the dish whenever they held a dinner party, and news of the recipe soon spread between the chefs of Hollywood and beyond.

Pizza: How a Dish from Naples Conquered the World

Pizza, the signature Italian dish that is a favourite in just about every country in the world, wasn't actually invented in Italy. The ancestor of the modern dish was created thousands of years ago by the ancient Greeks and Persians. It is said that soldiers of the Persian king Darius I (521–486 BC) baked a type of flatbread – in an improvised oven made by placing their shields over their camp fires – which they covered with cheese and dates. The ancient Greeks, meanwhile, served a similar type of bread, which they covered with cheese, herbs and olive oil. Indeed, it is thought that there could be an etymological connection between the Greek **pitta** and the Italian 'pizza', which is believed to have evolved from the Old German *pizzo*, meaning 'to bite'. The first recorded use of the word was in AD 997 in a Latin text from Gaeta, a southern Italian port near Naples, which has remained the home of the pizza ever since.

Pizza was a cheap and filling way to eke out the contents of a bare larder and the people of Naples were famously poverty-stricken. In 1830, the French writer and food expert Alexandre Dumas, père (1802–70), wrote how the Neapolitan poor subsisted on pizza during the winter and that it was typically flavoured with 'oil, lard, tallow, cheese, tomato or anchovies'. Today, pizzas are topped with a wide range of ingredients – including spicy meats from India and the Far East and, for the more adventurous, kangaroo and crocodile from Down Under – although the Neapolitan style still predominates. Here are four modern favourites:

MARINARA

Topped with tomato, oregano, garlic and olive oil, **marinara** is the oldest and most basic type of Neapolitan pizza. The full name – *pizza alla marinara*, or 'sailor-style pizza' – reflects its seafaring origins. This was a dish that might well have been prepared by *la marinara*, the sailor's wife, for her husband, either to sustain him on a sea voyage or to feed him on his return. These days some chefs interpret the name to mean a sauce or topping containing seafood, but that does not reflect the original, authentic version of the dish.

MARGHERITA

Another type of Neapolitan pizza, made with a topping of tomato, mozzarella, basil and olive oil, links an Italian queen with the country's poorest city. Margherita Maria Theresa Giovanna of Savoy, born in Turin on 20 November 1851, was the daughter of Ferdinand, Duke of Genoa, and his wife, Elizabeth of Saxony. With such a privileged background, it is hardly surprising that Margherita's future was planned long in advance, and on 21 April 1868, aged just sixteen, she was married to Umberto, the heir to the Italian throne. Margherita became queen in 1878 when Umberto succeeded as the second King of Italy, now a unified country (see CARBONARA), and her passionate patronage of the arts and outspoken support for organizations such as the Red Cross earned her the respect of the young nation.

Indeed, she was held in such affection that the third highest mountain in Africa was named after her, Margherita Peak (which you could translate as 'Mount Daisy' as that is the meaning of her name in Italian), and she is also commemorated in a culinary way. It was a visit by the popular queen to Naples in 1889 that prompted Raffaelle Esposito, owner of the Pizzaria di Pietro, to prepare a special meal in her honour. Using the colours of the new national flag, green, white and red, Esposito combined cheese and tomato (white and red) with basil (green) to create what has become one of the world's biggest-selling pizzas, and the base ingredients for most of the others. He called it **pizza Margherita** (daisy pizza, in other words, although that doesn't sound quite as appetizing) after his queen. And so it's been called ever since.

CALZONE

The pizza equivalent of a PASTY or a savoury turnover, the **calzone** has all the normal filling of a pizza but is folded in half, which makes it much easier to eat on the move. In reference to its less-than-glamorous looks, *calzone* means 'trouser leg' or 'drooping sack'. In America, where this form of pizza is very popular, it is typically served with marinara sauce for dipping.

THE AMERICAN

It was the arrival of thousands of Italian immigrants in America in the last two decades of the nineteenth century that introduced the rest of the world to pizza. At first it was served as a street food, as it had been in Italy, but once the first pizzeria opened in Little Italy, New York City, in 1905, pizza spread like wildfire. The first pizza vendors sold versions of the dish they had eaten in their home country, but soon all kinds of variations slipped in. A favourite topping was pepperoni, the American version of the spicy salamis of

Naples and southern Italy: it became so popular that a cheese and pepperoni pizza is now known throughout the world as an **American**. (And with the addition of another American ingredient, the jalapeño pepper – see CHILLI PEPPER – it becomes the **American hot**.) It is estimated that US citizens eat an average twenty-three pounds of pizza, per person, per year. And that makes the pizza second only to the HAMBURGER as their favourite food.

14
Chinese Takeaway

Chinese Food for Thought

Dim Sum: Afternoon Tea Chinese-style

When Spring Rolls into Summer

Peking Duck: A Very Rich Snack

Thousand-year-old Eggs: Could This be
the World's Oldest Dish?

The Less than All-American Story of Chop Suey

I find chopsticks frankly distressing. Am I alone in thinking it odd that a people ingenious enough to invent paper, gunpowder, kites and any number of other useful objects, and who have a noble history extending back 3,000 years, haven't yet worked out that a pair of knitting needles is no way to capture food?

BILL BRYSON

Chinese Food for Thought

To Western eyes, Chinese cuisine is hugely varied and complex, its delicacies ranging from a soup made out of bird's nests to sweet-and-sour pork. One way of understanding how it all works is to explore how the two major philosophies that have indelibly influenced Chinese culture – Taoism and Confucianism – have affected the way Chinese people cook and enjoy their food.

TAOISM

Taoism is based on the teachings of Lao Tse, who lived around the sixth century BC and was said to have been a teacher of Confucius. It revolves around the concept of the Tao, the guiding force behind the universe that holds everything in balance and which incorporates the principles of yin and yang, opposing yet complementary forces that are present in everything, including food. Taoists believe that either yin or yang predominates in a particular food, 'yin' foods having cooling properties and 'yang' foods warming ones. For a dish to be properly balanced, therefore, it is important to get the right mixture of yin and yang elements. Cooking methods come into the equation too, boiling and steaming being regarded as 'yin' techniques and frying and roasting as 'yang'.

Based on these concepts, meals should be carefully prepared and balanced and gluttony and snacking avoided (for more on this, see the origins of DIM SUM). As well as being better for the health, the idea of not eating too much may hark back to a belief in a golden age where people didn't need to eat at all but simply got by on the cosmic 'qi' or energy of yin and yang. Raw food shouldn't be consumed to excess either, as Taoists believe that it creates internal weakness from too much cold energy in the stomach. For this reason, all vegetables have to be prepared in various ways, steamed or stir-fried at the very least. The health benefits of a dish are important, too, food being regarded as preventative of disease, and every ingredient in a dish should contribute to its overall healthiness. Ginger is a particular Taoist favourite, for instance, taken both as a digestive aid and to help reduce high blood pressure. With so much to take on board, the Taoist chef must be reaching for the ginger at every opportunity.

CONFUCIANISM

Confucius (551–479 BC) was a philosopher whose teachings still remain crucial to the Chinese state of mind. Born into a period of anarchy and constant war, all his teachings were focused on establishing a sense of balance and order in the world. He believed in the importance of education and self-improvement and that people should cultivate themselves morally so that they refrained from doing wrong, living in harmony with each other. And he attached great importance to food, which he saw as one of the three essential requirements for a successful society (the other two being an army and mutual trust). Confucius stressed that for a meal to be both nutritious and a pleasant experience, each dish should have the right blend of colour, flavour, aroma and texture – something that remains central to Chinese cuisine today. As in Taoism, ingredients should be balanced: the fatty richness of PEKING DUCK, for instance, offset by a salad of spring onions, and sweet flavours counterbalanced by sour. It was he who taught the Chinese that it was barbaric (and dangerous) to bring knives to the dining table. And ever since then, Chinese food has been served in bite-sized pieces and eaten with knitting needles. Another food-related principle that the great thinker adhered to was never to eat alone: meals should be a shared activity, with people enjoying each other's company as well as the food. Interestingly, he also taught that an excellent cook must first become an excellent matchmaker.

Dim Sum: Afternoon Tea Chinese-style

The culinary art of **dim sum** began centuries ago, as a form of refreshment for the merchants and traders along the Silk Road, the route connecting China's lucrative silk trade with the Middle East, Africa and Europe. Teahouses cropped up along the way to provide travellers with a place to rest. At first, it was considered inappropriate to combine TEA with food, because it was believed it might lead to excessive weight gain, which was against Taoist teachings (see 'Chinese Food for Thought', page 265). But when it was later decided that tea aided digestion, teahouse owners began adding various light snacks, which became hugely popular and evolved into the tradition of dim sum.

Literally translated as 'touching the heart', because it is only meant to be a snack not a main meal, dim sum typically consists of small steamed items, such as dumplings of pork or prawn, SPRING ROLLS, meatballs or rice wrapped in lotus leaves, all served in bamboo steamer baskets. This form of Cantonese TAPAS is served in restaurants at any time of day between sunrise and the main evening meal and is always taken with tea. In fact, the Chinese invitation to go and partake of dim sum is 'let's go and **yum cha**', which actually means 'let's drink tea', so closely are the two activities related. One, it seems, always goes with the other. (In

Australia, yum cha has even become the preferred term for dim sum.) Not unlike the English pub, where a pint of lager and a bag of crisps are tablemates.

When partaking of dim sum, it is customary to pour tea for your fellow diners before filling your own cup. They will then thank you by tapping their bent index and middle fingers together on the table. The Chinese have a legend about the origin of this gesture, according to which an emperor went in disguise to drink tea with a friend outside the palace. While at yum cha, the emperor poured his companion some tea, which was deemed a great honour. The companion, not wanting to give away the emperor's identity in public by bowing, instead tapped his index and middle fingers on the table as a coded sign of his appreciation.

Dim sum became more widespread during the Song Dynasty (AD 960–1280), when teahouses flourished all over China. By the time Marco Polo arrived in 1271, teahouses and dim sum were an established part of the Chinese culture, and when the great explorer finally returned to Europe in 1295, he introduced some Chinese artefacts (see PASTA) and traditions, and wrote about many more, but dim sum wasn't among them. Indeed, it wasn't discovered by Westerners until relatively recently, via Chinese immigration to the West. From around the nineteenth century, Chinese communities began appearing in every major city around the world and 'Chinatown' became the place where most immigrants settled. It would have been on a visit to their local Chinatown that Westerners encountered the delights of dim sum for the first time.

These days, the range of dim sum dishes is vast and includes sweet as well as savoury items. As it is a style of food, not a particular dish, chefs can be as imaginative as they please and use any manner of frying, boiling or steaming to create the dishes. The essence of dim sum remains the same, however:

everything is served in small portions. Dishes are prepared fresh each day and wheeled around on trolleys, enabling customers to select whatever they like the look of each time the trolley passes by. Their bill is then calculated as they leave by the number, size and colour of the plates they hand back. It is a system that can be open to abuse (less scrupulous customers hiding or stealing the plates after finishing with them), so servers often keep a tally of the dishes consumed.

When Spring Rolls into Summer

Spring rolls consist of a mixture of meat, seafood or vegetables wrapped in a layer of thin, unleavened dough and deep-fried. They were originally served as special snacks with TEA (see DIM SUM) when relatives and friends came to visit. Because of its rich golden colour when fried, a spring roll is likened to a gold nugget and thus associated with prosperity and good fortune. The English name, which dates back only to 1943, comes from the tradition of serving them on the first day of the Chinese New Year, which is also the first day of spring in the lunar year. But if you order spring rolls in a Vietnamese restaurant, you'll get the healthier raw version – anathema to the Chinese (see 'Chinese Food for Thought', page 265) – made with rice paper, prawns and fresh herbs, and also known as **summer rolls**.

Peking Duck: A Very Rich Snack

One of the world's great delicacies, roast duck has been a favourite dish in China since antiquity, but **Peking duck** as we'd recognize it today came about somewhat later – during the latter part of the Ming Dynasty (1368–1644), after China had changed its capital from Nanjing to Peking (now Beijing) in 1421. Previously the birds that had been roasted were the small ducks living in the canals around Nanjing, but the relocation of the capital had an unexpected side effect. Feeding on the grains that fell overboard from barges travelling between Nanjing and Peking, the ducks gradually became larger, evolving over the years into a new variety of larger, plumper birds that were then domesticated by Chinese farmers. This meat had so much more fat in it that when roasted, the dish was transformed into a marvel of savoury crunchiness. The Chinese then started force-feeding the duck in order to increase its fattiness further (see also FOIE GRAS).

Peking duck, as traditionally eaten by the wealthiest Chinese, consists of just the crisp salted skin, caramelized into a beautiful glossy brown in a long process which takes a whole day. To the Chinese, the dish is all about the taste, the texture and the expense, not the nutritional value. The meat of the duck was simply used as the means to cook and flavour the skin and was then, like the pastry of a medieval pie (see 'A Brief History of the Pie', page 39), given to the servants to eat. Once exported to the West in the twentieth century, the many fans of the dish (known as *canard laqué* in French, literally 'varnished duck') misunderstood the preferred Chinese approach and relished both the skin and meat of the duck. Traditionally served with pancakes, spring onions and hoisin sauce, the dish is very popular in Britain, where it is perhaps better known as **crispy aromatic duck**.

Thousand-year-old Eggs: Could This be the World's Oldest Dish?

Thousand-year-old eggs are the result of a process that, appropriately enough, dates back thousands of years. The

Chinese worked out that by coating duck, quail or chicken eggs in alkaline clay they could be preserved for many years. This was apparently discovered when a Chinese man, using slaked lime as mortar for the construction of his new home, discovered perfectly preserved duck eggs buried in the mix and then screwed up the courage to taste the contents. Liking what he tasted, he then set out to produce more, adding salt this time to improve the flavour and thereby creating the recipe for the present Far Eastern delicacy.

Originally it took at least one hundred days of curing to produce the blackened eggs (leading to their alternative name of **century eggs**), although that process has been refined and they can now be mass-produced in only a few weeks. They are sold in huge quantities across the Far East, particularly as street food, and are always served on special occasions such as national celebrations or wedding banquets. In Hong Kong a variation of the dish consists of blackened eggs coated in fishmeal and breadcrumbs. Deep-fried and served as a snack, these sound very like SCOTCH EGGS to me.

The eggs produce a pungent odour of ammonia, leading to the notion that the original method of preservation was a three-month soaking in urine. Although modern tests have proved this unlikely, the myth still persists, embodied in the Thai name for the dish, *khai yiow ma*, or 'horse piss eggs'. The Chinese are by no means the only people to have 'ancient' dishes. In France there is a traditional recipe for hundred-year-old pâté, for instance, while the English have their hundred-year-old PLUM PUDDING.

One of life's most perplexing questions is **What came first, the chicken or the egg?** It troubled the great Greek philosopher Aristotle (384–322 BC), who said: 'If there has been a first man, he must have been born without father or mother – which is repugnant to nature. For there could not have been a first egg to give a beginning to birds, or there should have been a first bird which gave a beginning to eggs, because a bird comes from an egg.' The Bible comes down firmly on the side of the chicken, describing, in Genesis 1:21, how on the fifth day of Creation God made 'every winged fowl after their kind'. Scientists, meanwhile, have looked at evolution and concluded that the egg came first. And to the obvious question of 'Well, what laid it then?' the answer is 'Not a chicken'. It was a bird, though, the ancestor of the chicken, the Red Junglefowl (*Gallus Gallus*), a tropical member of the pheasant family from India and the Far East. As fossil evidence confirms, wild fowl lived alongside dinosaurs (who also hatched from eggs) and other prehistoric species, so it doesn't take a great leap of imagination to conclude that the Red Junglefowl could have crossbred with another ancient species (the Grey Junglefowl has been suggested) to produce the new breed now used all over the world for its meat and eggs. The offspring of this union would have been the first chicken – after it had pecked its way out of the egg, of course.

The Less than All-American Story
of Chop Suey

Traditionally seen as an American parody of Chinese food, **chop suey** is surrounded by all kinds of stories about how it was first invented. They all feature a harried immigrant cook forced against his wishes to cook a meal – depending on the version of the story, either by drunken gold miners, angry railway builders or a visiting Chinese dignitary – at an hour when only scraps were left in his kitchen. He stir-fried these all together into a kind of hash and, when asked by his satisfied customers what the dish was called, announced it was *chop suey*, which was his joke as it is Cantonese for 'odds and ends'. (In Mandarin, the name of the dish means cooked animal offal or entrails, which, assuming the cook had them to hand, may not have pleased his American customers quite so much.)

It turns out, however, that chop suey was actually an authentic dish from Toisan, a rural district south of Canton, home of most of the earliest Chinese immigrants to California. The name is *tsap seui* (which does indeed mean 'miscellaneous scraps') and it is made up of leftover vegetables and bits of meat stir-fried together. After all, as the most pressing reason for immigration to America was severe poverty, it's not unlikely that the earliest Chinese settlers in Gold Rush California would have been accustomed to reusing and eating scraps and leftovers. (See also BUBBLE AND SQUEAK and KEDGEREE.)

15
Christmas Dinner

Who Invented Christmas Dinner?

Why Do We Have a Christmas Ham?

Feast Your Mince Pies on This

Should It be Goose or Turkey for Dinner?

Where on a Turkey is the Parson's Nose?

Brussels Sprouts: The Vegetable
We All Love to Hate

The Pudding They Tried to Ban

Celebrating Twelfth Night with
King Cake and Hot Punch

Christmas at my house is always at least six or seven times more pleasant than anywhere else. We start drinking early. And while everyone else is seeing only one Santa Claus, we'll be seeing six or seven.

W. C. FIELDS

Who Invented Christmas Dinner?

When talking about feasting, what better subject to be tackling than the traditional **Christmas dinner**. It is the most important (and calorific) meal of the year for most of us, but why is it that we feel obligated to gather relatives around that we don't like very much and spend the day feeding them – if only in the hope they explode?

Part of the reason may lie in the fact that it belongs to a tradition of sociable merrymaking that goes back a very long way. Midwinter feasts are a feature of all cultures and religions: generally held on or around the shortest day of the year (21 December), they celebrate the fact that spring isn't far off, with its promise of new life. In Neolithic and Bronze Age times, the winter solstice was immensely important because communities could not be certain that they would actually survive the winter. The feast was an offering to the gods to ensure that they would survive the starvation common in the months between January and April. Tribes slaughtered most of their older cattle so they would not have to be fed during this period, hence it was almost the only time of year when fresh meat was available. The celebrations also had a valuable psychological purpose, cheering people up at the darkest point of the year. Even when life became easier and more civilized, the feasts still continued.

The Romans had celebrated the festival of Sol Invictus (the Unconquered Sun) on 25 December and when the Christian Church came to formalizing its feast days, it pragmatically picked that day as Jesus's birthday, which, of course, it wasn't – the actual date isn't known. As Syrus the Scriptor commented in the late fourth century:

> It was a custom of the pagans to celebrate on the same 25 December the birthday of the Sun, at which they kindled lights in token of festivity. In these solemnities and revelries the Christians also took part. Accordingly, when the doctors of the Church perceived that the Christians had a leaning to this festival, they took council and resolved that the true Nativity should be solemnized on that day.

Traces of these fire festivals can be found in aspects of the Christmas tradition that survive to this day: the Yule log that was kept burning for the twelve days of the festival, still commemorated in the log-shaped French Christmas cake known as the **bûche de Noël**; the candles Victorians fastened to their Christmas trees, today represented by much safer fairy lights; and of course the setting alight of the CHRISTMAS PUDDING.

The first recorded Christmas feast took place at Rome in AD 336 and a few years later, in 350, Pope Julius I formally adopted the date as the time to celebrate the birth of Christ. Festivities continued from 25 December until 6 January and the Epiphany (see also TWELFTH NIGHT), marking the visit of the Magi or Three Wise Men to the infant Jesus. Basically, it was a two-week party, a tradition that has remained part of the Christian way of life ever since.

Legend has it that it was on Christmas day that King Arthur drew Excalibur from the stone, thus proving that he was the rightful king of England, and Arthurian Christmas feasts swell the pages of medieval literature. The fourteenth-century poem *Sir Gawain and the Green Knight* begins in the midst of Christmas revelry at Camelot, where King Arthur, the Knights of the Round Table and their ladies celebrate 'for fully fifteen days, with all the feasting and merrymaking they could think of; such sounds of mirth and merriment, glorious to hear, a pleasant uproar by day, dancing at night'. The lavishness of medieval feasts is legendary. As one historian noted in 1398: '[King Richard II] kept his Christmas at Lichfield, where he spent [used] in the Christmastime 200 tunns of wine, and 2,000 oxen with their appurtenances.'

These celebrations, with their thinly veiled paganism, have had their detractors, however. In 1583, the Scottish Presbyterians decided that there was no biblical foundation for a Christmas feast day. Christmas only became an official holiday in Scotland once again in 1958. In 1644, Oliver Cromwell's Puritan Parliament banned its celebration – even the word 'Christmas' was abolished, with its overtones of the Catholic Mass. Cromwell wanted 25 December to be a purely religious anniversary in which people contemplated the birth of Jesus rather than ate and drank too much. In London, soldiers were ordered to patrol the streets and take, by force if necessary, food being cooked for a Christmas celebration. Traditional Christmas decorations like holly and festive dishes like MINCE PIES and Christmas pudding were also banned. However, with the return of Charles II, the Act of Uniformity (1662) overturned the ban, enshrining in law the ceremonies and rites of the Book of Common Prayer, and as the Church of England began to re-establish its authority, Christmas was once again celebrated with all its previous revelry.

The Puritans, who had already been leaving England in droves for over fifty years to set up a more godly new world, weren't entirely averse to a celebration, however. In 1621, to thank God for the success of their very first harvest, the pilgrims of Plymouth Colony held a festival known as the 'First Thanksgiving'. Celebrated on 13 December, Thanksgiving took over from Christmas as the midwinter festival of the new settlers. Then, in 1863, Abraham Lincoln moved Thanksgiving to the end of November, leaving a sufficient breathing space before Christmas, which now could be properly celebrated once again.

Why Do We Have a Christmas Ham?

In the same way that the Norse word for their pagan midwinter festival – Yule – is used almost synonymously with Christmas, the inclusion of a ham alongside TURKEY for the CHRISTMAS DINNER shows how the Christian festival has absorbed elements of other midwinter feasts. It was a Norse tradition to eat wild boar at Yule as a tribute to Freyr, the god of farming, weather and fertility, while the Romans ate boar during their midwinter festival, Saturnalia, held in honour of their god of agriculture, Saturn. A wild boar is associated with another figure in classical mythology, Adonis, who died after being gored by one and who shares certain characteristics with the story of Jesus, in that a cult of rebirth was associated with him (after his death he was reborn in the form of a flower, the anemone) and his birthday was celebrated on the same day, 25 December.

The **Christmas ham** is also linked with the Boar's Head Feast, which still takes place, although much more rarely than it used to, and is connected with the ancient tradition of serving a boar's head at a banquet, where it would have been the central dish. The wild boar is a ferocious beast and to have its head on a platter meant that you had vanquished a formidable enemy. In Christian symbolism, the boar's head came to represent the triumph of the Christ Child over sin. The tradition of sacrificing a boar and presenting its head at a Yuletide feast is described in the oldest Christmas carol in English, 'The Boar's Head Carol' (first printed in 1521), which is sung at the feast as the boar's head is carried in on a platter. The current festival originated at Queen's College, Oxford, where it is still observed every Christmas. The college has its own story, recounted in 1868 by William Henry Husk, who recorded how the tradition arose in

> commemoration of an act of valour performed by a student of the college, who, while walking in the neighbouring forest of Shotover and reading Aristotle, was suddenly attacked by a wild boar. The furious beast came open-mouthed upon the youth, who, however, very courageously, and with a happy presence of mind, thrust the volume he was reading down the boar's throat, crying, *Græcum est* [with the compliments of the Greeks], and fairly choked the savage with the sage.

Feast Your Mince Pies on This

The **mince pie** dates back to the Middle Ages when, as the word mince*meat* suggests, it was a savoury dish. It emerged not as a confection or a dessert, but as a way of preserving meat as winter drew in. Because of shortages of fodder, surplus livestock (see CHRISTMAS DINNER) were slaughtered in the late autumn. The meat was chopped up and cooked with spices and dried fruits, then sealed in a 'coffin' – an airtight pastry-case (see 'A Brief History of the Pie', page 39). The resulting pies – which were large, not the small, snack-sized things that we're familiar with – could then be used to feed hosts of people, particularly at the festive season. The earliest type, known as a *chewette*, contained chopped meat or liver mixed with diced hard-boiled egg and ginger. Gradually the filling became enriched with dried fruit until, as time went on, it predominated and the meat was replaced with suet (see

STEAK AND KIDNEY PUDDING). By the sixteenth century, 'minced' pies as they were known had become a Christmas speciality. So much so that when Oliver Cromwell was banning Christmas celebrations in 1644 (see CHRISTMAS DINNER), he specifically abolished mince pies too. That particular law has never been repealed, so it is technically still illegal to eat mince pies at Christmas – which is a great excuse to bear in mind if you're feeling too full to eat another thing but you don't want to hurt your mum's feelings after she spent half the morning making them.

Should It be Goose or Turkey for Dinner?

The traditional main dish at Christmas was once **goose**. That was because, like other migratory fowl, geese appeared and disappeared at crucial times in the yearly cycle, so eating them accompanied ceremonial events in the solar and agricultural year. People have linked geese to the changing seasons since antiquity, when different cultures around the world would sacrifice the goose to the gods in thanks for the harvest, then feast on its flesh afterwards. Goose was served at the Celtic Samhain, or Halloween, the Norse Yule (see CHRISTMAS HAM) and the Christian Michaelmas. In the Middle Ages there was even a festival known as Wayzgoose, a traditional printers' fête, held at around Michaelmas (the autumn equinox) to mark the end of summer and the beginning of working by candlelight. The master printer would hold a feast for his apprentices and journeymen, with roast goose as the main dish.

The shift from goose to **turkey** at Christmas was due to those Puritan settlers in America and their Thanksgiving celebrations (see CHRISTMAS DINNER). With characteristic hypocrisy, even they didn't want to ban Christmas celebrations altogether, so they moved the date and called it something else, a tradition still alive in America in modern times. Turkeys are native to northern America, where they live in flocks, roost in swamps and feed on wild berries and seeds. They are awkward in flight and easy to catch (see the box below and PARSON'S NOSE) and that made them a perfect food source for early settlers. The colonists initially confused the birds with guineafowl, which were exported from northern India and other parts of Asia via Turkey to Europe and consequently known as 'Turkey hens' or 'Turkey cocks'. Hence the American bird became known as a turkey, a term that, ironically, stuck to this species rather than the one actually imported via the country of the same name.

American settlers served turkey at Thanksgiving, making it the seasonal dish. And in much of the Western world today, turkeys have replaced geese at the Christmas feast. But interestingly, these two birds share the same symbolism. Just as the people of the Old World associated geese with the solar year, so the Native Americans connected turkeys with the sun. According to a Hopi creation myth, it was a male turkey that first tried to raise the sun in the sky, burning his head in the process. And that, apparently, is why turkeys are completely bald.

To talk turkey means to have a full and frank discussion. European settlers in America developed a taste for the local delicacy and soon the gobbler was in high demand. As a result, all serious discussions with the Native Americans became known as 'talking about turkey' and the phrase passed into common usage, eventually crossing the water back to Britain. An alternative suggestion for the origin of the phrase comes from turkey hunting. Hunters would attract their prey by making gobbling noises, in imitation of the bird. Apparently the daft creatures would then return the call and so reveal their whereabouts to the hunter.

Going ***cold turkey***, by contrast, is considered to be the best way to wean a person off an addiction to something, generally hard drugs. The expression was first recorded in the 1930s, from the observation that the skin of a person withdrawing from drugs is pale and clammy and covered in goose pimples – like the skin of a plucked turkey. American Beat writer William Burroughs goes a step further, suggesting in his book *Junkie* (1953) that human skin, during the period of withdrawal, resembles that of a turkey that has not only been plucked, but also cooked and left to cool. That is one explanation, but not all etymologists agree, some believing that the expression goes back further, to 1910, and a comparison between a meal of cold turkey, which requires minimal preparation, and withdrawing from heavy drug use without preparation.

Where on a Turkey is the Parson's Nose?

The fleshy protuberance at the end of a dressed TURKEY is known anatomically as the pygostyle (from the ancient Greek 'rump pillar') and covers the part of a bird's spine to which the tail feathers are attached. Millions of years ago, this is what gave the ancestors of modern birds an advantage over those with completely mobile tails, as the rigid structure was much better for flight control. (Not that turkeys are exactly noted for their flying ability; it's why they made such easy prey for the European settlers in America.) In addition to the turkey, the pygostyle can be found on chicken, GOOSE and duck alike, and is considered a delicacy by some when roasted until crisp. The French refer to the meat near it as *sot-l'y-laisse*, meaning 'only a fool would leave it'. Its swollen appearance is thanks to the oil glands a bird uses when cleaning itself, and has led to its common name, **parson's nose** – or the **pope's nose** or **sultan's nose**, depending on who you feel like insulting – based on the notion that it looks like a snooty parson with 'his nose in the air'. The expression dates back to the Middle Ages at least, as indicated by a carving that appears on the misericord (underside) of a seat in the choir stalls at St Mary's Church, Nantwich. Dating from around 1400 and portraying a fowl with a minister's face on its rear end, the image is said to have been carved by the craftsman in retaliation for not being paid by the vicar for his work.

Brussels Sprouts: The Vegetable
We All Love to Hate

Another foodstuff seen as integral to CHRISTMAS DINNER but disliked by almost everyone is the **Brussels sprout**. Sprout supporters claim that, cooked correctly, they are delicious and that the dislike stems from overcooking as it releases the glucosinolate singrin, which gives out the sulphurous odour redolent of canteens in Hell. Detractors, on the other hand, maintain there is no correct way to cook them. Jane Grigson in her *Vegetable Book* (1978) suggests that sprouts have been grown in Flanders since the Middle Ages, even featuring at wedding feasts of the Burgundian court in the fifteenth century, but that mysteriously they didn't catch on, not becoming known outside Belgian borders until the end of the eighteenth century. Luckily for Belgian national pride, the country has managed to redeem its culinary reputation with its simultaneous invention and perfection of FRENCH FRIES.

The Pudding They Tried to Ban

The earliest prototype of the **Christmas pudding** was a form of pottage – scraps of beef or mutton boiled with vegetables, dried fruit, wine and spices. Although thickened with breadcrumbs, the resulting dish, as its name suggests ('pottage' is another word for a stew or soup), was very liquid. It was much loved by Henry VIII, however – who was first fed the dish, legend has it, at a woodcutter's cottage while on a winter's hunting expedition – and who then insisted it be served on feast days throughout the year, especially at Harvest Festival.

Its development has a lot in common with mincemeat (see MINCE PIES), the meat gradually being replaced over time with more and more dried fruit and the wine with brandy. With the addition of prunes from the time of Elizabeth I, it became known as 'plum pottage' and then, increasingly, as **plum pudding**. During the seventeenth century, it became an unlikely hate object for radical Protestants, who were repulsed by the flaming of the pudding which, according to the Catholics, symbolized the Passion of Christ but which they saw as a throwback to the pagan fire festivals. Oliver Cromwell called it 'a lewd custom ... unfit for God-fearing people' and banned plum pudding, along with all other Christmas celebrations (see CHRISTMAS DINNER). When in 1714 George I, sometimes known as the Pudding King, requested that plum pudding be served at the meal celebrating his first Christmas after taking the throne, the Quakers' reaction was more extreme. They branded it as 'the invention of the scarlet whore of Babylon', but, like the Futurists' stand against PASTA, their hostility only served to increase the popularity of the dish.

With the arrival of the pudding cloth in the seventeenth century (see also STEAK AND KIDNEY PUDDING) came the distinctive spherical shape of the traditional pudding. (Prior to that, puddings – sweet or savoury – had to be boiled in the stomach lining or gut of a slaughtered animal; just like HAGGIS, in other words.) It was the Victorians who acknowledged the plum pudding had become Christmas pudding by formally changing its name, the first recipe for it appearing in Eliza Acton's *Modern Cookery for Private Families* in 1845.

Here's the perfect Victorian description of the serving of a
Christmas pudding (from Dickens's *A Christmas Carol*, of
course), from two years earlier:

> Mrs Cratchit left the room alone – too nervous to bear
> witnesses – to take the pudding up and bring it in ...
> Hallo! A great deal of steam! The pudding was out of
> the copper. A smell like a washing-day. That was the
> cloth. A smell like an eating-house and a pastrycook's
> next door to each other, with a laundress's next door
> to that. That was the pudding. In half a minute Mrs
> Cratchit entered – flushed, but smiling proudly – with
> the pudding, like a speckled cannon-ball, so hard and
> firm, blazing in half of half-a-quartern of ignited
> brandy, and bedight with Christmas holly stuck into
> the top.

Traditionally, the pudding should be made on the last Sunday before Advent, known as 'Stir-up Sunday' from the opening words of the Collect for the day in the Book of Common
Prayer: 'Stir up, we beseech thee, O Lord, the wills of thy
faithful people; that they, plenteously bringing forth the fruit
of good works, may of thee be plenteously rewarded.' Every
family member should take it in turn to stir the pudding, from
east to west, in honour of the Magi and their supposed journey in that direction. In another reference to the New Testament, the pudding should be prepared with thirteen ingredients – to represent Christ and his twelve Apostles.

The tradition of inserting silver coins or trinkets into the
Christmas pudding is an ancient one, deriving from pagan
rituals in which lots were drawn to predict good fortune (see
COLCANNON and KING CAKE). Silver charms were a Victorian favourite: traditional items included a boot, bell, wishbone, thimble, ring, button and horseshoe. The boot indicated

travel, the ring impending marriage and the wishbone the granting of a wish; the thimble was seen as bad luck, predicting spinsterhood. Silver sixpences and threepenny bits were also put in puddings, conferring good luck upon the finders. Following the Second World War, when coins were no longer made of silver but a copper alloy that reacted during the cooking process, the tradition of placing little surprises in Christmas puddings became rarer. The modern, health-and-safety approach is to wrap coins in foil before adding them, which somehow isn't quite the same.

Celebrating Twelfth Night with King Cake and Hot Punch

The sixth of January, also known as Epiphany (see CHRISTMAS DINNER), is the the last day of the twelve days of Christmas. The evening before it is known as Twelfth Night. In many European countries, a special pastry or cake made with dried fruit, known as the **king cake**, is baked for the occasion. In France, for instance, this is called the *galette/gâteau des rois*, in Spain the *roscón des reyes* and in Portugal the *bolo rei*. Traditionally, a bean is inserted – more likely a little plastic trinket these days – into the cake mix, just as coins or trinkets were formerly cooked in a CHRISTMAS PUDDING. The lucky person to come across the bean in their portion of cake is then crowned king or queen for the evening.

This calls to mind the Three Kings of the Nativity story, who arrived to pay their respects to the infant Jesus on the twelfth day after his birth, but the tradition is actually much older, pre-dating Christianity itself. Twelfth Night used to mark the end of the winter festival that began at the end of October with the Celtic festival of Samhain (now Halloween) and the ancient Roman festival of Saturnalia. In the Celtic tradition, on the final day of the festival the world would turn upside down for the evening, presided over by the Lord of Misrule – now represented by the person who finds the bean in the cake. This topsy-turviness is reflected in Shakespeare's play *Twelfth Night* (1601) with Viola, one of the central characters, dressing as a man and the servant Malvolio believing that he can court a noblewoman, thanks to the machinations of Feste the clown, who presides over events as the mischievous Lord of Misrule.

Part of the Twelfth Night celebrations was the tradition of wassailing – going from house to house wishing the occupants well (a practice that evolved into carol singing) and in return receiving **wassail** (derived from Middle English *wæs hæil*, 'be in good health!'), a hot, spiced PUNCH served in a special cup called a wassail bowl. Needless to say, the revellers would get increasingly the worse for wear as the evening progressed, which probably accounts for the lyrics of the sixteenth-century wassailing carol 'We Wish You a Merry Christmas', in which the singers demand 'figgy pudding' (a form of Christmas pudding) and 'a cup of good cheer' and then insist:

> We won't go until we get some;
> We won't go until we get some;
> We won't go until we get some, so bring some out here!

Try singing that outside my house on a cold winter's night, dear singers. You will certainly get some.

16
The Sweet Trolley

Pavlova: The Cold Dessert that Inspired a Hot Debate

The Tragicomic Tale of Poire Belle Hélène

Fools Rush in Where Angels Fear to Whip

Boodle's Orange Fool: Relished by Gentlemen Only?

Peach Melba: The Pudding that Defrosted a Diva

School Dinner Favourite: Spotted Dick

Crêpes Suzette: Pancakes for a Prince?

With this Nesselrode Pudding You're Really
Spoiling Us, Ambassador

Survival of the Sweetest: How Trifle
Outlived Its Evolutionary Rivals

Tarte Tatin: A Culinary Reversal of Fortune

Apple Brown Betty: One Pudding that
Definitely Didn't Get Lost in Translation

From Arab Delicacy to All-American Treat:
The Story of Ice Cream

Treacle Tart: The Intriguing Origins of Its Chief Ingredient

It's not improbable that a man may receive more solid satisfaction from pudding while he is alive than from praise after he is dead.

PROVERB

Ice cream is exquisite. What a pity it isn't illegal.

VOLTAIRE

Pavlova: The Cold Dessert that Inspired a Hot Debate

Anna Pavlova (1881–1931) may well be the most famous ballerina in dance history, synonymous with one of ballet's most enduring roles, that of the Dying Swan, created for her while she was a principal dancer at the Imperial Russian Ballet. Pavlova fell in love with ballet when she was just eight years old after seeing a performance of *The Sleeping Beauty*. Her mother took her to audition for the Imperial Ballet School but, frail and small for her age, she wasn't finally accepted until three years later. Once there, however, she trained obsessively and with the help of extra tuition the tiny dancer graduated in 1899, at the age of eighteen.

Pavlova went from strength to strength, her debut performance in Pavel Gerdt's *The False Dryads* earning her high praise, not least by one noted critic and historian who complimented her on her 'natural ballon, lingering arabesques and frail femininity'. It was this frail femininity coupled with a graceful energy that led to her quickly becoming a favourite with both the adoring public and ballet masters alike. She was also the first ballerina in history to go on tour around the world, even as far afield as New Zealand and Australia, where her first appearance was described as the 'Chief Event of 1926'.

The public of both countries were enraptured. 'She does not dance, she soars as though she has wings,' was how the New Zealand press described her during that first tour, in 1926. 'Exquisite Pavlova!' cried the Australians. On her second tour of the continent, in 1929, the Australians were so excited that one reporter noted: 'A symphony of silence! But who, seeing the famous ballerina for the first time as she stood on deck at Fremantle yesterday, could apply that description. It was Babel itself.'

It was in honour of Pavlova, and her visits to the Antipodes, that the famous dish bearing her name was invented. Consisting of a wide disc of meringue covered in whipped cream and fresh fruit, **pavlova** is so called because its built-up sides are thought to resemble the frothy layers of a tutu and the strawberry and passion fruit slices thought to resemble the rose decorations upon her outfit. The dish is said to have been created in New Zealand, but the Australians disagree, saying that it originated in their country. With numerous claims and counter-claims on both sides, it's a culinary tug of war that has persisted for many years.

According to the Australians, the pavlova first appeared in 1934, three years after the dancer's death. Mrs Elizabeth Paxton, owner of the Esplanade Hotel in Perth, asked the head chef, Bert Sasche, to devise something special for the menu. After a month of experimenting, Sasche presented the now-famous dessert to his boss with the words, according to Paxton family legend, 'It's as light as Pavlova', a clear reference to the dancer who was once their guest. Sasche stood by this claim for the rest of his life, although he did admit that the dish wasn't entirely original, explaining in a magazine interview in 1973 that he had based it on an existing recipe. Indeed, it's possible that he may have seen a recipe for meringue cake that appeared on 2 April 1935 in *Women's Mirror*, submitted by a lady from New Zealand.

Meanwhile, Pavlova's biographer Keith Mooney supports the idea that the dish originated in New Zealand, claiming that it was the creation of a young chef at a hotel in Wellington who had fallen in love with the ballerina during her first tour in 1926. Since the publication of *Anna Pavlova: Her Life and Art* in 1982, Australian food historians have argued that while the dessert seems to have been invented in New Zealand, it was only named after her later, in Australia, as borne out by Australian cookbooks, which didn't include pavlova until the 1940s.

And so the debate raged on, with each side refuting the other's claims, until 2008 and the publication by Dr Helen Leach, a culinary expert at the University of Otago in New Zealand, of *The Pavlova Story: A Slice of New Zealand's Culinary History*. Since then, the Australians have gone a little quiet on the subject as Leach, in her research for the book, managed to unearth evidence for a pavlova in a New Zealand women's magazine from 1929. She also discovered a recipe for the dish in the *Rangiora Mothers' Union Cookery Book*, a New Zealand publication of 1933, while Mrs McKay's *Practical Home Cookery Book* of 1929 includes a recipe for three dozen 'little pavlovas'. So unless the Australians can come up with an earlier, printed recipe, then I'm afraid this debate appears to be over, sport.

The Tragicomic Tale of Poire Belle Hélène

Jacques Offenbach (1819–80) was a German-born French composer, one of the first to write operettas – a form of opera that is light in both its music and subject matter – of which his *Orpheus and the Underworld* (1858) is perhaps the most famous, chiefly on account of its *galop infernal*, better known these days as the music that accompanies the cancan. Satirical and witty, the operettas of Offenbach were incredibly popular both in France and throughout the English-speaking world. Hence when his *La belle Hélène* ('The Beautiful Helen')

– recounting the story of Helen of Troy whose elopement with Paris kicked off the Trojan War – opened at the Théâtre des Variétés on 17 December 1864, it was guaranteed to be a success. But when it became known that the French soprano Hortense Schneider – as scandalous as her fictional counterpart, she was rumoured to be the mistress of the Prince of Wales – had accepted the role of Belle Hélène, it became an instant sensation and enjoyed a run of seven hundred performances.

To mark the success of the operetta, distinguished French chef Auguste Escoffier (see PEACH MELBA and SOLE VÉRO-NIQUE) created a dish in its honour, **poire belle Hélène** – a poached pear served with vanilla ICE CREAM and coated with chocolate. The shape of the pear could be said to suggest womanly curves while the coating of chocolate makes the chosen fruit stand out from all others, just as Helen of Troy or Hortense Schneider – known to her legion of admirers as La Snédèr – stood out among women.

La belle Hélène and other works enjoyed huge popularity during the 1850s and 1860s, but in 1870 things took a sudden dive for Offenbach whose life began to resemble a tragic rather than a comic opera. When war broke out between France and Germany (Prussia), he was accused by the French press of being a secret agent for the German chancellor Bismarck (see BISMARCK HERRING) and was forced to flee to his native country, where the press, in turn, accused him of being a French spy and a traitor. Offenbach then fled with his family to Spain, but when he returned to Paris, he discovered that his operettas were no longer popular as, satirical in content, they were considered to have undermined Napoleon III and his armies, leading to their defeat. Hounded by the police and reviled by his once adoring audience, Offenbach was forced into bankruptcy in 1875 and escaped to America, where several successful runs of his works helped recoup his financial losses, enabling him to lead a comfortable life until his death in 1880. These days few may have heard of Offenbach, the most celebrated and creative composer of his generation, but millions will have eaten one of France's classic desserts, named in his honour, *poire belle Hélène*.

Fools Rush in Where Angels Fear to Whip

A traditional English pudding, a **fool** consists simply of raw or cooked fruit – usually acidic fruit like raspberries or rhubarb – that is either mashed or puréed and then folded into whipped cream. Originally synonymous with TRIFLE, the name may be a play on words, alluding simultaneously to 'fool' in the sense of a dimwit and to the French verb *fouler*, meaning 'to crush' or 'to press' (hence all the mashing and puréeing). The earliest recipe for it dates back to the mid seventeenth century, although one of its most popular forms, **gooseberry fool**, may date back earlier, possibly to the fifteenth century. We could be in punning territory here too, as some etymologists suggest 'gooseberry' may be associated with the actual bird (i.e. 'berry of the GOOSE'), which is in turn a traditional expression for a fool, giving 'fool's fool' as the name of the dessert. Another popular version of the dish, dating from the seventeenth century, is **Norfolk fool**. Containing no fruit, this must be the most foolish fool of all.

Boodle's Orange Fool:
Relished by Gentlemen Only?

A gentleman, by definition between the seventeenth and nineteenth centuries, was a man of independent means, his comfortable lifestyle supported by the income from a generous inheritance. The activities of a gentleman in times of peace were socializing and gambling – never working. Before the opening of Whites in 1693, gentlemen would gather together to play cards and drink, generally in taverns of varying degrees of ill-repute. This first gentlemen's club provided a haven for upper-middle-class Englishmen, a place to dine and socialize with men (never women) of the same social status. Whites was an instant success, becoming extremely exclusive and hard to join. Only the idle rich were welome; anyone with a proper job, including senior judges and politicians, wasn't eligible.

Seventy years later, William Petty, 2nd Earl of Shelburne (1737–1805) – a future prime minister of Great Britain (see also WHITEBAIT) – decided to set up his own establishment. Shelburne wanted something rather different, a specifically Tory club for gentlemen to discuss politics and play cards. The place was run with extreme efficiency by Lord Shelburne's imperturbable head waiter, Edward Boodle, after whom the club was named. Boodle was not a gentleman, of course, but he was a gentleman's confidant and Boodle's quickly established its name as the club to which no scandal was attached – even the coins were dirt-free, boiled in water before being given to members. Strict protocol was adhered to: servants wore black knee-breeches, there was a more informal dining room called the 'dirty room' for those wishing to dine in less than the proper attire, and, as with Whites, women were not allowed on the premises except to clean it. All this formality and respectability meant that over time Boodle's became the epitome of the gentlemen's club, known as an impenetrably male stronghold. In Oscar Wilde's play *An Ideal Husband* (1895), the confirmed bachelor Lord Goring is deemed to be 'the result of Boodle's Club' and, in a barbed comment by a female adversary, Mrs Cheveley, to reflect 'every credit on the institution'.

Over the years, Boodle's has remained one of the better-known gentlemen's clubs. Among the famous names associated with it, Ian Fleming was a member and Blades, the fictional club to which James Bond belongs, is modelled on it. It is also known for its signature dish. Rich, comforting and delicious, just like the club itself, **Boodle's orange fool** – a layer of sponge covered in whipped cream mixed with orange and lemon zest – is more of a TRIFLE than a FOOL and can now be enjoyed by everyone, regardless of sex or status.

Peach Melba: The Pudding that Defrosted a Diva

Auguste Escoffier (1846–1935) was a French chef, restaurateur and writer, a key figure in the development of modern French cuisine. In the 1880s, he formed a partnership with the equally celebrated César Ritz (founder of the Ritz Hotel in London), the two of them being called upon by Richard D'Oyly Carte (see SOLE VÉRONIQUE) to run the Savoy Hotel, where Escoffier devised some of his most famous dishes. Aside from being the most respected chef in London during the 1890s, Escoffier was also an avid opera fan (see also POIRE BELLE HÉLÈNE) and legend has it that he forged a friendship with one of the greatest opera singers of her era, Dame Nellie Melba (1861–1931), when she was staying at the Savoy.

One evening in 1893, the Australian singer, and reputed drama queen extraordinaire, remarked to Escoffier that she loved ice cream but was unable to eat it in case it froze her vocal cords. Never averse to a challenge, the chef went straight to his kitchen and set about experimenting with ICE CREAM mixed with different types of fruit and sauces, in the hope that these might render the dish less chilly. He soon hit upon his favourite combination, peaches and vanilla ice cream smothered in raspberry sauce (although alternative versions of the story ascribe the sauce to a later version of the dish). In a dramatic flourish, the chef later presented his new creation in an ice sculpture of a swan, in reference to *Lohengrin* and its story of the Swan Knight. Melba was so enchanted by the dish that she was soon demanding it at restaurants and hotels the world over. Since then, **peach Melba** has proved such a hit that it was recently shortlisted by a national television competition as one of the world's greatest dishes, while a National Peach Melba Day (13 January) has been declared in America. (See also MELBA TOAST for another dish inspired by the diva.)

School Dinner Favourite: Spotted Dick

You can all stop laughing in the back now and settle down – this is a serious subject. No book about traditional English food could be complete without looking into why my favourite pudding, as a schoolboy, was called **spotted dick**. The first clue must lie in one of the ingredients, currants, which provide the 'spots'. The next clue comes from the shape of the dish: the suet dough is rolled up into a sausage shape, which, like the resemblance of the frankfurter to a dachshund (see HOT DOG), may have given rise to its alternative name, **spotted dog**. But the most likely reason lies in the derivation of the word 'dick', which, like 'dog' and 'duff', was a colloquial word for 'pudding'. In fact, it's easy to see how the word 'pudding' could over time have been corrupted into 'puddink' and 'puddick' and then eventually shortened to 'dick', a recipe for 'spotted dick' first appearing in print in 1850.

In Ireland, the dish consists of sweet soda bread mixed with currants and raisins, and is known variously as **railway cake**, spotted dog, spotted dick or, presumably, spotted mick. The pudding continues to be popular in both countries, although there have been worrying moves among the more prudish to rechristen it 'spotted Richard'.

Crêpes Suzette: Pancakes for a Prince?

Like many of the world's best dishes, **crêpes Suzette** – pancakes covered in Grand Marnier and flambéed – was created by accident at the Café de Paris in Monte Carlo. During a stay in 1895, the notorious womanizer the Prince of Wales (see POIRE BELLE HÉLÈNE) was dining with one of his mistresses when a fourteen-year-old waiter, Henri Charpentier (1880–1961), made a mistake as he prepared the princely plateful. Charpentier described the incident himself in his autobiography *Life à la Henri*, published during the 1940s:

> It was by accident as I worked in front of a chafing dish
> that the cordials caught fire. I thought it was ruined.
> The Prince and his friends were waiting. How could

I begin it all over? So I tasted it and it was, I thought, the most delicious melody of sweet flavours I had ever tasted, and I still think so. That accident of the flame was precisely what was needed to bring all those various instruments into one harmony of taste ... He ate the pancakes with a fork but used a spoon to capture the remaining syrup. When he asked me for the name of what he had eaten with such relish, I told him it was to be called Crêpes au Prince. The Prince recognized ... that this was a compliment designed for him, but he protested with mock ferocity that there was a lady present. She was alert and rose to her feet and holding her little skirt wide with her hands she made a curtsey. 'Will you,' said His Majesty, 'change Crêpes au Prince to Crêpes Suzette?' Thus was born and baptized this confection, one taste of which, I believe, would reform a cannibal into a civilized gentleman. The following day I received a present from the Prince, a jewelled ring, a panama hat and a cane.

With this Nesselrode Pudding You're Really Spoiling Us, Ambassador

This popular pudding – an iced dessert of creamy custard mixed with chestnut purée and candied fruits – is said to have been invented in 1814 by the travelling chef of the prominent Russian diplomat and gourmet Count Karl von Nesselrode

(1780–1862). Nesselrode was obviously as obsessed with chestnuts as Parmentier was with potatoes (see page 152) as his name has become shorthand for their presence in any sweet dish: **Nesselrode pie**, **Nesselrode tart** and **bombe Nesselrode** all contain the nut.

The son of a count of the Holy Roman Empire, von Nesselrode joined the diplomatic service during the Napoleonic Wars as Tsar Alexander I's ambassador to Berlin, where he was tasked with reporting on French troop movements. In 1814, he was promoted to state secretary, serving as the head of Russia's official delegation at the Congress of Vienna, and for the next forty years distinguished himself as a leading European statesman, a key figure in the politics of the continent. But it was his attempts to expand the Russian Empire into the lands vacated by the dwindling Ottoman Empire that saw conflict with Britain and France and their own empire-building and that, in turn, led to the devastating and unnecessary Crimean War (1853–6). This means that Nesselrode was responsible, if indirectly, for its great victories (or defeats, depending on which side of the conflict you were on), including the Battle of Balaclava, a triumph overall for the British despite the ill-fated Charge of the Light Brigade. I wonder what he would have made of it had he known he would be remembered by history chiefly for a creamy chestnut pudding.

Survival of the Sweetest: How Trifle Outlived Its Evolutionary Rivals

Hedgehog pudding, tipsy cake, tansy, syllabub, flummery, junket, trifle: the only popular survivor of these favourites of the eighteenth-century banquet today is the rich cold pudding known as **trifle**. The word comes from the old French term *trufle*, meaning something whimsical or of little consequence. The first trifles were very much like FOOLS, and for many years the two terms were used almost interchangeably. Indeed, a recipe for 'Foole' appearing in a recipe book by Joseph Cooper, cook to Charles I (1600–1649), bears a closer resemblance to the modern trifle, consisting as it does of a thin layer of bread soaked in 'sack' (dry white wine) and covered in custard flavoured with rose water. (See also BOODLE'S ORANGE FOOL for another trifle-like dish.)

By the middle of the eighteenth century, trifles had expanded to absorb macaroons soaked in sweet wine, covered with custard and topped with syllabub (milk or cream sweetened with sugar and lightly curdled with wine), this last addition eventually replaced with whipped cream. At this point, trifle shared the culinary limelight with a number of similar dishes, including the aforementioned tipsy cake (soaked in alcohol, surrounded by custard or syllabub and dotted all over with slivered almonds) and hedgehog pudding (a variation on tipsy cake, with the almonds poking out like spines). But the trifle eventually upstaged its rivals, absorbing the almonds as decoration on top of the syllabub/whipped cream.

How trifle became a lastingly popular pudding may well be for reasons of thrift: it offered a delicious way to use up stale cake, custard and fruit (a much later stage in the evolution of the trifle) plus any other leftovers from a week's worth of puddings. This may also be why the Italian version is jokingly called *zuppa inglese* (English soup), because the British were renowned in their country for two things: recycling all leftovers into soup for the next day (see MULLIGATAWNY); and an obsessive love of puddings.

Tarte Tatin: A Culinary Reversal of Fortune

Most cultures have their own recipe for apple pie. In America it has even become key to their sense of national identity, and everything would be 'as American as apple pie', if they had their way (see the box on page 210). But the French version, the **tarte Tatin**, is commonly recognized as one of the best in the world. And like BAKEWELL TART, it was invented by accident. The Hôtel Tatin in Lamotte-Beuvron, France, was run by a pair of unmarried sisters, Stéphanie and Caroline Tatin, during the late 1800s. Usually everything ran very smoothly but, one day, the apples for a traditional pie were left cooking in sugar and butter for too long, and burned. Stéphanie Tatin, who was in charge of the kitchen, tried to save the dish by pressing a disc of pastry on top of the apples and putting the pan in the oven. She then turned the contents of the pan out on to a plate, creating a sort of upside-down tart in the process (except that now it was the right way up, of course). To the sisters' amazement, the hotel patrons raved about the resulting dish, with its topping of buttery, caramelized apples, and a classic was born, ensuring fabulous advertising for the hotel forever afterwards.

Tarte Tatin immediately became a signature dish of the Hôtel Tatin and the recipe, and its unusual cooking technique, soon spread throughout the surrounding Sologne region. But it became an international sensation when Louis Vaudable, the legendary owner of Maxim's Restaurant in Paris, was served a slice when travelling through Sologne. He immediately made the tart a permanent fixture on the menu of his restaurant, where it is still served to this day.

Apple Brown Betty: One Pudding that Definitely Didn't Get Lost in Translation

The early European settlers of America were very good at improvisation, but they had to be. In the absence of key ingredients and suitable cooking apparatus, they were obliged to use whatever came to hand. Their attempts to cook their favourite steamed puddings resulted in a series of sloppier (but very tasty) desserts, all similar to crumbles. The settlers definitely had a sense of humour about the aesthetic failings of their new dishes: calling one 'slump' was in direct reference to how the traditional pudding reacted to their more basic cooking apparatus, and christening another 'cobbler' reflected how they had had to cobble ingredients together to make the dish. Yet they were so fond of these dishes that they often served them for breakfast, or even as the first course for dinner. It was not until the late nineteenth century that they became primarily desserts.

One favourite of these baked desserts was the **apple brown betty**, which became very popular during the American Civil War (1861–5). It consisted of alternate layers of thinly sliced apples and breadcrumbs, which meant that it was easy to prepare on the move and robust enough not to fall apart. The first mention in print was in the *Yale Literary Magazine* in 1864 where brown betties appeared on a list with coffee, tea and pies as items to be given up during military training. On Monday 11 July 1938, the *Daily Times* newspaper in Rochester, New York, published a recipe for brown betties, suggesting they were named after a young English lass called Betty Brown, who had emigrated to North America during the early 1800s. But the real reason behind the name may well be yet another joke from the settlers: apple brown betty was their rather more down-to-earth version of the European favourite **apple charlotte** ...

If someone gets their ***just deserts*** it is generally thought that they had what was coming to them; they got what they deserved. The confusion over the origins of this phrase lies in the spelling of 'deserts'. It looks like the word that means a vast sandy place in Egypt, but sounds like that SPOTTED DICK and custard we might have after dinner, which is why the phrase is often explained as 'Well, he deserved a pudding like that after what he did'. But this is wrong. The *Concise Oxford Dictionary* gives three definitions for the word 'desert': (1) to 'callously or treacherously abandon'; (2) 'a waterless, desolate area of land with little or no vegetation, typically covered with sand'; and (3) 'a person's worthiness or entitlement to reward or punishment'. It is this third definition that explains the phrase 'just deserts', meaning an appropriate reward or (more usually) punishment for someone's actions, and nothing at all to do with spotted dick or indeed any other kind of dessert, just or otherwise.

From Arab Delicacy to All-American Treat: The Story of Ice Cream

Today we take it for granted but, in the days before refrigeration, the possession of ice in hot climates or throughout the summer was a luxury that could only be afforded by the very rich. From ancient times, special buildings known as ice houses were contructed to store ice and snow gathered during the winter, keeping it frozen during the blazing summer months. The Persians introduced these and it was they who, around 400 BC, first put the ice to culinary use. Mixing ice with rose water, saffron and fruits, they made a chilled dessert that became the precursor of the **water ice** or **sorbet**. (They also made fruit drinks chilled with snow called 'sherbets', from which the word 'sorbet' derives.) The Romans also stored ice and snow, which they too used for making iced drinks and desserts. Such was his passion for these that, in AD 62, the emperor Nero, famed for his extravagance, sent slaves to the Apennine Mountains to collect snow for an iced dish flavoured with honey and nuts. It was the Arabs who first made water ices into a dairy dessert, sweetening the milky liquid with sugar rather than fruit juices to create an early form of **ice cream** that became very popular in Baghdad, Damascus and Cairo.

The Chinese may very well have invented their own proto-types of sorbet and ice cream at the same time as the Persians and Arabs (a frozen mixture of milk and rice was reputedly used in China around 200 BC), but the story that, like PASTA, the recipes and techniques were brought back to Italy by Marco Polo is very unlikely to be true. What is irrefutably the case is that, by the sixteenth century, Italy had become the home of the frozen dessert, which Catherine de Médicis then introduced to France via her team of Italian chefs (see EGGS FLORENTINE). But while Europe preferred water ices, the perfecting of ice cream was down to the English, who were much more interested in a frozen version of their favou-rite thick, rich custards. The first recorded English use of the word dates back to 1672, where it is listed as a key dessert for special occasions, and the first recipe to 1718. From the mid eighteenth century onwards, while still an expensive delicacy, ice cream began to appear more frequently in cookbooks. Hannah Glasse included a recipe in her 1751 edition of *The*

Art of Cookery (see YORKSHIRE PUDDING), for instance, while in 1768 *L'Art de bien faire les glaces d'office*, a work entirely devoted to the subject, was published in France.

Ice cream was introduced to America by Quaker colonists, who brought their ice cream recipes with them. Benjamin Franklin, George Washington and Thomas Jefferson were all known to have been fans of the dish. It took American energy and egalitarianism to realize the full potential of ice cream, and from the first time it was formally served at a banquet in 1744, they proceeded to make it their national dish. Confectioners sold ice cream at their shops in New York and other cities during the colonial era. This was received so enthusiastically that, on both sides of the Atlantic, ice cream came to be regarded as an entirely American concoction, so much so that in museums and antique shops early ice cream makers and moulds from Europe were mislabelled as American.

ICE CREAM SODAS AND SUNDAES

Two variations of ice cream, the **ice cream soda** and the **ice cream sundae**, are both genuinely all-American creations, however. The first is believed to have been the invention of a Philadelphia soda vendor, Robert M. Green, in 1874. According to the story, it was a particularly hot day and Green, having run out of ice for the drinks he was selling, tried substituting it with vanilla ice cream from a neighbouring vendor. His new creation caught on and the drink sold so well that it soon became the national institution that it is today. Meanwhile, Green was so proud of his invention that he instructed in his will that the words 'Originator of the Ice Cream Soda' be carved on his tombstone.

The ice cream sundae emerged slightly later, reputedly the creation of two competing ice cream parlour owners in Wisconsin, although there are rival claims from elsewhere in America. Ed Berners in Two Rivers discovered almost by accident in 1881 that the chocolate sauce he used for making sodas made a delicious topping for ice cream, and went on to create a number of ice-cream-and-sauce combinations, which he called the Flora Dora, the Mudscow and the Chocolate Peany. But it was George Giffy, in nearby Manitowoc, who hit on a name that stuck. He started serving these special ice creams to parishioners after church on Sundays. Then one weekday a little girl ordered a dish of ice cream 'with stuff on it'. On being told that Giffy only served it on Sundays, the child was supposed to have replied: 'Why, then it must be Sunday, for that's the kind of ice cream I want!' Keen to avert the brewing tantrum, Giffy quickly made the dish for her and from then on called it a 'Sunday'.

Treacle Tart: The Intriguing Origins of Its Chief Ingredient

And finally, to complete this menu of desserts, we have Harry Potter's favourite tart. Consisting of shortcrust pastry filled with a mixture of **golden syrup** and breadcrumbs, **treacle tart** is generally served hot with a dollop of thick cream – although at my school that was runny custard. Golden syrup is a form of pale **treacle**, the generic name for a syrup made during the refining of sugar cane. Used today primarily for sweetening dishes, treacle was employed in former times as a medicine to treat venomous bites and stings; indeed, the word evolved from the Old French *triacle*, meaning 'antidote to poison'. The Romans used honey in the same way but at some point between the demise of their culture and the dawning of the European Age of Discovery in the fifteenth century, honey was replaced by treacle as the great healer of the Middle Ages. Around the seventeenth century, as the new sugar plantations began sending their product back to Europe by the fleet load, treacle lost its mythical medicinal status and began to be used primarily as a sweetener and dessert filling. One enduring legend involving treacle is that it was actually mined in remote parts of England from treacle deposits. The story appearing to lend credibility to this obscure claim is that Oliver Cromwell's Puritan army buried millions of barrels of molasses during the mid seventeenth century and that over time these have leaked and created great underground treacle lakes. An alternative explanation refers to prehistoric sugar plantations that have become fossilized and can now be mined in the same way as coal, or tin. It is an interesting theory but, sadly, not true.

The invention of golden syrup is rather better documented, however, known to be the creation of Scottish businessman Abram Lyle, who discovered in 1883 that this byproduct of the sugar refined at his east London factory made a delicious syrup that could be used as a spread or in cooking. A deeply religious man, he is said to have chosen the slogan that appears on the iconic green and gold tins, 'Out of the strong came forth sweetness'. Accompanying the image of a lion's carcass surrounded by bees, the words are from the Old Testament (Judges 14:14), relating to the story of Samson who, on his travels, killed a lion and, coming across its body again later, discovered that a swarm of bees had made a comb of honey inside the carcass. In 1921, Lyle merged with the sugar refiner Tate to become Tate & Lyle, now the only cane sugar refiner in the UK and the largest in Europe. The company still sells more than a million tins of golden syrup each month, its brand, registered as a trademark in 1904, deemed to be the oldest in Britain.

17
The Cheese Course

What was Little Miss Muffet Eating?

Brie: Blessed are the Cheesemakers

Parmesan: Much Admired and Secretly Imitated

What's the Most Insulting Way to Serve
Cheese on Toast?

Fondue: The Cheesy Alpine Classic

Defining Cheddar: Hard Cheese to the
Rest of the World

Port Salut: When It Pays to Keep Silent

The Ancient Art of Making Cheese into a Cake

Cheese Rolling: An Energetic Way to
Serve Double Gloucester

A Selection of Biscuits to Accompany the Cheese

I saw a figure leap with great rapidity behind the trunk of a pine…

'Who are you?' I asked.

'Ben Gunn,' he answered, and his voice sounded awkward, like a rusty lock. 'I'm poor Ben Gunn, I am; and I haven't spoke with a Christian these three years … But, mate, my heart is sore for Christian diet. You mightn't happen to have a piece of cheese about you, now? No? Well, many's the long night I've dreamed of cheese – toasted, mostly – and woke up again, and here I were.'

ROBERT LOUIS STEVENSON, *Treasure Island*

What was Little Miss Muffet Eating?

A major change brought by the development of organized farming around 7000 BC was that animals were suddenly no longer seen merely in terms of their meat. And as soon as humans began to milk their domesticated animals, the issue of how to preserve this delicious, nutritious but rapidly rancid liquid became a pressing concern. It's likely the earliest type of cheese was a form of sour milk, a simple result of the observation that milk left in a container turned solid, especially in hot temperatures. However, according to one widely told legend, **cheese** was an accidental discovery, similar to that of STEAK TARTARE and originating in the same part of the world, Central Asia. To sustain himself on a long journey across the desert, a nomad once filled his saddlebag with milk, tying it to his saddle. After several hours of galloping in the hot sun, he stopped to quench his thirst, only to find the milk had separated into a thin, sour watery liquid and solid white lumps. The rennet in the sheep's stomach, from which the saddlebag was made, had caused the milk to set, turning it into a form of cheese. Otherwise known as **curds and whey**, this is the very snack Little Miss Muffet was eating when she sat down on her nursery rhyme tuffet. And it is this that provides the basis for all our favourite cheeses.

The modern type of cheese that most resembles this basic early form is **cottage cheese**. It became a popular staple in Europe in the late Middle Ages, when rural workers became expert in deriving nourishment from almost anything. And from a nutritional point of view, cheese is a most valuable food, concentrating as it does most of the nourishment of the milk: the solids extracted from milk to make cheese contain virtually all of the fat, vitamins and proteins. The workers would salvage any leftovers from cheese and butter making, which they took home and turned into a cheese that was so simple to create that it could easily be made in any dwelling, however humble or poorly equipped. The technique for making cottage (or cottager's) cheese was brought by early European settlers to America, where it also went by a rather less appetizing name, as indicated in *The Dictionary of Americanisms* (1848): 'Smear-Case is a preparation of milk made to be spread onto bread, hence its name but otherwise known as Cottage Cheese.' Deriving from the German *Schmierkäse* ('spreadable cheese'), **smearcase** reflected the mix of nationalities among the colonists. But as America's many German settlers became increasingly anglicized, the name was eventually dropped in favour of 'cottage cheese'. The Amish – who trace a direct line to their Swiss forefathers and continue to speak a form of German – remain resistant to all forms of anglicization and modernization, and their recipe for CHEESECAKE is still called **smearcase cake**.

Brie: Blessed are the Cheesemakers

In Homer's *Odyssey*, Circe when trying to seduce Odysseus serves him cheese. The Greeks and Romans were obsessed with cheese and cheese making features in many of their writings and mosaics. By AD 300, cheese trade and export was well underway along the Mediterranean seaboard and throughout Europe. But when the Roman Empire fell to the Barbarians (around AD 410), the Dark Ages began and cheese all but disappeared.

Luckily for us, the early Christian Church, as we've seen

with CHRISTMAS DINNER, had a great eye for the most attractive parts of pagan life and eventually monks in early monasteries all around Europe revived the practice of cheese making. Removed from the commercial pressures of the outside world, monasteries offered great opportunities for innovation and the monks greatly improved techniques for cheese ripening and ageing. One type to emerge during these times was **Brie**, the famous soft French cheese with its distinctive doughy white crust. Originating in the Brie region of northern France in around 770, it is the subject of a well-known legend. According to a ninth-century biography of the first Holy Roman Emperor, Charlemagne (742–814), who conquered and Christianized vast tracts of Dark Age Europe, he was travelling through the region and stopped at a bishop's residence for dinner.

> Now on that day, being [Friday], he was not willing to eat the flesh of beast or bird; and the bishop, being by reason of the nature of the place unable to procure fish upon the sudden, ordered some excellent cheese, rich and creamy, to be placed before him. Charles … required no better fare: but taking up his knife cut off the skin, which he thought unsavoury, and fell to on the white of the cheese. Thereupon the bishop, who was standing near like a servant, drew close and said: 'Why do you do that, lord emperor? You are throwing away the very best part.' Then Charles … on the persuasion of the bishop put a piece of the skin in his mouth, and slowly ate it and swallowed it like butter. Then, approving the advice of the bishop, he said: 'Very true, my good host,' and added: 'Be sure to send me every year two cart-loads of just such cheeses.'

For his pains, the bishop was awarded an 'excellent estate' to add to the Church lands, while Brie went on to become one of the most defining French cheeses.

Big cheese is a colloquial expression for the most important person. During the early nineteenth century, 'cheese' was a common slang term used by Londoners to describe anything genuine or popular. John Camden Hotten's *The Slang Dictionary*, first published in 1863, describes 'cheese' as 'anything good, first rate, genuine and pleasant'. Used in this sense, the word has nothing to do with the dairy product but appears to have been a corruption of the Persian word chiz, meaning 'item' or 'thing'. As Sir Henry Yule explains in *Hobson-Jobson*, the famous Anglo-Indian dictionary (see POPPADOM), *chiz* was commonly used by Anglo-Indians in the form 'real *chiz*', to describe something (or someone) that was the best of its kind. In America in the early twentieth century, this phrase was corrupted further to 'big cheese', following on from a whole range of 'big' phrases describing the best of something, including ***big fish***, ***big bug*** and ***big banana***. The phrase is not entirely complimentary, however, with overtones of other 'cheese' expressions, such as ***cheesed off*** (to be annoyed) and ***cheesy*** (cheap or inauthentic). Deriving perhaps from the strong odour of the actual substance, 'cheesy' could equally have evolved as an ironic application of *chiz* ('chizzy') to indicate something showy and tasteless.

Parmesan: Much Admired and Secretly Imitated

There is a mountain in Boccaccio's *Decameron* that is made entirely of grated **Parmesan**, on which there live people who do nothing but make MACARONI and RAVIOLI. Made in Italy from the Middle Ages, chiefly in the area of Parma (from which its name derives), Parmesan was the favourite cheese of both Napoleon and Samuel Pepys, who famously buried his Parmesan, 'as well as [his] wine and some other things', in order to preserve it from the ravages of the Great Fire of London in 1666. The playwright Molière (1622–73), suddenly stricken by a fatal illness, waved aside the conventional bowl of medicinal broth, and called for Parmesan, which he devoured with such enthusiasm that there were cheese crumbs all over his deathbed. Although it failed to revive him, Parmesan had and still has a reputation as being good for the health – as well as being highly nutritious, its long ageing process makes it easy to digest and it is believed to encourage the development of 'friendly' bacteria in the gut. Over the years, Parmesan has acquired many admirers outside Italy, and as the proverb goes, 'Imitation is the sincerest form of flattery'...

FARMERS' HAND CHEESE

Described as an 'Italian-style hard cheese', **Farmers' Hand** follows the same recipe as Parmesan cheese only it's made with British cow's milk. Crowned 'Best British Modern Cheese' in 1998, Farmers' Hand is made at Bookham Farm in Heathfield, East Sussex, where the producers are forbidden to use the name 'Parmesan' for their cheese as it is trademarked. Only cheese from the Emilia-Romagna area of northern Italy, made using the traditional methods and ingredients, can be

called Parmesan (or, more properly, Parmigiano-Reggiano).
But the English are a resourceful lot and this European cheese
policy is directly responsible for the unusual name of this
award-winning cheese. Try saying 'Farmers' Hand Cheese'
out loud several times. Now you may never need use the word
'Parmesan' again.

What's the Most Insulting Way
to Serve Cheese on Toast?

Essentially cheese on TOAST with added ingredients, **Welsh
rabbit** or as some people insist, **Welsh rarebit**, has become
the subject of fierce debate: should it be 'rabbit' or 'rarebit'.
Many a wager has been placed on the outcome, especially by
the Irish, who really shouldn't be getting involved in the first
place. But they're probably looking on with amused disinter-
est at this bit of culinary discord between the English and
the Welsh.

As the Welsh enthusiasm for devolution shows, the English
have traditionally scorned them as poor, inept and not always
trustworthy, as reflected in an old nursery rhyme: 'Taffy was
a Welshman, Taffy was a thief; / Taffy came to my house
to steal a joint of beef ...' So when a new dish of melted
cheese on toast was devised in the eighteenth century, it was
jokingly called Welsh rabbit, meaning that a Welshman, too
poor to have meat, would be obliged to use cheese instead.
It is in a similar vein to the dig at the Scots represented
by **Scotch woodcock**, actually scrambled egg on toast with
anchovies and nothing to do with the meat of a bird. The earliest written reference to Welsh rabbit can be traced to 1725
and the diary of John Byrom (1692–1763), an impoverished
poet and the inventor of shorthand, a coded language he used
for his journals. In one entry he sourly noted: 'I did not eat
of cold beef, but of Welsh rabbit and stewed cheese.' It was

Francis Grose, sixty years later in his *Classical Dictionary of the Vulgar Tongue* (1785), who first used the term rarebit: 'A Welsh rabbit is bread and cheese roasted, i.e. a Welsh rare bit.' He was thus trying to extend the joke further, stressing that for the Welsh cheese on toast was a rare treat. The subsequent preference for calling the dish 'rarebit' became popular because it softened the crudity of the old insult and gave the dish an unusual and thus rather more genteel name.

The Welsh, who are as fond of the snack as the English, have come up with a couple of stories to explain the derivation of the dish and claim its origin for themselves. The first describes how Welsh wives, seeing their menfolk returning from the hunt empty-handed, would tactfully set cheese before the fire to melt to make up for the lack of game for supper. The second claims that the dish was invented by an imaginative Welsh monk who poured wine over a slice of toasted bread and crumbled a mild Caerphilly over the top, holding it close to the fire in order to melt it. The Welsh also point out that the eighteenth century was a time when appetizers were known as 'fore-bits', because they were served in advance of the meal, while the savouries traditionally served at a meal's end (including cheese on toast) were consequently called 'rear-bits', which, when said with a thick Celtic accent, comes out as 'rarebit'.

However, all the earliest recipes and mentions of the dish are English: Hannah Glasse's famous cookbook *The Art of Cookery* (see YORKSHIRE PUDDING) even has three different rabbits – Welsh, English (with added red wine) and Scottish (uncooked). Which brings us back again to the notion of the name being an insulting reference to the Welsh, rather than a dish originating in Wales. It could simply reflect the age-old way that one nation likes to insult its immediate neighbour, which has given rise to such expressions as **going Dutch**, for someone too mean to pay for their guest's meal, or **French leave**, departing without saying goodbye. In this spirit, it is

easy to see why the English may have taken to assuming the
Welsh were unable to catch even the poor man's staple of a
rabbit for his supper and therefore had to live on bread and
cheese alone. And when the English were eating bread and
cheese themselves, the meal became known as the Welsh rabbit, largely as an insult to their neighbours.

Fondue: The Cheesy Alpine Classic

Cheese fondue was originally a Swiss peasant recipe: up
in the Alps the peasants relied very heavily on the produce
of their herds and on cheese in particular. Fondue offered
a clever one-pot cooking method for using up scraps of
cheese and bits of stale bread – for dipping in the cheese
sauce once it had been made. The word derives from the
French verb *fondre* ('to melt'), and simply means 'melted'.
Most Swiss would agree that a proper fondue is made with
a blend of cheeses – hard Gruyère with a semi-hard cheese
like Emmental or raclette – plus white wine, a little kirsch,
a spoonful of flour to prevent curdling and a sprinkling of
salt, pepper and nutmeg. However, the dish might have
remained an overlooked regional delicacy if it were not
for the intervention of French gastronome and cheese
enthusiast Jean Anthelme Brillat-Savarin (1755–1826). His
classic book *The Physiology of Taste* (published in 1825,
two months before his death) has a rather strange entry on
fondue, describing it as 'a soup … that consists of frying eggs
in cheese in proportions revealed by experience' – a recipe
which incidentally has been condemned by Swiss authorities
as being for scrambled eggs with cheese rather than a true
fondue. Nevertheless, the dish became so popular that it
was picked up and highly recommended by Mrs Beeton in
her *Book of Household Management* in 1861. Such was his

passion for cheese that Brillat-Savarin has one named after him – a very creamy, Brie-like soft cheese from Normandy. And it was he who came up with the unforgettable saying that 'a dinner without cheese was like a beautiful woman with only one eye'.

To grin like a Cheshire cat means that you are feeling extremely pleased with yourself and therefore smiling very broadly indeed. It's an expression that immediately calls to mind the Cheshire Cat in Lewis Carroll's *Alice's Adventures in Wonderland* (1865), in which the cat, perched on a branch, gradually disappears until only its grin is visible. But where did Carroll get the inspiration for his grinning feline? There are suggestions that the idea may have come from a carving of a cat on St Wilfrid's Church tower in Grappenhall, a village near Daresbury, Cheshire, where the author was born. Or that it may relate to the image of a cat or lion with a strange smile said to have appeared on the coat of arms of a prominent Cheshire family, the Grosvenors. If that's the case, then other people must have been similarly inspired as the expression appears in a much older work, *The Classical Dictionary of the Vulgar Tongue* (1788) by Francis Grose, which contains the entry: 'He grins like a Cheshire cat; said of anyone who shows his teeth and gums in laughing.' Another suggestion connects the phrase with **Cheshire cheese**, which, it is believed, used to be sold moulded in the shape of a cat that looked as though it was grinning – no doubt having seen off a few mice keen to sink their teeth into the cheese. As bits of the cheese were cut off the 'body' of the cat, only its head would remain, just like that of its fictional counterpart.

Defining Cheddar: Hard Cheese
to the Rest of the World

Originally from the village of Cheddar in Somerset, **Cheddar cheese** has been produced since at least 1170, when the records of King Henry II (1133–89) reveal that he ordered 10,500 pounds of the cheese to be sent to him in London. Going forward a few centuries, the man credited with having invented the 'defining formula' for it, and hence regarded as the 'father of Cheddar cheese', was dairyman Joseph Harding (1805–76). It was he who introduced a more scientific approach to the process of cheese making, insisting on strict hygiene and temperature control, techniques that form the basis for commercial cheese making today. Indeed, such was his faith in his production process that he would say: 'Cheese is not made in the field, nor in the byre, nor even in the cow; it is made in the dairy.'

Harding was then consulted by cheese makers from America, who took his ideas with them across the Atlantic and his techniques were adopted by other countries, too; hence a Cheddar-like cheese is produced in every corner of the globe. Cheese calling itself 'Cheddar' is made in a multitude of places, although to be a true Cheddar, it traditionally had to be made within thirty miles of Wells Cathedral. As with PARMESAN, the European Union has granted Cheddar a 'protected designation of origin' status whereby only **West Country Farmhouse Cheddar** is officially recognized, a label that can be applied only to the traditionally made product of four designated English counties: Dorset, Somerset, Devon and Cornwall. Any other Cheddar cheese you come across (and supermarkets are full of them) is simply not authentic. So now you know.

Port Salut: When It Pays to Keep Silent

A semi-soft French cheese with a distinctive orange crust, **Port Salut** was created during the nineteenth century by Trappists, an enclosed order of Catholic monks who observe the Rule of St Benedict (living communally under the authority of an abbot). Their original abbey was built in 1122 by Rotrou III, comte du Perche, as a memorial to his wife, an illegitimate daughter of Henry I who had drowned with half the royal family in the English Channel on 25 November 1120 in what became known as the *White Ship* disaster (as famous in its day as the sinking of the *Titanic* in the last century). A few years later, Rotrou extended the building, turning it into a monastery, which he then offered to the monks of a nearby abbey, renowned at the time for their piety. In 1140, the monastery of La Trappe was raised to the status of abbey and a group of contemplative French monks lived there for the next two centuries until 1337 when their peace was shattered by the outbreak of the Hundred Years' War.

In 1376, La Trappe was looted and burned by wandering soldiers and again in 1465, at which point the monks were forced to abandon the abbey. It then lay in ruins until the sixteenth century, when it was finally rebuilt. This led to an improvement in the abbey's fortunes, especially under a new abbot, Armand de Rancé, who was installed in 1662 and who introduced an austere programme of reform that led to the foundation of the Trappist order (named after the abbey). As well as strict adherence to St Benedict's Rule, with its vows of stability, fidelity and obedience, the monks now adopted a rule of silence. Although Trappists do not have to make a vow about this, silence is generally observed and consequently a sign language has evolved to enable them to communicate with each other.

In 1789, the monks found their peace threatened once again, this time by revolutionary soldiers, and once again had to abandon La Trappe. After twenty years in exile – during which they learned new skills, including cheese making, in order to survive – they eventually found a new home, settling by a ford in the River Mayenne in the north-west of France. On first discovering the site, the monks are said to have exclaimed: '*Ici est notre salut!*' ('Here is our salvation!'). Which is why they named their new abbey – and later their delicious new cheese – Port Salut (Port of Salvation).

The Ancient Art of Making Cheese into a Cake

The ancient Greeks lived on a frugal diet of wheat, olive oil and wine, so it's easy to see where their obsession with cheese came from. They gave it to their children as a treat – 'little cheese' was a special term of endearment. Their earliest cheese was a simple sheep's milk cheese that they stored in brine to save it from the blistering summer heat. Still a staple of the Greek diet, **feta** has been produced for centuries, although its name, deriving from the Italian word *fetta*, or 'slice', didn't become current until the seventeenth century. The blandness of feta makes it a highly versatile cheese, delicious in both savoury and sweet dishes, including **cheesecake**, which also dates back to antiquity – made by the ancient Greeks and served on special occasions. Historians believe that it was even served to the athletes during the first Olympic Games in 776 BC, presumably as part of the athletes' dietary regime, which consisted chiefly of cheese. Wedding cakes of that era were almost invariably made with cheese, while at Argos it was customary for the bride to bring little cheesecakes covered in honey for serving to the bridegroom's friends. The Romans were quick to pick up on the Greek dish, the earliest mention appearing in Cato the Elder's *De agri cultura* ('On Farming') around 160 BC, in which the author describes making a cake (*libum*) closely resembling the cheesecake of today. So the next time you eat a slice (*fetta*) of cheesecake, pause for a moment to think just how long people have been tucking into them.

Cheese Rolling: An Energetic Way to Serve Double Gloucester

Every year, on the spring bank holiday, the good folk of the village of Brockworth near Gloucester hold a contest at Cooper's Hill, one that began as a small local festival and grew into a much publicized event attended by thousands of visitors from all over the world. Nobody remembers exactly how or why it started or what inspired the villagers to gather at the top of the hill and roll a large cheese down the steep, uneven slope and then go charging after it at breakneck speed to see who can reach the bottom first. The cheese in question is **Double Gloucester**, the locally produced variety of hard cheese that is typically manufactured in large cylindrical blocks. After rolling down the hill, this is awarded to the first contestant over the line. Ideally, it would be awarded to the person who catches it, but as the cheese can reach speeds of up to seventy miles an hour, this is perhaps a tall order. Needless to say, injuries are commonplace and the seven-pound cheese frequently strays offline and flattens an unsuspecting spectator. Even so, each year hundreds of people take part, often after

What Caesar Did for My Salad

discussing tactics in the nearby Cheese Rollers public house, considered by many to be responsible for much of the 'over-enthusiasm' among competitors and for the need to position a St John's ambulance at the bottom of the hill.

The Cooper's Hill Cheese Rolling and Wake (to give the contest its full title) is known to have been an established event as far back as the early 1800s. And it may go back further – to Roman times or beyond, perhaps as part of a pagan fertility ritual (hence the modern festival taking place on a spring bank holiday). During the food rationing of the Second World War, a wooden substitute was used, with a small wedge of cheese secured inside, just to keep the competition, as well as the cheese, rolling on from year to year.

To sum up the event, it appears to consist of a bunch of young men throwing themselves off a steep hill after a runaway cheese and racing each other to the Accident & Emergency Department. And quite why anybody would want to eat cheese that has careered down Cooper's Hill at speeds approaching the national limit is beyond me, especially if it drew the blood of an unsuspecting bystander along the way.

A Selection of Biscuits to Accompany the Cheese

Good cheese needs something to show it off to best advantage, like the frame around a painting. Hence, at the end of a meal, cheese is frequently served with savoury biscuits, usually quite plain, in order to complement its creamy richness. One of the most familiar kind are **water biscuits**, thin and hard with a flaky texture and golden brown bubbles all over the surface. Made using only flour and water, with no fat, they are baked in a very hot oven to create their distinctive bubbly brown surface. What may amaze the hosts of smart dinner parties serving them up with a platter of choice cheeses is that they are the descendants of SHIP'S BISCUIT, the detested and notoriously weevil-ridden staple diet of sailors until the twentieth century. Originally produced in the nineteenth century, they became known as **water crackers** in America due to the crackling sound they made during baking, the term 'cracker' then being applied to similar types of plain biscuit.

Oatcakes were a traditional staple food of the inhabitants of the Lake District, the Pennines and Scottish Highlands. Oats were used because this was the only cereal that would ripen in the cold wet climate of these upland areas. As Samuel Johnson observed, somewhat sardonically, in the definition of oats in his *Dictionary of the English Language* (1755), it is a 'grain, which in England is generally given to horses, but in Scotland supports the people'. In parts of Scotland, cooking the **Beltane bannock**, a type of oatcake, is a popular custom. Beltane was the second of the four fire festivals of the pagan year and oatcakes were traditionally baked in the embers of the festival bonfire. It's said that if you eat one on Beltane morning (1 May), your crops and livestock will be guaranteed abundance.

The coarse, crumbly and slightly sweet biscuit we know as the **digestive** is so called because the sodium bicarbonate contained in the early recipes for them back in the nineteenth century was believed to give the biscuit antacid qualities. It turns out that this is a bit of a misnomer, however, as the digestive has no particularly digestion-improving properties and is thus banned from sale in America under that name.

A biscuit that was actually first introduced as a diet item, is the **Bath Oliver**. Invented by Dr William Oliver (1695–1764) of Bath, at about the time the town became a health resort, these hard dry biscuits are said to have emerged as a substitute for **Bath buns** (also created by Oliver, it is said) when he found that these were too fattening for his rheumatic patients. Although the biscuits proved just as fattening, of course, when his patients discovered that they tasted best accompanied by high-calorie cheese. As a lasting tribute to their creator, true Bath Olivers have an imprint of the good doctor in the middle of each biscuit.

The final item in this selection is not strictly a biscuit, although it is often served with cheese. Buoyed by his success with PEACH MELBA, and his growing friendship with Dame Nellie, Auguste Escoffier came up with another dish in her honour. During her stay at the Savoy Hotel, the singer was complaining of feeling ill one morning, apparently unable to eat her breakfast TOAST. Escoffier, who had been standing by her table, quickly took a sharp knife and – despite what must have been an obvious temptation to anyone in the company of a whingeing diva – applied it to the toast instead of the singer herself. He carefully sliced the toast through the middle, producing two thinner pieces that were easier for the great lady to swallow. And only half as fattening, which went down well with the singer, who was always trying to lose weight. Ever since that morning at the Savoy Hotel in 1897, **Melba toast** has gained in popularity, especially when it was discovered that it made the perfect accompaniment for soup or pâté, not to mention cheese.

Further Reading

Blake, Anthony, and Crewe, Quentin, *Great Chefs of France* (H. N. Abrams, 1978)

Burrow, John, *A History of Histories* (Allen Lane, 2007)

Chapman, Pat, *Curry Club Balti Curry Cookbook* (Piatkus Books, 1997)

David, Elizabeth, *English Bread and Yeast Cookery* (Viking, 1977)

— *French Country Cooking* (John Lehmann, 1951)

— *French Provincial Cooking* (Penguin Books, 1960)

— *Mediterranean Food* (John Lehmann, 1950)

Davidson, Alan, *The Penguin Companion to Food* (Penguin Books, 2002)

Grigson, Jane, *English Food* (Macmillan, 1974)

— *Fish Cookery* (David & Charles, 1973)

— *Vegetable Book* (Michael Joseph, 1978)

Kulansky, Mark, *Salt: A World History* (Penguin Books, 2002)

Lee, Christopher, *This Sceptred Isle* (Penguin, 1998)

Montagné, Prosper, *Larousse Gastronomique: The World's Greatest Cookery Encyclopedia*, ed. Jennifer Harvey Lang, third English edition (Clarkson Potter, 2001)

Odya Krohn, Norman, *Menu Mystique: The Diner's Guide to Fine Food & Drink* (Jonathan David, 1983)

Saulnier, Louis, *Le Répertoire de la cuisine*, tr. E. Brunet, seventeenth edition (Leon Jaeggi & Sons, 1982)

Shaida, Margaret, *The Legendary Cuisine of Persia* (Interlink Books, 2002)

Smith, Drew, *Modern Cooking* (Sidgwick & Jackson, 1990)

Swinnerton, Jo, *The Cook's Companion* (Robson Books, 2004)

Tannahill, Reay, *Food in History* (Penguin Books, 1973)

Wilson, C. Anne, *Food and Drink in Britain* (Constable, 1974)

— (ed.), *Traditional Food East and West of the Pennines* (Edinburgh University Press, 1991)

Index

Please note that page numbers in bold refer to the main entry for a type of food or food-related item.